UNBECOMING WOMEN

GENDER AND CULTURE

Carolyn G. Heilbrun and Nancy K. Miller, Editors

GENDER AND CULTURE
A Series of Columbia University Press

Edited by Carolyn G. Heilbrun and Nancy K. Miller

In Dora's Case: Freud, Hysteria, Feminism
Edited by Charles Bernheimer and Claire Kahane

Breaking the Chain: Women, Theory and French Realist Fiction
Naomi Schor

Between Men: English Literature and Male Homosocial Desire
Eve Kosofsky Sedgwick

Romantic Imprisonment: Women and Other Glorified Outcasts
Nina Auerbach

The Poetics of Gender
Edited by Nancy K. Miller

Reading Woman: Essays in Feminist Criticism
Mary Jacobus

Honey-Mad Women: Emancipatory Strategies in Women's Writing
Patricia Yaeger

Subject to Change: Reading Feminist Writing
Nancy K. Miller

Thinking Through the Body
Jane Gallop

Gender and the Politics of History
Joan Wallach Scott

The Dialogic and Difference: "An/Other Woman" in Virginia Woolf and Christa Wolf
Anne Hermann

Plotting Women: Gender and Representation in Mexico
Jean Franco

Inspiriting Influences
Michael Awkward

Hamlet's Mother and Other Women
Carolyn G. Heilbrun

Rape and Representation
Edited by Lynn A. Higgins and Brenda R. Silver

Shifting Scenes: Interviews on Women, Writing, and Politics in Post-68 France
Edited by Alice A. Jardine and Anne M. Menke

Tender Geographies: Women and the Origins of the Novel in France
Joan DeJean

Modern Feminisms: Political, Literary, Cultural
Maggie Humm

Versions of the following chapters have appeared in whole or in part elsewhere and are reprinted with the permission of the original publishers:

Chapter 3, "The Humiliation of Elizabeth Bennet." Originally published in *Refiguring the Father: New Feminist Readings of Patriarchy*, Patricia Yaeger and Beth Kowaleski-Wallace, eds. (Carbondale: Southern Illinois University Press, 1989).

Chapter 5, "*The Mill on the Floss*, the Critics, and the *Bildungsroman*." Originally published in *PMLA* 108, no. 1 (January 1993). Copyright © 1993 by The Modern Language Association of America.

UNBECOMING
WOMEN

British Women Writers and
The Novel of Development

Susan Fraiman

COLUMBIA UNIVERSITY PRESS

NEW YORK

COLUMBIA UNIVERSITY PRESS
NEW YORK   CHICHESTER, WEST SUSSEX

Copyright © 1993 Columbia University Press
All rights reserved

Library of Congress Cataloging-in-Publication Data
Fraiman, Susan.
  Unbecoming women : British women writers and the novel of
development / Susan Fraiman.
    p.   cm.—(Gender and culture)
  Includes bibliographical references and index.
  ISBN 0-231-08000-X
  ISBN 0-231-08001-8(pbk.)
  1. English fiction—Women authors—History and criticism.
2. Women and literature—Great Britain—History.   3. Bildungaroman.
I. Title. II. Series.
PR830.W6F73   1993
823.009'9287—dc20   92-26024
                                                              CIP

∞

Casebound editions of
Columbia University Press books
are printed
on permanent and durable
acid-free paper.

Book design: Teresa Bonner
Printed in the United States of America

c 10 9 8 7 6 5 4 3 2 1
p 10 9 8 7 6 5 4 3 2 1

For My Parents
and
Eric

CONTENTS

PREFACE

A book on the novel of development might seem a book invested, by definition, in notions of linear progress and coherent identity. Certainly the form and most discussions of the form have tended to invoke a purposeful youth advancing toward some clarity and stability of being. "Development," it has been said, emerged as a dominant idea in relation to Enlightenment confidence in human perfectibility, to Romantic views of childhood as prelude to creative manhood, and to the nineteenth-century general preoccupation with historicity. Out of these ideological contexts, and from the influence they continue to exert in the twentieth century, arose what English-language critics have variously named the "novel of development," "novel of formation," "apprentice novel," or *Bildungsroman*." It is one project of this book to raise questions about these generic formulations and the understanding of development on which they rely. The *unbecoming* of my title is intended to push back against conventional assumptions about becoming and stories of becoming, and this pressure is obtained in large part by focusing on *women*.

The women I discuss—Frances Burney, Jane Austen, Charlotte Brontë, George Eliot, and several conduct-book authors—wrote in

England during the Georgian and Victorian periods. My readings of their variations on growing up female suggest that a heroine's progress toward masterful selfhood is by no means assured, even in apparently comic texts. What Burney's subtitle calls "a young lady's entrance into the world" might be more accurately described as a young lady's floundering on the world's doorstep. Yet if *Bildung* in the classic sense proves difficult for my female protagonists, it cannot simply be shrugged off so as to map a girl's destiny along altogether different lines. The improbability of the *Bildung* plot may even serve to heighten its appeal, for the heroine and for female writers and readers alike. In critical terms, I would say its aggressive trajectory continues to inform the texts under discussion, to be relevant as both foil and goal; in theoretical terms, I would argue that "progressive development" and "coherent identity" are, to some extent, enabling fictions whose limited availability to women has hurt us, and I therefore hesitate to give them up entirely. At the same time, the tendency of these fictions to exclude the female does mean that women may be less apt to see them as natural or inevitable, may be more apt to treat them ironically, and must of necessity formulate the developmental process in other ways.

I would like to imagine the way to womanhood not as a single path to a clear destination but as the endless negotiation of a crossroads. Women take various routes depending on what class of woman they are; each woman, at the same time, is divided among several routes, so that she lives her gender as a continuous movement in contradictory directions, some more sanctioned than others. Thus becoming a woman may be thought of as, in Judith Butler's rephrasing of Simone de Beauvoir, "an incessant project, a daily act of reconstruction and interpretation" (131). It is a lifelong act continuing well past any discrete season of youth, and it involves a struggle among diverse narratives: official and also oppositional stories of arriving at adult "femininity." (While something similiar may be said of achieving "masculinity," the single, surging story line remains nevertheless more plausible for men.) I hope to get from this formulation more than a sense of how painfully confusing it is to apprentice for womanhood: the mixed signals one receives, the double standards for women in different social positions and for the same woman at different times, the residual criteria for femininity at odds with emergent ones. I want, in addition, to derive a sense of how confused and inconsistent, how partial and basically shoddy the construction of femininity is—in a way that leaves room for alternative formations, for some degree of rude and rebellious agency within a complex set of constraints.

With this view of becoming female in mind, the following chapters turn to women's novels and conduct books in search of the divergent narratives, the rival ideologies, that constitute femininity at a specific place and moment. I look to these texts not for a female version of one figure's private formation but for a wrestling with the range of discursive possibilities for becoming a woman in a given culture. While I am offering above all a way of reading for development—a postmodernization of the *Bildungsroman*, if you will—the texts I discuss may yield all the more readily to this approach for having been written during that extended period in the course of which development as a notion, the novel as a genre, and gender as a ruling social category were all being defined and, in the process, debated. It is also significant to my choice of texts that the novel and conduct book were both immensely popular forms in these years, and that each of the novels I treat (with the possible exception of *The Mill on the Floss*) was, in its author's lifetime, her most popular book; the centrality of these works to their culture's discourse about femininity is inseparable from my purposes. Yet the popularity, say, of *Pride and Prejudice* and *Jane Eyre* should not be taken to imply that these works are inherently more conservative than the less beloved and more openly defiant *Persuasion* or *Villette*. I hope my readings will dispute this common assumption by putting special emphasis on the "counternarratives" of these novels—those dissenting stories that cut across and break up the seemingly smooth course of female development and developmental fiction. As the following chapters will demonstrate, these counternarratives involve "unbecoming women" in two related senses. First, they account for growing up female as a deformation, a gothic disorientation, a loss of authority, an abandonment of goals. Second, they tell this story—alongside conventional stories— in what I see as a spirit of protest, challenging the myth of courtship as education, railing against the belittlement of women, willing to hazard the distasteful and indecorous.

This book, then, addresses and attempts to complicate the issue of female development in a number of overlapping ways. It is about the embattled development of female characters; it is about the novel of development as a genre and how women writers might challenge received definitions; it is also very much about the development of feminist criticism in the United States—its recent controversies and many contributions. The gynocritical readings at the heart of the book and each of its chapters could not have been written without the gorgeous explosion of feminist theories and interpretations that occurred throughout the 1980s as this project was taking shape. These analyses of women's writing are framed, as the entire book is framed, by metacritical considerations most fully elaborated in chapters 1 and 5. There I explore differences among feminist approaches as well as the differences made by feminist interventions into genre criticism and literary studies generally. This book is, finally, also bound up with my own development as a woman and feminist in the academy, and here I would like briefly to describe some of the critical assumptions and agendas underlying my arguments in the pages to come.

I begin, and this study begins, with the investment in women's writing so powerfully articulated in the late 1970s and early 1980s by such American critics as Elaine Showalter, Sandra Gilbert and Susan Gubar, and Nancy K. Miller, among a great many others. My purpose in this case is less to recuperate neglected works (though such an impulse is present in my treatment of conduct materials by women) than to appreciate the peculiarity and off-centeredness of even canonical female texts: the marks of gender and gender resentment obscured by traditional readings and pointing in the direction of new interpretive paradigms. One need hardly scratch the surface to perceive the significance for the novelists I discuss of *writing as women*: witness Burney's unproduced plays, Austen's self-deprecating anonymity, and Brontë's and Eliot's use of male pseudonyms. For these novelists, as for the female courtesy writers of chapter 1, gender (along with class, nationality, and a host of other social positionings) was not only a symbolic construction but also a closely lived reality and material condition of their writing. This is not to imply that works by these women are simple transcriptions of their female experience—much less that they are uniformly imbued with some essentially "feminine" quality. I would say, however, that we may distinguish them by the intensity of their talk about female destiny, their dense accumulation of cultural discourses regarding the "feminine," and above all by their stake in those discourses that construe women as active subjects. The historical particularity as well as multiplicity of these discourses, the fact that some ideologies and not others were in circulation as these women took pen in hand, sets my texts off from "feminine writing" monolithically conceived. At the same time, the special *interest* of these writers in testing Georgian and Victorian truisms about womanhood—their preoccupation with and ability to benefit from such an inquiry—gives their work a demonstrably gendered accent. Following Mary Poovey, Judith Lowder Newton, Hazel Carby, Cora Kaplan, and others, I am attracted, then, to a feminist historicism that counters the essentializing tendencies of some 1970s American feminist criticism even as it reclaims the referent abandoned by poststructuralism. It is, one might say, precisely an attention to history—to the details of a certain moment— that at once explodes any universal notion of Woman, and puts flesh and blood on the frame of "gender," making visible its real and specific meanings for women day to day. Such an attention is perhaps one way of (a)voiding the debate over essentialism that, as Teresa de Lauretis notes, has all too often been an exercise in ranking feminisms, asserting the theoretical correctness of antiessentialist stances and disparaging others accordingly (255–70).

So I am after a poetics of women's writing, which chapters 1 and 4 begin to situate historically. This said, however, I should repeat that I look to women's writing for new modes of interpretation and see this book primarily as a model for *reading as a woman*—less a genealogy of the female novel of development in its historical contexts, than a critique of old explanations in favor of another instrumentality. The view I am proposing depends, I have suggested, on a poststructuralist sense of identity as conflicted and provisional, involving not one but many developmental narratives. Going further, I would say that these narratives do not simply proceed toward the destination of adulthood but go on themselves to constitute the adult self, which is always fluid and emergent. My readings in effect disperse the individual into a set of trajectories, suspend her in a series of ongoing stories. In my recasting of the novel of development along these lines I depart, however, from the poststructuralist in at least two ways. First, as I have stressed in the paragraph above, the developmental narratives I trace do not refer only to themselves or each other but finally, in some grossly mediated way, to the plotting of women's lives in history. Second, my emphasis on open-endedness over closure, on contradiction over consistency, should be distinguished from what, in some poststructuralist readings, amounts to a favoring of indeterminacy seemingly for its own sake—a kind of aesthetics of "mess." For me, once again, the appeal of ideological disarray is the room it leaves for oppositional impulses; dissent is made possible not by entering some fourth dimension beyond ideology, but by recognizing that no ideology is singular or seamless, that there are always voices disputing the dominant view, if only we would hear them. So while I see my texts as highly ambiguous, serving as well as betraying the regime of female propriety, I choose for political reasons to tease out the feminist content, to privilege the resisting stories or counternarratives. Indeed, such a choice is arguably what defines my strategy as feminist, setting it apart both from poststructuralism and from that new historicism in which dissent is always already policed.

These are some of the personal presuppositions at work in the following chapters. They are not, of course, actually personal or original any more than the narratives I treat are merely private fantasies. The stories I tell about myself are meaningless outside the institutions, occasions, and people who have helped to shape them and who precede this book in every important sense. I am glad for the opportunity, at long last, to acknowledge them here. The Women's Studies Program at Barnard College first gave me the chance to teach students who, when they weren't out demonstrating, were pushing me to think more clearly about all kinds of women's issues. The University of Virginia granted me two Faculty Fellowships for Summer Research and a Fourth Year Research Assignment, and these were crucial to the project's completion. The University of Virginia's Regent's College Program enabled me to spend a renovative semester teaching in London and spending time in the British Library. The Jane Austen Society of North America provided an unusually well-informed audience for some of my ideas about *Pride and Prejudice*. A special session on women and the *Bildungsroman* at the 1988 MLA helped me to see where my readings were tending in theoretical terms; I am grateful to copanelists Linda Hunt, Elizabeth Langland, and particularly to Carol Lazzaro-Weis, who was responsible for the session's title, now the title of my first chapter. I am

also indebted to the Virginia Feminist Theory Group, which, in its
many incarnations, has been a key source of intellectual stimulation
and political support.

At various stages, a number of people generously commented on all
or part of this manuscript. For their careful and perceptive readings, I
want very much to thank Jonathan Arac, Alison Booth, Rachel Brownstein, Paul Cantor, Ralph Cohen, Beth Kowaleski-Wallace, Joseph Lit-
vak, Pat Spacks, Garrett Stewart, and Patsy Yaeger. Thanks are also due
to Virginia Germino and Gena McKinley for their scrupulous help in
preparing the manuscript. It is impossible to express, much less ever
begin to repay, the debt I owe to my teachers. Carol Kay first inspired
me with her brilliance and encouraged my early efforts. Carolyn
Heilbrun and Nancy Miller have, separately and together, supported
me at every step and given me, or so it seems, the very language I speak.
As for Debbie McDowell, Debra Nystrom, and Jahan Ramazani, their
smartness and friendship have been invaluable, and I thank them.
What I owe to Eric Lott is difficult to say, since it gets harder all the
time to tell where his ideas end and mine begin. For his collaboration in
everything, my thanks are boundless and my debt ongoing.

UNBECOMING WOMEN

CHAPTER ONE

Is There a Female *Bildungsroman?*

THIS is a book about girls entering the world, about how that difficulty is narrated by four women novelists writing in England between 1778 and 1860. Among the questions it raises are some concerning generic classification: what kind of novels are these, and how do they fit into the usual box marked "apprentice novel" or "novel of development" or, that mystifying term, *Bildungsroman?* I want to begin therefore by stating some of my assumptions about the practice of genre criticism. According to Northrop Frye, "the poet's intention to produce a poem normally includes the genre, the intention of producing a specific kind of verbal structure" (246). We may take Frye to represent that view of genre as something the poet deliberately "puts in" and that the critic at some later date "finds." The discovery may be mixed, a generic ore rather than pure substance, but it is seen to inhere patiently in the text. I am intrigued, however, by a passing remark Frye makes about Anthony Trollope—that his "novels" were read during World War II as "romances" (307)—for here he implies that genres are not in fact static and that what critics think they are reading depends on when they are reading it, on the agendas and antagonisms of a particular time. This is to say that Frye's essentialist theory of genres leans, at points such as this, in a poststructuralist direction, toward a view of genre as not found but invented by critics to specific explanatory ends. Such a view collapses Tzvetan Todorov's famous distinction between "historical" and "theoretical" genres by insisting that all generic categories are to some degree theorized. It argues that critics never just stumble across "the novel" and carry it gently, still intact, into the museum of literary history. Rather, they construct a theory of the novel that selects a few features of certain texts as fundamentally defining, and while these are rendered legible and meaningful, other features and other texts recede from sight. Nor is there any such thing as a strictly theoretical genre in Todorov's abstract, "scientific" sense, since critical workers occupy a place in history and society that necessarily inflects their generic schema. [1]

It is this view of genres as constructed and ideologically laden, particularly as it has been elaborated by feminist and Marxist critics, that informs the present study. [2] I will be assuming, for example, that genre criticism plays a key role in canon formation both by policing individual categories and by maintaining hierarchical relationships among categories; that it regulates not only which texts we read but also, by alerting us to some elements over others, how we are able to read them. The point is not that we should struggle free of genre altogether—as some champions of postmodern writing have implied[3]—for writing (like everything else) can hardly escape the discursive habit of sorting into "kinds," is indeed only readable in terms of these kinds. What we can do, however, is examine the patterns of inclusion and exclusion fostered by a given category, consider the explanations it is capable of yielding, identify the ideas and values on which it relies and that it reproduces, and evaluate these in relation to our own political commitments. My preliminary purpose here is an ideological analysis of the category *Bildungsroman* as it has been used in discussions of the English novel. I do this by way of clearing some space for my own readings of novels about female development—readings that suggest a swerve from ruling definitions of the genre. Frye remarked that "the forms of prose fiction are mixed, like racial strains in human beings, not separable like the sexes" (305), apparently rejecting gender as a figure for genre. I, however, will be taking for granted that the forms of prose fiction are frequently in some sense "female" or "male." Certainly the *Bildungsro-*

man has been defined in terms of works by, about, and appealing to men. One goal of this project, like that of much feminist criticism, is to see how attention to works by, about, and appealing to a female readership transforms our thinking about narratives of growing up.[4] Yet this is not to perceive the sexes as essentially "separable," and if our lived gender is more complex than this, so inevitably is fiction. What I produce from novels by Frances Burney, Jane Austen, Charlotte Brontë, and George Eliot is never an entirely "other" story of becoming adult—in Nancy K. Miller's phrase, never an "exclusive alterity" ("Emphasis," 342). Instead I will be tracing out a messy rivalry of stories, many significantly "female," others engaged by and struggling with the conventional *Bildungsroman.*

II

The term *Bildungsroman* is said to have been suggested by Friedrich von Blanckenburg's discussion of *Bildung* in his 1774 "Essay on the Novel," and Karl von Morgenstern actually coined it around 1820 in two lectures on the "Essence" and "History" of this contemporary form. But the person most often associated with its origin is the philosopher Wilhelm Dilthey, whose 1870 biography of Friedrich Schleiermacher certainly popularized, if it did not actually introduce, the German genre. Elaborating on this in 1906, Dilthey offered what has become the most frequently cited definition of the type.[5] Most important, in both 1870 and 1906 he yoked the *Bildungsroman* firmly to Goethe's 1795 novel, *Wilhelm Meisters Lehrjahre.* Subsequent theorists of the German *Bildungsroman* include Hans Heinrich Borcherdt (1955), Fritz Martini (1961), Hartmut Steinecke (1975), and Martin Swales (1978), to name only a few. At what point, however, and on what terms did the *Bildungsroman* begin to organize our thinking about the British novel? How was its transposition from one national literature to another accomplished and with what ideological consequences? We could, of course, return all the way to Thomas Carlyle, who in 1824 translated Goethe's novel as *Wilhelm Meister's Apprenticeship.* But while Carlyle made Goethe (hitherto known primarily for *The Sorrows of Young Werther*) more widely available to the English, the gathering around Wilhelm Meister of his "English kinsmen," the explicit nomination of an

English family of texts seen to descend from *Wilhelm Meister*, did not happen for another hundred years. Focusing on this neglected moment of the *Bildungsroman*'s emergence into English critical discourse, I hope to offer a vantage point from which to look back toward Dilthey and Carlyle as well as forward to common usage in the Anglo-American academy.

In 1930 Susanne Howe published *Wilhelm Meister and his English Kinsmen: Apprentices to Life*. The term *Bildungsroman* would still not appear in English-language dictionaries or literary handbooks until the 1950s, yet the novels Howe affiliated with the German paradigm—by Carlyle, Edward Bulwer-Lytton, Benjamin Disraeli, John Sterling, G. H. Lewes, J. A. Froude, Geraldine Jewsbury, and Charles Kingsley—would lay the groundwork for ensuing English claims to Goethe's legacy. In fact since Howe, these claims have generally been assumed rather than systematically argued; casual appeals to the English genre have been many, formal attempts to codify it few. And those formal studies that do exist, notably G. B. Tennyson's essay (1968) and Jerome Buckley's book, *Season of Youth* (1974), owe much to Howe—if not for their selection of texts, then for the principles underlying their selection.[6] But I will concentrate on Howe not only because she put into place a working definition of the English category; more than this, her landmark book also began to test the limits of this definition.

We may begin with Howe's rendering of *Bildungsroman* as "apprentice novel" (rather than as the more literal "novel of formation"), for this decision has several implications. *Apprentice* refers, first, to Carlyle's translation of Goethe's title. While insisting that for the English Goethe is mediated by Carlyle, it nevertheless perpetuates the German tradition of citing *Wilhelm Meister* as originary text—the significance of which will be apparent shortly.[7] Second, *apprentice* refers to a vocational practice and chronology. Its meaning for Goethe is illustrated by a passage from his *Ferneres über Weltliteratur*, which Howe reproduces:

> Let everyone ask himself for what he is best fitted, that he may develop himself zealously for this, and by means of it. He may regard himself as an apprentice, then as a journeyman, and finally, but only with great caution, as a master.   (Howe, 25)

Mapping the apprentice novel in terms of this straightforward sequence, Howe defines it as an inherently optimistic form. G. B. Tennyson, too, will later stress that it posits a single, well-marked, "right" path and a protagonist who, finding this path, climbs predictably from stage to higher stage (137). Thus *apprentice* implies not only youth and inexperience, but also (what Wilhelm's patronym spells out) eventual *mastery* (Howe, 4). Becoming a master requires guidance, and Howe, like Jerome Buckley, further notes that *mentors* are necessary to the student of life (Howe, 3; Buckley, 19). While the *Bildungsroman* is usually distinguished by German scholars from the *Erziehungsroman* with its focus on formal schooling, in *Wilhelm Meister* the true mentors turn out to be members of a secret society who supervise Wilhelm's development in an organized, quasi-institutional way.

Finally, as the passage above suggests, apprenticeship seems to imply *choice*. It does not, as it did for so many years under the guild system, mean being indentured to one's father's trade, born to a particular kind of work and social status without having much to say about it. Nor does it mean the later, less familial, industrial relation of worker to capitalist and the hardly chosen binding of man to machine instead of master. Rather, Wilhelm and his kinsmen look around, ask themselves where their unique talents lie, and self-consciously determine to cultivate those talents. As Howe puts it, the form represents the hero "choosing his friends, his wife, and his life work" (4) and chronicles his educative wrong choices en route to right ones. Thematized thus, at least one of the genre's ideological functions seems clear: emergent in the late eighteenth century as surplus labor was being ever more efficiently extracted, this representation of apprenticeship helped to construct the normative, middle-class man whose skills and labor are his own. Whatever impact capitalization actually had on the organization of work, the Wilhelm Meister narrative participated in a mythology of vocational choice, of the worker as free individual—in effect rationalizing the shift from the first, residually feudal scenario to the second, factory-based one. [8] The continuing relevance of this mythology should be obvious, and perhaps it begins to explain the appeal of Goethe's paradigm for many twentieth-century American critics.

It may come as no surprise that another bit of ideological work accomplished by Howe's paradigm (influenced by Dilthey and elaborated by Tennyson and Buckley) is to define development in emphatically masculine terms—for the contemporaneous heroine's relation to choice, mentors, and mastery is rather different. Her finding of friends, her picking of work are both subsumed by the single, all-determining "choice" of a husband, and even this (turning down a Mr. Collins, seeing through the blandishments of a Wickham) is a mostly negative prerogative. The myth of bourgeois opportunity has little place for the middle-class female protagonist, and to reinvent the genre around her is to recognize a set of stories in which compromise and even coercion are more strongly thematized than choice. Of course the Wilhelms and Pips get buffeted around as well and feel themselves in the hands of some higher power, but willful self-making is still the keynote of their stories, and self-regard is still the decisive factor. The heroines I will consider have, by contrast, a clearer sense that formation is foisted upon them, that they are largely what other people, what the world, will make of them. The typical girl also has trouble with mentors. She rarely has a formal education, mothers are usually either dead or deficient as models, and the lessons of older men are apt to have voluptuous overtones; though she may spend the whole novel in search of positive maternal figures, it is too often true that her one mentor is the man who schools her in order to wed her. And finally, consequently, when the mentor is a husband and when apprenticeship reduces to a process of marital binding, it never leads the heroine to mastery but only to a lifetime as perennial novice. That the usual parameters of Georgian and Victorian womanhood preclude the goals of progress and mastery suggests to me that the female "apprentice" novel is split at the root, divided over what female formation is and uncertain about what it should be. The following chapters construct the novel of development precisely in terms of conflict and uncertainty, of dissenting narratives that break away and stray beyond the bounds of Howe's formulation and of those modeled after hers.

I would like to look more closely at Howe's description of the classic developmental path. First and foremost, like those precursor genres the picaresque and romance (5), it involves travel.[9] As Howe says, "Going somewhere is the thing. And there—in all sorts of tempting variety— is your story" (1). Whether a soldier like Xenophon's Cyrus, a bourgeois boy on a bohemian ramble like Wilhelm, or one of Bulwer-Lytton's dandies on a grand tour of Europe, the hero begins his *Bildung* by leaving home and going abroad—a point repeated by Buckley, who gives it an oedipal twist (*Season*, 17–20). Needless to say, middle-class heroines can do this only at the risk (or in the aftermath) of infamy; as Burney's last novel, *The Wanderer*, argues, if the roaming protagonist happens to be a woman, the subtitle of her life is sure to be *Female Difficulties*. Mobility is difficult for women not only in their own stories but also in Howe's male-centered texts, where static female figures, "more or less symbolic of the stages he has reached on his pilgrimage" (50), measure out the hero's progress. [10] This making of women into milestones is, moreover, replicated and further naturalized by Howe's own recounting of the lives of male writers. She writes of Goethe, for example, stalled on *Wilhelm Meister*: "The connection with Frau von Stein was broken; Christiane Vulpius, according to many opinions, was not adequate to share Goethe's ideas about his literary work" (48); and similarly of Carlyle in the spring of 1819: "He had not met Jane Welsh as yet. . . . [He] was still languishing a little for Margaret Gordon, and reading Kant and Fichte and *Faust*" (84).

As their serial encounters with women suggest, for Wilhelm and his peers heterosexual adventures are favored in the world's curriculum. Buckley says that "at least two love affairs or sexual encounters, one debasing, one exalting" are typical of male *Bildungsromane* (17), and Howe notes that "both [Wilhelm and Wieland's Agathon] are irresistibly attractive to women. They have a way of letting things happen to them" (30). In the formation of their female counterparts, by contrast, sex plays a less positive role. In fact the female protagonist's progress, at least until the twentieth century, is generally contingent on avoiding the abyss of extramarital sexuality, on successfully preventing "things" from happening to her. Her paradoxical task is to see the world while avoiding violation by the world's gaze. [11] Appearance on the theatrical stage, for instance, an important chapter in Wilhelm's story, contributes to a heroine's development only insofar as she resolutely shuns it, as Fanny Price does in *Mansfield Park*. It is true that Goethe himself was ambivalent about theater; while it is Wilhelm's ultimate mission in an earlier version of *Meister* (*Wilhelm Meisters Theatralische Sendung*), in the final edition theater is but the brief means to a nobler end, and later *Bildungsromane* seem to drop it entirely. I would argue three things, however. First, theater remains a nonetheless significant trope in *Wilhelm Meister*, central to a cluster of essentially Romantic themes. Second, Howe and her followers, looking reflexively to Goethe, have invariably seized on this Romantic cluster (if not on theater itself) in characterizing the English *Bildungsroman*. And third, for a variety of reasons, not least among them its aura of immorality, this Goethean motif becomes highly problematic in the context of novels about bourgeois female development.

During his theatrical interlude Wilhelm dedicates himself to Shakespeare, starring in the company's production of *Hamlet* and evincing, in his devotion to the bard, the reverence for "genius" characteristic of the Romantic period in general. And while Tennyson and Buckley both remark that in England the *Bildungsroman* does not arise until the early Victorian period (Tennyson, 139; Buckley, 13), Buckley follows Howe in depicting its heroes as "more sensitive and more gifted than the average young man" (Howe, 6), reiterating just this Romantic infatuation with the anomalous artist. In fact, much of Buckley's book goes to proving the autobiographical nature of the English *Bildungsroman*, so that its protagonists tend to be writers or artists of some kind, and the category itself slides into the *Künstlerroman* (13). If critics of the English genre look back to Goethe for his elevation of poets to a spiritual elite, they do so also for his culture's interest—again like Wilhelm's own— in self-staging, in taking one's formation into one's own hands, theatricalizing one's life. Yet both this cult of the genius and this mania for narrating one's own origins run up hard against nineteenth-century views of proper female development. For a girl taught that to be exceptional is to be morally suspect, that "the happiest women," in George Eliot's words, "have no history" (*The Mill on the Floss*, 335), such Romantic notions are only partly available. Of course, there were women cultivating their genius and scripting female destiny at this time, Austen and Eliot among them, but the conception of artistic selfhood augured by Wilhelm's identification with Shakespeare was, nevertheless, distinctly male. Indeed as Marlon Ross, among a host of critics now exploring the gender politics of the Romantic period, has argued:

> Romanticism is historically a masculine phenomenon. Romantic poetizing is not just what women cannot do because they are not expected to; it is also what some men do in order to reconfirm their capacity to influence the world in ways socio-historically determined as masculine. The categories of gender, both in their lives and in

their work, help the Romantics establish rites of passage toward poetic identity and toward masculine empowerment.   (29)

Wilhelm Meister has, in short, been delivered over to a Romantic ideology about the forging of poetic identity that turns out to be intrinsically male, and the effect of continually harking back to this text is to elide the other kinds of more hesitant and conflicted narratives that may bring young girls to womanhood. I would argue, further, that the Anglicizing and Victorianizing of Goethe by Carlyle only intensifies this effect. For Howe tells us that what Carlyle drew from *Wilhelm Meister* was a lesson in "the sane and corrective power of action" (10), so that he tips the German ideal of balance between the inner and outer life in favor of the latter. If the figure of Hamlet is offered as a prototype for the young Wilhelm, Carlyle's *Meister* is the story of a Hamlet who shakes off his moodiness and turns from introspection to useful work. And though Wilhelm is never so reflective as the character he plays, he still encounters the interpolated "Confessions of a Beautiful Soul" as a cautionary tale; Howe notes that this dead woman's autobiography, tracing her departure from the material world on a path of exclusively spiritual development, serves as a negative example for Wilhelm (55). As a result of her intervening story, the contemplative, unworldly, too earnestly spiritual, not to mention writerly, is gendered *female*, and Wilhelm reaches manhood by looking down this path in awe—before going another way. It is tempting to see this as a staging of the male writer's own anxiety as he himself displays traits commonly coded as "feminine"; at the very least, it specifies the masculinity of the work-oriented *Bildung* Carlyle gleaned from Goethe, while it repudiates female development as ghostly, reclusive, and short. [12]

Tennyson's and Buckley's extension of Howe's basic paradigm to the works of writers (particularly Dickens) more central to the conventional English canon was also an attempt to shift the category itself, previously of "marginal interest" (Tennyson, 142), closer to the center of the critical lexicon. While making broader claims for its occurrence, they followed Howe's precedent of deriving the form from Goethe and, reinforcing this derivation while heightening the genre's incantatory power in English-speaking circles, reverted to the untranslated German term. [13] The continual fetishizing of *Wilhelm Meister* as originary

text, even by many revisionist critics, has not only defended as normative the single path of middle-class, male development described
above, eclipsing all others; not only established a canon of overwhelm-
ingly male-authored and male-centered texts; it has also to a large degree fetishized Wilhelm himself. Indeed, as Howe's title suggests,
there has been a tendency to think of the tradition as a family not of
texts but of personages: Wilhelm and his kinsmen. The effect of this has
been to define the genre in terms of a single heroic figure and to privilege an approach that emphasizes character. Thus, while critics note
the influence of the picaresque on the *Bildungsroman*, the predominant
models for reading it have been the confession, the autobiography, and
the biography, with their interest in psychology over episode. [14] At the
risk of simplifying a good many richly textured arguments, I would say
that discussions of the genre have generally made it coextensive with
the experience of the *Bildungsheld*, equating it with the destiny of this
one figure, whose movements are tracked, detectivelike, to the exclusion of other movements or meanings.

Such a strategy of reading grows logically out of what has been seen
as the *Bildungsroman*'s essential faith in the ability of individuals, however laboriously tried, to weather "plot" and affirm the sovereignty of
"character." Yet as I have suggested, the stories of middle-class female
protagonists rarely demonstrate this faith; on the contrary, they tend to
insist that personal destiny evolves in dialectical relation to historical
events, social structures, and other people. More than this, I find in my
four novelists a blurring or decentering of the "major" narrative by alternative stories of female destiny, so that each text is less the telling of
one life than a struggle between rival life stories. In *Pride and Prejudice*,
for example, the often reiterated tale of Elizabeth's enlightenment as to
Darcy's true character and her own true feelings is countered, in my
reading, by the overlapping tale of her "humiliation." The "other" stories I assemble are typically demystifications of this kind—rewriting
the heroine's rise to happy maturity as a history of obstruction, imposi-
tion, and loss. In their tones of terror and rage, my counternarratives
imply that the disreputable gothic novel may account more plausibly
for the passage to bourgeois womanhood than the classic *Bildungsroman*. In addition, though less confidently, they may begin to reconceive
a girl's progress as the building of solidarity between women or as the

scaling of an intellectual summit. Yet it must be remembered that the critiques and potential compensations implied by these alternative stories are only tentatively offered, for the dominant narrative continues, simultaneously, to retain tremendous power and appeal. Novels by Burney, Austen, Brontë, and Eliot suggest that, riven by contradiction, female development (and perhaps development generally) may be mapped onto antagonistic plots that are never finally reconciled.

Women writers (including three of my four novelists) and even several of my points about them are actually imminent in but also—with obvious effort—suppressed from Susanne Howe's analysis. Jane Austen surfaces on the very first page (regarding Howe's association of *Bildung* with travel) only to be set aside and indefinitely postponed: "After all—putting aside for the moment Miss Austen's *Emma* and a few other magnificent exceptions—no one can learn much of anything at home" (1). Austen reappears later, again as an exception to the rule, the only figure during the Romantic period unreceptive to foreign, and particularly German, influence (127). Madame de Staël, whose *Corinne* must have suggested itself as a splendid female *Künstlerroman*, comes up only in relation to Carlyle: he had read her *Germany* and remarked on her death that she was "very ugly and very immoral" but still the "loftiest" female soul of her day (83). Charlotte Brontë is mentioned because she received letters from George Lewes proving his critical acuity (224); *Jane Eyre*, difficult to ignore in this context, is cited because Geraldine Jewsbury read the novel and apparently preferred Lewes's *Ranthorpe* (240). (It is true that Dickens and Thackeray are also omitted, but their absence is carefully accounted for [14].) And finally George Eliot, the one woman whose *The Mill on the Floss* made it into subsequent canons (those of Wagner, Tennyson, and Buckley), is literally suspended in parentheses and effectively superseded by Goethe: "Before he saw Germany again (in company with George Eliot, many years later), Lewes had evidently read and studied Goethe carefully" (222).

I am persuaded that the frequent recurrence and forcible bracketing of these women amounts to an underlying, alternative narrative of female destiny in Howe's own text, which continually challenges the official premises of her study. Only with the treatment of Jewsbury does it finally break into the open, and at this point (much as Howe would link Jewsbury to Lewes instead of Brontë) two pieces of the pattern I associate with female developmental fiction begin to be discernible. First, the primacy of relations between women in such fictions is neatly displaced from Howe's treatment of the novels onto her framing account of Jewsbury's own formation, in which Jane Carlyle figures significantly. Though embarrassed by its "childish" emotionality, Howe describes Carlyle's friendship as "the one great, abiding joy of [Jewsbury's] life" and comments gratefully on its preservation in letters (242). Second, unlike any of the works previously discussed by Howe, Jewsbury's *Zoe* (1845) and *The Half Sisters* (1848) are both explicitly bifurcated texts. Split between the destinies of two characters, they support my claim that formation for women, because uniquely controversial, tends to occasion narrative disunity. Howe goes so far as to remark that Jewsbury brought to the conventional form "her own passionate interest in the position of women, and gave the old pattern some fresh material to work upon" (251), and in this Howe begins to articulate the feminist project at hand. Texts interested in women do indeed rework the old *Bildungsroman* pattern, providing us as critics with fresh material and unsettling the ways we routinely think about narratives of development.

In the following chapters I will be reading some of this material not for how it pictures the dawning of coherent female selfhood, but rather for how it positions young women amid many incoherent and class-specific notions about girls becoming women. Instead of reconceiving the genre in terms of the different road taken by the female individual, I suggest we locate its multiple narratives within a larger, cacophonous discourse about female formation. I want, in short, to rephrase the usual questions—"How does the hero of this novel come of age? What are the stages that mark his passage to maturity?"—as "What are the several developmental narratives at work in this novel and what can they tell us about competing ideologies of the feminine?" To speak, as I will, of *plural formations* is to apply the lessons of recent critical theory in two respects: first, by seeing "integrated" selfhood as the clashing, patchwork product of numerous social determinations, the "I" as basically unstable and discontinuous; and second, by acknowledging that formation is differentiated in terms of, say, class, country, race, and time as well as gender, so that in this sense, too, it is no longer possible to speak of a uniform fiction of female development. The rival narratives I discuss in *Jane Eyre*, for example, correspond to the bivalent class status of the governess. Finally, while I will be looking at "female" texts whose high degree of internal conflict seems to reward the approach I propose, I ultimately offer it as well for a reconsideration of "male" texts, which may evince greater, but by no means total, consensus about what makes a man.

III

If Howe is right that Austen was less indebted to German models than her male contemporaries, on what discourse did she draw (and to what did she contribute) in wondering what would become of her Elizabeths and Emmas? In the section that follows I want to look briefly at the narration of female development by a selection of "conduct" or "courtesy" books written between the 1760s and 1840s and to suggest that these popular guides, as much if not more than *Wilhelm Meister* and its kindred texts, mark out a discursive context for the novels that concern me here. Only for Eliot is *Wilhelm Meister* a primary intertext, and her imagination also continues to be shaped by those representations popularized by conduct books and similar materials addressed to women. And perhaps this is the time to jettison once and for all the notion of a "female *Bildungsroman*"—by uncoupling these two terms to release our discussion of female developmental fiction from so much Goethean baggage and relinquish the appeal to any single, authoritative because originary, novel of formation, whether female or male. We recur to the *Bildungsroman* from now on as but one among many narrative models; attractive but problematic for female protagonists, it is invoked by my women writers only to be broken up and dispersed by other arguably more compelling accounts of entering the world. I turn to conduct literature then—in particular to the works of Sarah Pennington, Ann Murry, Hester Chapone, and Sarah Stickney Ellis—to identify an additional, widely available, and demonstrably salient set of stories about coming into womanhood. Without attempting a comprehensive survey of courtesy literature (much less the range of related genres, which might include diaries, educational dialogues, ladies' magazines, sermons, and children's fiction), I offer the works of these four women to sketch out in some preliminary way, as well as to historicize, the contradictory narratives I find in my four novelists.

My precedents for introducing conduct books directed toward women into a discussion of women's novels are several. In 1950 Joyce Hemlow first called attention to these influential didactic texts, arguing that novelists such as Burney "attempted to justify and dignify their new art by including [in their novels] the reputable and useful matter of the courtesy books" (757). Hemlow even calls *Camilla* (1796) a "courtesy novel," and notes that while novelists sought to gain respectability by incorporating material from courtesy books, so courtesy book writers sought to trade on the popularity of novels by employing novelistic devices (757). Some writers, Wollstonecraft and Edgeworth for example, tried their hand at both genres. If the eighteenth-century novel was, in general, highly permeable—emerging as a genre by scavenging from (and corrupting) others—then we should think of women's conduct books and novels as particularly contiguous and interpenetrating forms. In keeping with this point, Nancy Armstrong has recently implicated courtesy literature along with the rising novel in what she sees as a domestication or "feminization" of culture beginning in the late eighteenth century and coincident with the making of the middle class. Key to this argument is the fact that, as Hemlow observes, courtesy books for women reached a peak between 1760 and 1820 (although many continued to be reprinted well into the Victorian era)—just as the novel of manners was coming into being (732). Armstrong adds that, until the end of the seventeenth century, most courtesy literature was written for aristocratic men (61). From the genre's subsequent proliferation and redirection toward middle-class women, it seems clear that bourgeois womanhood was under especially intense construction at this time, and that novels as well as conduct books were part of the attempt to articulate and manage this new icon.

While I coincide with Hemlow and Armstrong in emphasizing the continuity between these two kinds of contemporary texts, their overlapping interest in female formation and their collaboration in producing a notion of the "feminine" bound up with notions of the middle class, I would challenge the view of both forms as simply and unanimously invested in the emergent ideal, what Mary Poovey has called the "proper lady."[15] For while acknowledging the many, mixed sources on which the discourse of domesticity drew, Armstrong claims the ideology of femininity offered by conduct books was able "to suppress the very conflicts so evident in the bewildering field of dialects comprising this body of writing" (69). She argues not only the internal coherence of this ideal but also its uniformity across works, thereby justifying her treatment of "these quite different texts as a single voice and continuous discourse" (94). This "single voice" is assumed to be that of the dominant culture, so that for Armstrong, as for the majority of critics, "conduct-book morality" is synonymous with a grim conservatism. I will be arguing, by contrast, that conduct books, like novels, are often profoundly inconsistent in relation to female formation, that they characteristically contest the dominant narrative as it appears in both their own and other works.

As my choice of guides implies, I would distinguish here between those written by women (usually addressed to daughters, nieces, or female students) and those by male professionals such as the Reverend James Fordyce or Doctor John Gregory—the former seem to me particularly compelled out of the beaten path and into other developmental ways. In addition, I agree on the one hand with Armstrong's major, crucial point that domestic fiction and guidebooks contributed to the class formation of the bourgeoisie: by formulating as "feminine" an ethic based on inner moral worth as opposed to inherited status, they produced the conception of subjectivity on which middle-class identity and hegemony would be based (14). Yet I want on the other hand to insist that even as their modeling of gender worked to reorganize society in class terms, these texts could hardly help enforcing ideologies of femaleness and maleness that were *lived as such*, inescapably, from day to day. Indeed Armstrong tends to forget that gender does more than simply code class: it is one of the most deeply felt ways in which class status is played out.[16] I look therefore to conduct literature for versions of a struggle among constructions of the feminine that are always lived concurrently with those of class; for some sense of what could be thought about female development at a particular time, a rough guide to the landmarks and limits of this discursive terrain; and for the preview it offers of the play among developmental narratives in *Evelina* (1778), *Pride and Prejudice* (1813), *Jane Eyre* (1847), and *The Mill on the Floss* (1860) that is the subject of subsequent chapters.

My sampling of conduct books by and for women indicates two major nodes of conflict, two areas of dense ambivalence about how to plot a girl's life. One area concerns what we could loosely call affiliation: the desire for dyadic, familial, and also wider communal ties. The other area has to do with ambition, especially the ambition to study, to gain intellectual authority, and perhaps to write.[17] I begin first with affiliation and its usual reliance on the trajectory of courtship, marriage, and motherhood. Not surprisingly, this heterosexual series is largely taken for granted by each of my texts—with the significant exception of Murry, to whom I will return later—and by the courtesy books and novels of the period in general. Most guides not only recommend a sequence closing with the marital and maternal, but also, novel-like, reproduce this sequence in their own structures. It is not unusual to move, as Sarah Ellis does in *The Daughters of England* (1842), through such topics as "Taste, Tact, and Observation" to "Love and Courtship," which, as the tenth of twelve chapters, occupies the position of climax or goal, reached presumably by means of taste and tact. Hester Chapone's *Letters on the Improvement of the Mind*, first published in 1772 and reissued continually until as late as 1877, included in many editions after 1777 an appended "Letter to a New-Married Lady," so that even the story of mental improvement appears to culminate with marriage. Lady Pennington's book of maternal advice—which went into seven editions in the years 1761–1790 and, like Chapone's, reappeared throughout the first half of the nineteenth century—acquired in 1817 an "Additional Letter On the Management and Education of Infant Children." Its effect is similarly to drive the events and energies of girlhood to the finish line of wife- and motherhood.

The very shape of these narratives supports an ideology of romance that rigidly equates female maturity and gratification with the married state, and Chapone, "recommending your husband to be your first and dearest friend" ("New-Married," 122), is not alone in seeing the conjugal relation as primary. Yet, as in the novels that concern me here (which, except for *The Mill on the Floss*, all lead to the altar), a great deal of space in Pennington, Chapone, and Ellis is devoted to the difficulties and risks involved in finding and wedding this "first and dearest friend."[18] As Chapone laments (addressing her niece):

> Young women know so little of the world, especially of the other sex, and such pains are usually taken to deceive them, that they are every way unqualified to choose for themselves, upon their own judgment. Many a heart-ach [sic] shall I feel for you, my sweet girl, if I live a few years longer!   (*Letters*, 93–94)

Ellis seconds this despairing view that young women can hardly make a knowing choice of husband, that men are all too likely to deceive, and wives to suffer:

> "But how are we to know a man's real character?" is the common question of young women. Alas! there is much willing deception on this point. Yet, I must confess, that men are seldom thoroughly known, except under their own roof, or amongst their own companions.   (230)

The safest procedure, advises Ellis, is to infer how a man will treat his wife from how he behaves with his mother and sisters (230).

Lady Pennington worries similarly lest her daughters pledge obedience to a man whose surface "Good Humour" has been mistaken for genuine "Good Nature" (60–62). Anticipating the abused mother/heroine of Mary Wollstonecraft's *Maria* (1798), Pennington warns that a bad-hearted husband is "the worst of all temporal ills—a deadly potion, that imbitters every social scene of life" (68). Like Ellis, she prays her daughters may be spared this by consulting

> the simple, unpolished sentiments of those, whose dependent connections give them an undeniable certainty—who not only see, but who hourly feel, the good or bad effects of that disposition, to which they are subjected. By this I mean, that if a man is equally respected, esteemed, and beloved by his tenants, by his dependents and domestics . . . you may justly conclude, he has that true good nature. (63–64)

Compare this with Elizabeth Bennet's reasoning about Darcy in *Pride and Prejudice*, and the resemblance reinforces our sense that Austen and Pennington were using and shaping a common language:

The commendation bestowed on him by Mrs. Reynolds was of no trifling nature. What praise is more valuable than the praise of an intelligent servant? As a brother, a landlord, a master, she considered how many people's happiness were in his guardianship!—How much of pleasure or pain it was in his power to bestow!—How much of good or evil must be done by him! (170–71)

Ellis would be glad to know that Darcy's kindness as brother to Georgiana and nephew to Lady Catherine are also major factors in Elizabeth's calculations.

But all this is only an attempt to load the dice in what Pennington describes as a losing gamble: "So great is the hazard, so disproportioned the chances, that I could almost wish the dangerous die was never to be thrown for any of you!" (56) In fact, all three writers first hold out hope for conjugal satisfaction—telling girls to choose carefully—and then proceed to assume that, at the very least, male tenderness will wane and infidelity probably ensue. Urging resignation to this likely circumstance, they offer an array of consolations. Chapone emphasizes religion and suggests that children may help to fill the void: "For their sakes life will still be valuable to you" ("New-Married," 120). She also urges "uniform adherence to your duty," and says that prospects brighten if the straying spouse is sick, in which case dutiful attendance "may at length regain his heart" ("New-Married," 119). Ellis agrees that one's own faithfulness and integrity are key, though she admits, "It may be called a cold philosophy to speak of such consolation being available under the suffering which arises from unkindness and desertion" (228). Ellis's strategy for reviving male interest is to hoard one's love: "You will want it to re-awaken the tenderness of your husband," she explains, "when worldly cares and pecuniary disappointments have too much absorbed his better feelings" (237). Pennington, too, describes jealousy as useless (80–82) and counsels "patient submission" in "dealing with a morose tyrannical temper" (71), but she alone draws the line at demands that would compromise one's principles. Sounding again surprisingly like Wollstonecraft's Maria, she informs her daughters: "All commands repugnant to the laws of christianity, it is your indispensable duty to disobey" (69–70).

If Pennington spends ten pages on what makes a good husband and fifteen on what to do if he is cruel, I suggest that so the accent of my novelists' two-suitor plot may fall as much on the hazards of a Sir Clement or St. John as it does upon the merits of another. Jane Eyre's return to Rochester coincides with realizing that St. John proposes she yield to him her very existence. Moreover, if girls are so naive and men so deceiving as Chapone and Ellis suggest, who is to say that Jane's choice of Rochester over St. John or Evelina's of Orville over Clement is actually well founded? Sharing with courtesy literature doubts about the legibility of male character, the fictional texts I examine are similarly concerned about telling the good suitor from the bad. As I shall demonstrate in chapter 2, this anxiety is especially evident in *Evelina*, in which the dream of romantic progress coexists with the nightmare of circling from bad to worse. Though rarely so explicit or pragmatic as courtesy books, women's novels of this period exhibit a matching apprehension about courtship and its aftermath. Judging by the quotations I have cited, the romantic apprenticeship proceeds in both genres with a girl's aggrieved sense that marriage will place her, no less than his tenants, servants, and other female relations, at the legally sanctioned whim of a powerful man. As Pennington points to "the *good or bad* effects of that disposition, to which they are subjected," and as Elizabeth Bennet considers "how much of *pleasure or pain* it was in his power to bestow" (my emphases), the reader is alerted in conduct book and novel alike to a rift in the romantic plot: a split between one narrative that continues pleasurably along a gentle rise and another that slopes down or spins round into pain. And as I have implied, the second, dysphoric narrative is not associated solely with the rejected suitors or with the possibility of seduction; it also runs darkly along the road to marriage with an Orville, Darcy, Rochester, or Stephen Guest. Even in the ostensibly comic novels I discuss, both stories of female development, which we might loosely call the romantic and antiromantic, recur. In the readings that follow, I want at once to stress the tension between these crisscrossing stories and to dwell on the antiromantic—not because this story is more "real," but because, in relation to axioms about developmental fiction, its disconcerting virtues are those of the perverse.

These same conduct books can help to identify still another affiliative impulse at work in the novels, a narrative that more positively counters the heterosexual by drawing women to each other. In fact, Chapone flatly contradicts "Dean Swift" who "exhorts his fair pupil to make no friendships with any of her own sex" ("New-Married," 120). Dismissing this as "preposterous advice" (121), Chapone's section "On the Regulation of the Heart and Affections" discusses relations between women at great length and treats the choosing of female friends with at least as much seriousness as the choice of a husband. Regarded in her time as the emblem of propriety, Chapone, as mentioned, is careful to privilege the conjugal tie (*Letters*, 86; "New-Married," 122) and to warn of its peculiar irrevocability (*Letters*, 93); yet the fact remains that three-quarters of her "Affections" is devoted to ties between women. Taking the standard criteria for marriage as the criteria for female friendship, she recommends to her niece an older girl, twenty-three or twenty-four, in a position to instruct. Like a spouse, the friend should be religious and of good repute, understanding, and temper (*Letters*, 73–80); she should not be inferior in birth or education (81). Echoing Pennington's advice in a different context, Chapone instructs her niece to "observe [the friend's] manner to servants and inferiors—to children—and even to animals" (78). In the same vein, she urges fidelity to such a friend and warns against the pernicious effects of jealousy (85). Finally, she ends her "Letter to a New-Married Lady" in a way that implies the priority she gives to love and trust between women. After dutifully agreeing with Swift that one's husband should be "first and dearest," Chapone closes with a sentence whose effect is subtly to displace the official mate: "I shall therefore depend on his full consent to my having always the pleasure of styling myself/ Your faithful and affectionate friend" (122).

Here I would observe several things. First, Chapone's "depend," while implying humility, means not that she breathlessly awaits the husband's consent but that she assumes or even commands it. Second, she receives his consent only to discard it in favor of her own permission: *she* styles *herself* loyal friend. Third, with the intervention of "my," repeated by "myself," Chapone appropriates not only the husband's consent, but also his *pleasure* in friendship with the "new-married lady." Signing her name at the bottom of the page, she seems to say: Though he may be "first," my name is here at the end, it is I who am faithful to the last, my pleasure is for "always"—and certainly her earlier account of marriage seems to bear this out.

Chapone's story of the love between women is present in all of my courtesy texts, whose very terms of address rely upon the mother-daughter relation. But Ellis's chapter on "Friendship and Flirtation," agreeing with Chapone on the importance of fidelity to women friends, takes this mandate a step further. Whereas Chapone is interested in the couple, the mentor-student dyad, Ellis celebrates the *circle* of "young female friends, who love and trust each other, who mutually agree to support the weak in their little community, to confirm the irresolute, to reclaim the erring, to soothe the irritable, and to solace the distressed" (199). If this sounds like some kind of proto-support group, Ellis goes on to describe a process that second-wave feminists would surely call consciousness-raising:

> In the circle of her private friends, as well as from her own heart, she learns what constitutes the happiness and the misery of woman, what is her weakness and what her need, what her bane and what her blessing. She learns to comprehend the deep mystery of that electric chain of feeling which ever vibrates through the heart of woman, and which man, with all his philosophy, can never understand. (199)

Of course Ellis's 1842 text coincided with the swelling of the first wave of the women's movement, with the writing of pamphlets and gathering of rage that produced both the 1848 meeting at Seneca Falls and, as I argue later, the publication of *Jane Eyre* in 1847. Judging by the extraordinary series of metaphors that follows this passage, Ellis herself was not unaware that female community, based on a sense of collective disadvantage, may have radical political implications. Asserting that, through close friendship with a few women, "a measure of the same sympathy and tenderness is extended to the whole sisterhood of her sex," Ellis asks the following:

> What should we think of a community of slaves, who betrayed each other's interests? of a little band of ship-wrecked mariners upon a friendless shore, who were false to each other? of the inhabitants of a defenceless nation, who would not unite together in earnestness and good faith against a common enemy? (199)

The more urgent question underlying these questions—what should a community of oppressed people do?—is never explicitly posed, but an insurrectionary answer is silently assumed until, in the final lines, it is stated/disguised as a patriotic truism: they should (naturally) unite together against a common enemy. Ellis has already mentioned her abolitionist views (66), and here she invokes slavery as a convenient code for the subjection of women and an oblique reference to their struggle for emancipation. [19] I should stress that Ellis was no Lucretia Mott; she opens *The Daughters of England* by announcing that "as women . . . the first thing of importance is to be content to be inferior to men" (8). Yet even here she seems to argue less for inferiority than contentedness, leaving room for the chance that discontented women might dispute their status, as she herself apparently does just two hundred pages later. For each of these scenarios, articulating women to each other, leads inevitably to her conclusion that women are inferior only insofar as they betray one another—whereas "in their integrity, their faithfulness, their devoted affection [to one another], they rise to an almost superhuman eminence" (200). [20] This narrative of female identity and power located in loyalty to a group, of solidarity against a "common enemy," of individual destiny linked to a common plight, offers a dramatic challenge to the plot of private romance that more typically organizes female development. We might call it, in Eve Sedgwick's sense, a narrative of the female homosocial, and in chapter 4 I will argue it is one of the stories attempted by *Jane Eyre*. [21]

Ellis closes her chapter on the "Economy of Time" with two contrasting vignettes of a wife and mother getting ready for a journey. In one case the woman has been tardy, making her last moments frantic and inefficient, causing tempers to be lost and goodbyes to be rushed, leaving the household in disorder and affections in disarray. In the other case the woman has prepared in advance; she devotes the entire last day to calm rituals of farewell; she provides in turn for each member of the household and stores up abundant tenderness for the coming separation (39–41). All very well, we might say, and perhaps Ellis is right about packing the day before, but what strikes me finally is that in both of these scenes, whether frantic or calm, a carriage is waiting outside and *a woman is leaving*. Where is this woman going? What kinds of narratives are possible for her once she leaves the family circle and even the circle of women behind? I invoke Ellis's image to turn us now to that other node of conflicting stories about female destiny, this one concerning extradomestic, solitary, and scholarly ambitions usually framed in this period as "masculine," but according to conduct books and novels cherished, nonetheless, by women. For this purpose I call first upon Ann Murry's *Mentoria; or, The Young Ladies Instructor: in Familiar Conversations, on Moral and Entertaining Subjects. Calculated to Improve Young Minds in the Essential as well as Ornamental Parts of Female Education.*

Murry's conduct book was initially published in 1778; a sequel appeared in 1799, and by 1823 the original had gone into twelve editions. In 1801 Austen gave a copy to her beloved niece Anna (daughter of James), which is now on display at Chawton Cottage, but so far as I know the text has never before been commented on. The work consists of twelve dialogues between the governess Mentoria, her pupils Lady Mary and Lady Louisa, and their brother Lord George, home from Harrow and sitting in on dialogues four through twelve. They cover such typical topics as "Industry, Truth, and Sincerity"; "Politeness, Civility, and Gratitude"; "The Church-Service, and Nature of Parables"; and "Complacency and Cheerfulness." Yet Murry's handling of these strikes me as particularly bold, and so does her devotion of entire dialogues to "The Derivation of Words, and Geography"; "The Spartan Form of Government, and Plan of Education"; and "The Sciences, with an exhortation to acquire knowledge."[22] Chapone's *Letters on the Improvement of the Mind,* by contrast, addresses the "learned" languages, history, "abstruse" sciences, dancing, and handwriting all with great circumspection under the heading "On Politeness and Accomplishments." I want to argue, however, not that Murry is wholly anomalous; rather that she thematizes with peculiar clarity a woman's ambition for knowledge and tells with exceptional vigor the story of a girl aspiring to genius, thereby alerting us to a narrative more subtly and ambiguously present in other conduct books by women and available as well to novels of female development.

Although her late eighteenth-century society was, by all accounts, increasingly regimented by gender, Murry seems little concerned to demarcate a narrowly female sphere of education. Her Socrates, the masterful governess Mentoria, will not concede the mental inferiority of women or tout their talent for feeling over reasoning, and she says noth-

ing about apprenticing for marriage. In fact, Mentoria manages—
partly by directing her remarks to girls perhaps eleven or twelve—to
avoid altogether the matters of fashion, flirtation, and courtship, let
alone the minutiae of household economy treated at length by many
conduct books. The governess offers girls instead the "male" models of
Demosthenes, whose industry overcame his deficiencies as an orator (5–
9), and the Spartans, whose rigorous education made them exemplary
for courage and determination (192–98). Both models urge that excellence be pursued against all odds, in spite of apparent disability, fear,
and even public humiliation. For Demosthenes was hissed into silence
for his early, stammering speeches, but only "redoubled his assiduity,
and at last became one of the most eloquent men of the age" (7). In
Mentoria's account, Demosthenes devised a battery of heroic techniques: he declaimed with a mouthful of pebbles while climbing a
mountain, orated over the roar of a raging ocean, installed himself in a
device to break him of shrugging his shoulders, and kept to an under-
ground study for months, during which time "he shaved but one side of
his head, that he might not be tempted to appear in public" (6–7).
Spartan children are likewise admired for "the intense application with
which they pursued their studies" (195). Mentoria explains how they
were separated from their families and bravely went barefoot, almost
naked, their heads shaved (on both sides), until they were inured to
hardship (192).

Together Demosthenes and the Spartans put into the hands of Mary
and Louisa a map to intellectual mastery more often reserved for the
likes of George. At the same time, their examples seem calculated to
prepare girls for the obstacles that they, in particular, will encounter on
the steep path of mental development. As if to answer those who call
women "naturally" weak-headed, Mentoria tells stories in which nature—rocky ground, harsh elements, shrugging shoulders, stammering mouth—is triumphantly overcome by human industry and desire.
As if to counter the sneering comparisons of preaching women to dancing dogs, her stories show humiliation as a spur, eccentricity as a scientific method. The shaved heads of her protagonists seem not only to
figure this eccentricity but also, like the images of physical hardship, to
encourage a kind of monkish renunciation of the gendered body. Along
with Mary Wollstonecraft, who in *A Vindication of the Rights of Woman*

(1792) would call for national coeducation, Mentoria seems virtually to degender the curriculum as well as the narrative of scholarly achievement. When Mentoria recalls her exhortation to a boy at Eton—in which she charges him to work hard "And gain the depth of subjects most abstruse/Fair science is the clue by which we find/Th'intricate lab'rinth of the human mind"—she is asked whether these words apply only to young men. Her answer, whose unorthodoxy she registers in parentheses, is nonetheless clear: "They are (if I may be allowed the expression) *epicene* instructions, and in their tendency of general use to both sexes" (231–32).

Murry's identification of Mentoria and her instructions with a category beyond female or male is the final payoff for an act of appropriation staged and restaged in the course of her text. Mentoria claims for herself the "male" story of literary ambition and celebrity, for example, by quoting a few lines on "gratitude" by Milton—and then casually adding some recently penned lines of her own (54–55). As the dialogues proceed, Mentoria continues to stamp her lessons with the authority of iambic pentameter by citing a poet who is less and less often Milton, and ever more frequently . . . Mentoria. Lord George's arrival in time for the lesson on geography also occasions a polite struggle for the professor's chair. "I hope you will not think it lessens your consequence as a man, to be taught by a Governess, and have young ladies for your school-fellows and companions," Mentoria modestly begins. "Not in the least, Madame: I shall esteem myself much obliged to you for permitting me to partake of your instructions" (60), Murry has George say. A few pages later, Louisa suspects her brother already knows what an island is—but Mentoria, not George, sails on to describe its properties. When she concludes, George approves the definition, thereby assuming, for one tense moment, the professorial role. With his next words, however, he cedes the floor for good: "But I will not interrupt you," he says contritely to Mentoria, "as I suppose you will now tell us what a promontory is" (74).

Mentoria's most difficult and decisive struggle for access to the scholarly highroad involves geometry and "a gentleman, who was a great mathematician" (229). In the ninth dialogue, delighted by her teacher's rapid survey of triangles and hexagons, Lady Louisa declares that she should like to study geometry. But here Mentoria balks, reverting for the first and only time to axiomatic taboos against erudition in women: "It is not a part of female education," she informs her eager student. "Neither can you form a proper judgement from the sketch I have given" (216). Leaving open the question of whether Mentoria herself is privy to geometry's higher mysteries, the dialogue moves on to what is carefully termed a "cursory or slight view of *Astronomy*" (216). A dozen pages later, however, geometry returns, along with the story of a famous man who bored his companions with untimely displays of geometrical knowledge. Assenting to cream in his coffee, he would invariably say: "Yes, Ma'am, because the globular particles of the cream render the acute angles of the tea more obtuse" (229).

As if taking revenge on this geometrician for many such offenses at her tea table, Mentoria uses him to make two points. First, she corrects those like Doctor Gregory who advise women, "If you happen to have any learning, keep it a profound secret" (*Father's*, 26). "Knowledge ought not wholly to be concealed," Mentoria says, and her own example would seem to confirm this view. She goes on, however, to warn Louisa that showing off one's wisdom may become "pedantic and ostentatious" (228–29). Apparently on the verge of clichés about female modesty, Mentoria now introduces her *masculine* pedant. Throughout this text, the sound of separate spheres colliding is audible; at this enjoyable juncture one also hears the crash of double standards tumbling down. Second, Mentoria answers once and for all the question of her own intellectual status. Prompted by George's ensuing curiosity about the chemistry of tea and cream, Mentoria proves herself the great man's equal in knowledge of globulars:

> It is a generally received opinion, that all soft liquors, such as oil or cream, are composed of round or globular particles, which cause that smoothness in the taste; whilst, on the contrary, acids, such as vinegar or cyder, consist of acute or sharp particles, which make them irritate the palate: hence he supposed the richness of the cream would render the roughness of the tea more obtuse, which means blunt. (230)

So saying, she revises both her earlier proscription about women and geometry and the entire scenario: not only has the tiresome guest been humbled, but the tea-pouring hostess has taken his place as scientific

authority, and the tea table itself become a laboratory for female scien-
tists of the future. Mentoria's remarks about "epicene instructions" follow immediately on this revision.

In the final dialogue, Mentoria names herself a surgeon of the understanding. "I feel the pulse of your mind," she explains. "Thus you see I
exercise the medical function" (276). I would say, in sum, that the figure of the doctor may refer metonymically to the desire throughout
Mentoria to undergo a rigorous training, to master a body of knowledge, and to gain a public voice. It may figure, in short, the middle-
class woman's envy of the course of professional development only just
under construction in relation to middle-class men. This is the story
Brontë will later tell in *Villette*, whose "rising character," Lucy Snowe,
falls in love not only with Dr. John's Grecian beauty but also, as Kate
Millett observes, with his vocational success.[23] It is likewise the story
implied by Eliot's juxtaposition of Lydgate and Dorothea Brooke,[24]
and it does not end well; for notwithstanding Mentoria's triumph,
what appears in women's conduct books and novels is more often an
abandoned or otherwise ambiguous version of her climb to intellectual
predominance. Thus, even as *Pride and Prejudice* carries Elizabeth Bennet up the sweeping drive to Pemberley, it also takes her down the road
to knowledge, judgment, and the oracular authority of Demosthenes
(or Austen)—in humiliating reverse. Elizabeth's ceding to Darcy of
what I see as her authorial status is the subject of chapter 3. In Chapone,
too, Mentoria's narrative is considered but disowned, or thought to be
unavailable:

> The danger of pedantry and presumption in a woman—of her excit-
> ing envy in one sex and jealousy in the other—of her exchanging the
> graces of imagination for the severity and preciseness of a scholar,
> would be, I own, sufficient to frighten me from the ambition of
> seeing my girl remarkable for learning. Such objections are perhaps
> still stronger with regard to the abstruse sciences. (*Letters*, 156–
> 57)

Yet what exactly does Chapone "own" in this hesitating passage?
Cued by the slight uncertainties of "would" and "perhaps," I suggest
she confesses to contradictory feelings about "presumption in a woman." For Chapone seems actually to have "the ambition of seeing my girl

remarkable for learning," only to be frightened away from it. But what interests me most is the envy (or is it jealousy?) she admits to feeling in the presence of women like Mentoria. The same denied desire comes through her remark that certain ancient works "are universally said to be entertaining as well as instructive, by those who can read them in their original languages" (*Letters*, 167); as she refers her niece to those "well translated" (167), I hear a sigh that anticipates Maggie Tulliver, envious of Tom's wasted drilling in the classics. A similar wistfulness underlies Lady Pennington's observation that a "sensible woman will soon be convinced, that all the learning her utmost application can make her mistress of, will be, from the difference of education, in many points, inferior to that of a school-boy" (29). Though meaning to re-buke vanity in "reading ladies," the effect of this comment is actually to rebuke the absurd gap in learning between the most sensible, hard-working woman and the merest schoolboy, and to place the blame on their different educations. In Pennington as in Austen and Chapone, the story of Mentoria, the governess-as-pundit, occurs in conflicted forms as that which has been lost or prohibited, but also as that which stealthily returns as a wish, an envy, and perhaps a bitterness.

Chapter 5 will contend that a similar envy of the schoolboy's devel-opment is at work in *The Mill on the Floss*. In Eliot, however, Maggie's repeated exclusion from this boy's education produces a degree of es-trangement from it. Attraction to Tom's *Bildung* ultimately coincides, I believe, with skepticism, for *The Mill on the Floss* appears to perceive that Mentoria's strategy of male impersonation—taking over what Eliot would recognize as Wilhelm Meister's struggle for mastery—involves a ruthless individualism of which Maggie is morally as well as practically incapable. Like Goethe's and Carlyle's, the apprenticeship I take Murry to represent includes lessons in both class and national domination. Her fifth dialogue, continuing the survey of geography, develops telling correspondences between torrid, frigid, and temperate climates and the upper, lower, and middle classes. As Nancy Arm-strong might have predicted, the upshot of this intriguing thermal de-terminism is praise for the temperate bourgeoisie, whose "manners pre-serve the medium between the Northern barbarity and Eastern luxury" (136). There are some ominous remarks about international relations as well. Mentoria has earlier condemned Cortez for his "lawless" conquest

(110), yet here she situates England in a zone that just happens to be both the most comfortable and the most moral, conveniently rationalizing its still inchoate imperial project. The domination of darker peoples is intrinsic to Tom Tulliver's *Bildung* as it is to Mentoria's, but I will be arguing that Eliot criticizes as well as collaborates with this impulse. In fact, *The Mill on the Floss* may finally propose an alternative view of development, virtually implicit in the form of the novel and explicit in the epistolary or dialogic form of all but one of my conduct books. In all of these texts the projection of a girl's growing up into dialogue may invite an understanding of identity not as a matter of individual choice and conquest but as a complex set of social relationships.

I want to close this chapter by stressing once again the contradictions I find across the gamut of this period's developmental narratives by women. Lady Pennington's text was originally called "An Unfortunate Mother's Advice to Her Absent Daughters." But sometime after her death in 1783, the word *unfortunate* was dropped, so that the subsequent title promised simply "a mother's advice." This title—with the "unfortunate" under erasure, the mother's own sad history muted—nicely represents the double view of maternal destiny that produces discordant accounts of becoming adult in women's handbooks and fiction alike. Pennington's own marriage and motherhood were indeed unfortunate. Enraged when she inherited an independent fortune from her father, Lord Pennington accused his wife of what we can only assume was adultery, and though he offered little evidence, his claims cost Lady Pennington her reputation and her children, from whom she was separated (7). In Pennington, therefore, the counterpointed stories of female formation correspond to the mother's qualified but still conventional encouragement to marry and mother on the one hand and her own calamitous history and powerfully negative example on the other. A remarkably similar tension is central to *Evelina*, whose optimistic courtship-as-education narrative is crossed by the tragic story of Evelina's mother, who was betrayed, like Lady Pennington, by the man she married.

In another sense, too, the mother/mentor's example directly undercuts her lesson, for all of these female-authored texts are founded, and in their official capacities founder, upon the contradiction between

"proper lady" and "woman writer" that Mary Poovey has so compelling-
ly analyzed. Pennington may warn that a girl's reputation is of a delicacy "almost sullied by the breath even of good report" (vii), and Ellis may
shudder at how publication reduces a woman's spirit to "an article of
sale and bargain, tossed over from the hands of one workman to another, free alike to the touch of the prince and the peasant" (175)—yet
the extraordinary fame and popularity of both these writers, the high
visibility and wide circulation of their works, tell a different story. If
this other story of the woman writer is always present in the biographical circumstances hovering around these books, it also breaks on occasion into the texts themselves. One encounters it, for example, when
Ellis launches into an earnest digression on the art of good letter-
writing (200–5). Condemning "common-place" and demanding
"freshness," she echoes Samuel Johnson's famous admiration for Shakespeare's "just representations of general nature": "Common-place,"
Ellis asserts, "consists chiefly in speaking of things by their little qualities, rather than their great ones" (201). It can also be glimpsed when
Pennington, admonishing her daughters to use their time well, employs a suggestive metaphor:

> Look on every day as a blank sheet of paper put into your hands to be
> filled up;—remember the characters will remain to endless ages,
> and that they never can be expunged;—be careful therefore not to
> write any thing but what you may read with pleasure a thousand
> years after. (22)

This is, of course, what Evelina literally does, her almost daily letters
comprising the bulk of *Evelina*. Staging a woman in the act of writing,
Evelina, like Austen's *Love and Freindship* and other such epistolary novels and conduct books, implicitly poses its own production history—
the fact of female authorship—against its ambivalent rendition of what
I have been calling the Mentoria narrative.

There are conflicts about how and into what girls should grow not
only within individual texts but also, as I have mentioned, among their
various authors. In addition to rejecting Swift's advice about female
friendship, Chapone specifically challenges Dr. Gregory's recommendation that wives hide the full extent of their love: "a precept which
does no honour to his own sex," she argues, "and which would take

from ours its sweetest charms, simplicity and artless tenderness" ("New-
Married," 105). Austen wickedly mocks the whole of Fordyce's *Sermons*
by having Mr. Collins read from them "with very monotonous solemnity" until, after three pages, Lydia can no longer contain herself and
rudely interrupts (68–69). Austen looks back, as Chapone looks forward, to Wollstonecraft's more extended "Animadversions on Some
Writers" in which Gregory and, especially, Fordyce are singled out for
urging girls to become docile and dissimulating adults (92–100). "Idle
empty words!" Wollstonecraft cries, scorning Fordyce's comparison of
women to angels (95). She also criticizes Hester Thrale Piozzi and Mme.
de Staël, women who "argue in the same track as men" (102–3), but
pays her respects to Chapone, although they do not always agree (105).

Like the courtesy writers reviewed in this chapter, Frances Burney,
Jane Austen, Charlotte Brontë, and George Eliot may all be said to "argue in the same track as men," reproducing many orthodoxies about
middle-class female formation. Yet I hope in the course of this book to
show they argue in other, dissident tracks as well, some of which I have
referred to above as the antiromantic, female homosocial, and Mentoria
stories. The following chapter will trace the antiromantic narrative of
female development in *Evelina*; chapter 3 will argue that the antiromantic theme in *Pride and Prejudice* is at the same time a tragically
inverted version of the Mentoria narrative; chapter 4 will look at the
suppression but also uncanny persistence of the female homosocial narrative in *Jane Eyre*; and chapter 5 will read *The Mill on the Floss* as a failed
appropriation of the *Bildungsroman* that is finally a critique of this genre
and its values. To move on at this point to Burney, Austen, Brontë, and
Eliot is not to imply that these women, as novelists, were somehow
more capable than the less "literary" Pennington, Murry, Chapone, and
Ellis of offering alternative plots or articulating oppositional views. I
would say, rather, that all these writers, by dramatizing female development in contradictory ways, pointed to the "feminine" as a site of
ideological confusion, struggle, and possibility, thereby opening up
still more space for debate around this term. Unable to represent a girl's
entrance into the world as a simple, graceful passage, attending in diverse ways to its dangers and insisting on its deprivations, they man-
aged collectively to question the routines of growing up female and
male and at moments to imagine they could be otherwise.

CHAPTER TWO

Getting Waylaid in *Evelina*

EVELINA *or The History of a Young Lady's Entrance into the World* (1778), Frances Burney's first published work of fiction, has long been her most acclaimed, its seeming lightness and familiarity making it generally more acceptable than the darker books to come.[1] *Evelina's* theme of innocence abroad and epistolary form sit easily with traditional conceptions of the eighteenth-century novel; its domestic realism and satirical wit may be seen to anticipate if not directly to influence Jane Austen's shaping of the novel for the subsequent century. Much of *Evelina* is legible in terms of our expectations for comedies of manners.[2] Yet for all that is reassuringly known, elements of Burney's first novel remain disturbingly *unheimlich* to students of *Pamela* and *Emma*. There are in this text (as elsewhere in Burney) repeated episodes of unabashed brutality—victimizing most of the female characters and villainizing most of the men—innocently registered by its heroine in letters to her guardian. In addition there is what looks like a narrative of education, leading at last to greater wisdom and appropriate partnering, which appears at the same time to advertise its insufficiency.

Numerous feminist critics have noted the unfunny violence that slashes through Burney's ostensibly comic novels and have linked this to her representation of a particularly female vulnerability. Patricia Meyer Spacks admires Burney's depiction of a world "very real in its pressures, cruelties, and arbitrary benignities" (*Imagining*, 177). Rose Marie Cutting comments that "the cruelty which pervades Fanny Burney's fictional world has been viewed as a strange weakness, rather than as a manifestation of a feminine sensibility: she was, after all, describing a world in which women had little power" (520). Susan Staves adds that while Richardson's heroines suffer perhaps equivalent violence, it is less anonymous and more effectively opposed (370–71). Rather more bluntly, Judith Lowder Newton describes *Evelina* as "a chronicle of assault" (23), while Margaret Anne Doody calls Burney a "student of aggression and obsession" (*Frances*, 3). And more graphically still, Julia Epstein's examination of the 1812 "mastectomy letter" (detailing the removal of Burney's right breast without anesthesia) places this account of violence to the female body in line with earlier novelistic versions: "Long before her surgical ordeal in 1811 . . . Burney's writings had already depicted physical and mental pain to satirize the cruelty of social and behavioural strictures, especially for women, and to pillory the sentimental conventions of eighteenth-century fiction" (86).

As for the ending, a few critics have cheerfully seen Evelina's marriage to Lord Orville as a kind of diploma, certifying her success in the classroom of life.[3] Many, however, are troubled by a book whose subtitle suggests movement forward, and whose story leaves us doubting whether such movement has in fact occurred. Michael Adelstein, in his patronizing biography, blames "Fanny" for failing to achieve her alleged goal. She intended, he asserts, to recount the heroine's development and improvement. "But, in fact, Evelina is a static character who is little wiser at the end than in the beginning. . . . She has learned little about values, morals, or people, suggesting that a social education is all" (38). Toby Olshin takes up the same complaint, charging that "little moral change has been effected in the heroine" (38). Like Adelstein (and Freud, long on the shortcomings of the female superego), Olshin argues that "Burney falls short in . . . her understanding of ethical maturation. . . . Too readily, she dramatizes the easy rightness of received wisdom" (40). Adelstein and Olshin, remarking that Evelina masters etiquette but remains morally sophomoric, attribute this to Burney's own failure to conceive of growth in other than shallow terms.

Waldo Glock also contributes to this pattern of critics campaigning for "permanent change in Evelina—as the educational purpose of the novel would seem to require." Finding Evelina basically unaltered at the close, Glock judges her creator not morally so much as professionally lacking: "That Miss Burney was totally serious as a novelist remains questionable" (41). And finally, George Starr makes a more elaborate but essentially similar point in his "Notes on Sentimental Novels." He defines the sentimental novel as a form valuing stasis—idealizing innocence and resisting maturity—in sharp contrast to the *Bildungsroman* with its desire for growth and change. According to Starr, however, the work featuring a female protagonist is an exception, for there *Bildung* and stasis are no longer antithetical. In *Evelina*, for example, the heroine grows up to marry a father-figure who repositions her as "child"; as Starr rightly observes, her formation evidently consists of remaining immature (523–27). *Bildungsroman* and sentimental novel come together here, he concludes; or rather *Bildungsroman* is assimilated to sentimental novel. Starr resolves the conflict between *Evelina*'s impulse to educate and failure to do so by invoking what he posits as the ideology of Burney's day in regard to female destiny: the paradoxical equation of "womanliness" with girlish ignorance, of female *Bildung* with stasis. Whereas Adelstein, Olshin, and Glock think Burney was too dumb to see the conflict between *Evelina*'s contradictory propositions, the more historically-minded Starr suggests that for Burney, accepting the received equation, *there was no conflict*.

What never occurs to any of them is that Burney's novel might not be entirely congruent with the truisms of its day or—as I argue in my discussion of contemporaneous conduct materials—that these truisms might themselves be contradictory, offering divergent accounts of female destiny. Taking *Evelina* to be as artless as its heroine, all four critics regard this text as complacently univocal, incapable of narrative complexity or defiance. Consequently, they fail to consider the possibility that Burney's novel might recognize and in some sense designedly portray the conflict between an account of courtship as successful education, a female approximation of *Bildung*, and a rival account of courtship as antithetical to a girl's growing up—what I have described as an antiromantic narrative of female development. Far from being a *Bildungsroman* simply vanished into sentimental novel, *Evelina* may be a work revealingly at odds with itself, continuing to invoke and value some "masculine" notion of linear development, even as another geometry of obstructed female development emerges. My project in this chapter is to map the other developmental narrative in tension with the linear. I do this by bringing together the previously noted (female and male) critical strains: using an anatomy of violence to help make sense of an ending. I want to take up the observation that Evelina's "entrance" rapidly dead-ends, that the "woman" remains fundamentally a child, but argue that this points less to Burney's disability or to an ideological consensus than to an ideological debate ongoing in her text and in the contemporary discourse about female formation.

One side of this debate is evident in the very thoroughness of violence that Spacks et al. have indicated. Local sites of violence function, I suggest, as figures for the overall violence of the antiromantic narrative, identifying as rude arrest what Starr perceived as happy quiescence. Again and again the women in this novel are forcibly kept from doing what they would and made to do what they would not—Madame Duval dragged, dropped, and roped to a tree; elderly ladies raced and bet on like horses; Evelina herself so often ungently constrained—and the sum of these small imprisonings is a general, distinctly gendered, logic of impediment. Reading the end of *Evelina* through its many instances of women hindered or coerced, we may see the heroine's nuptial knot—tying off her education—as the culmination of this logic, continuous with all previous obstruction and restraint. It appears in this context as the ultimate waylaying of Evelina's destiny, at one with the waylaying of Madame Duval's coach. At the same time there is, as I say, a second, more obvious and less alarming narrative, in which Evelina does appear to grow wiser and more gratified: the romantic story of a girl for whom true love is knowledge and marriage signifies completion. Yet this progressive apprenticeship—the steady, improving climb so sought after by certain critics—is perceived to be only problematically available to the heroine. Its purposes, I suggest, are several. First, it disguises the less acceptable tale of blockage and frustration, providing a consoling cover story. Second, earnest as well as fraudulent, it registers the appeal of a soaring trajectory. And finally, it indicates the currency of such a trajectory as a female version of *Bildung*.[4] My object here is to show how in *Evelina* this climbing, linear narrative is drastically undercut—its developmental myth placed at an ironic remove—by the circling counterstory that leaves Evelina back where she began.

I want first to evince more specifically what I am calling the logic of impediment and to show how it drives the plot whose dizzying circularity this chapter will trace. Its principal effect is a satiric and sadistic rewriting of the fairy tale, so that the very man who saves the heroine from distress takes advantage of her trust and gratitude to assault her in turn. As prince turns repeatedly into dragon, rescue into recapture, and relief into trepidation, Evelina begins to doubt not only the world but also her own ability to interpret it. More than simply blocked, she is worn down almost, as she says, to death. This holding pattern is familiar from nightmares and gothic novels, and its presence in Burney causes Margaret Doody to place her in a quasi-gothic tradition.[5] Doody describes, for example, the heroine's mad scene in *Cecilia* as "a repetition and culmination of many previous scenes involving desire thwarted and anxious hurrying forward impeded" ("Female," 548). Speaking of *Cecilia* (1782) and *Camilla* (1796), Doody notes that, whereas in a (full-fledged) gothic novel such female terror is everywhere, in these two Burney novels it is relegated to fits of madness from which the heroine recovers or bad dreams from which she finally awakes.

What interests me about *Evelina*, by contrast, is the sane, waking terror it deals in. Like *Northanger Abbey* (and, as I will show, *Pride and Prejudice* and *The Mill on the Floss*), Burney's first novel locates danger to women neither in a peculiar state of consciousness nor in some dreary, implausible dungeon, but on the street and in the carriages, ballrooms, and domestic settings of the realist novel.[6] In addition to the sentimental and the gothic novels, both of which suggest the counterprogressive plot I find underlying *Evelina*, and beyond the courtesy books whose similarly anxious renderings of courtship we have already encountered, another intertext is relevant here. Nancy K. Miller has explored a related seriality of innocence abused in Sade's *Justine* (1792), calling attention to its reversal of eighteenth-century tales in which virtue is conventionally rewarded ("*Justine*," 216). Miller explains that because Justine's virginity is always reconstructable it is infinitely reviolable; the repetition of her abuse depends on the intractability of her innocence (224). Although no one is technically violated in *Evelina*, the continual threat and figuration of violation, the relentless pattern of persecution, seem curiously to anticipate Sade. What courtesy books imply and sentimental novels deny, the gothic and especially the Sadeian genres make explicit: the violence of a plot that both literally restrains its heroine and, refusing Evelina (like Justine) the benefit of her experience, holds her to a debilitating innocence.

II

I will offer three examples of the logic of impediment at work in *Evelina*, observing that this logic is no sooner shown than disowned, for just as the telling of female obstruction intensifies, the text habitually reverts to the nicer story of gratification and growth. In the first case Evelina and the Branghton sisters, having strayed into a dark alley at Vauxhall, are ambushed and encircled by a "riotous" party of drunks. As Evelina recounts, "Our screams were answered with bursts of laughter, and for some minutes we were kept prisoners, till at last one of them, rudely seizing hold of me, said I was a pretty little creature" (181). Struggling furiously, she manages to free herself only to be blocked by a new gang of gentlemen. One of them, she writes, "placed himself so directly in my way, calling out, 'Whither so fast, my love?'—that I could only have proceeded by running into his arms" (181). Her captors leer and tease until suddenly the aristocratic rake Sir Clement Willoughby, recognizing Evelina's cries, rushes forward to her rescue. As his friends applaud enviously—"Willoughby has all the luck!"—Sir Clement conducts the ingenuous heroine to a still darker alley where he offers the "protection" of his more private advances (180–84). One effect of this passage is to code the flattering language of courtship—phrases of endearment and possession such as "pretty little creature" or "my love"—as a vocabulary of assault. Another is to depict in vignette the "progress" of courtship as the barring of Evelina's way, forcing her into imprisoning arms. Here in small, then, is the very repetition of constraint, the same systematic interception of Evelina's impulse forward, which in my view characterizes this narrative as a whole.

But once displayed, such logic is, as I say, quickly covered over. Finding his victim unyielding, Sir Clement exacts her pardon with surprising ease, and even her anger toward him abates more quickly than seems right. The reason for this involves not only Evelina's vulnerable femaleness but also her precarious class position. Unacknowledged by her patrician father (Sir John Belmont), adopted by an obscure though gentlemanly cleric (Villars), and much ashamed of her "vulgar" maternal grandmother (Madame Duval), the heroine's social standing is conspicuously ambiguous. Thus when she and the noble Sir Clement rejoin her lowly relatives and the blatantly bourgeois Mr. Smith, Evelina's smarting sense of gender disadvantage is compounded by anxiety about class; it is no wonder that she takes advantage of a vacillating status to position herself, this time, on the side of power. Closing ranks with the man who has just deceived and assailed her, Evelina now joins Sir Clement in sneering at Mr. Smith. This alliance with nobility compensates Evelina for recent events, but only at the cost of denying their brutality. Identified with Sir Clement, Evelina leaves his indictment to Madame Duval, and even that brash grandmother, refusing to call Clement a gentleman, has difficulty voicing her suspicions: "I wonder, child, you would let such a—such a *person* as that keep company with you" (185). (Here she fulfills precisely that maternal duty she is alleged to shirk, as I explain later.) Sir Clement answers with a well-turned lie: "I believe you will not regret the honour I now have of attending Miss Anville, when you hear that I have been so happy as to do her some service" (185).

Evelina says nothing, and in this she allows him to revise their encounter, letting the record of her harassment give way to a more decorous version. She bows to this version to the extent of deciding, by the end of a letter that began with the attack at Vauxhall: "*Nothing* could be more disagreeable to me, than being seen by Sir Clement Willoughby with a party at once so vulgar in themselves and so familiar to me" (my emphasis; 192). Of course, Madame Duval and her noisy kin are easier targets because less privileged than Sir Clement. Further, Evelina's vulnerability in the alley had actually to do both with her femaleness and with assumptions about what class of female she is— "the prettiest little actress I have seen in this age" (181), one man says. It makes sense that Evelina should take shelter in snobbery. But if we are made to see this, we are also, and more forcefully, shown its effect: to obscure the routine abuse of lower-class women by ruling-class men behind the myth of chivalry and the fact of class prejudice. Nor does *Eve-*

lina let hostility toward Sir Clement dissipate entirely, for even as the heroine's anger is displaced onto her middle-class cousins, it is stammeringly revived by Madame Duval, who proceeds to keep up a tirade against that "person" for the rest of this letter. As Evelina remarks in closing, "There is no apprehension of his visiting here, as Madame Duval is far too angry to admit him" (192). Though seeming to speak about her grandmother, the Evelina who succeeded in rebuffing Sir Clement continues to insist that a woman's outrage can keep a man from entering. Throughout *Evelina*, a leakage of female anger from the furious story of women deterred will keep this narrative, however receded, in partial view.

In my second example, as in the first, the pattern of impediment is inflected by hierarchical class as well as by gender relations, although here the heroine's snobbery works to occasion instead of to conceal the incident. Evelina is sitting in the cheap seats, suffering terribly from her cousins' concern with money and indifference to opera.[7] Sir Clement's arrival promises escape, and she is desperate enough to ignore his ominous eagerness. Abandoning Madame Duval and believing the gentleman takes her to Mrs. Mirvan's more fashionable set, she ends up alone with him in his coach—taking the long way home. Once again, apparent liberation twists into a new captivity. Here, too, the "good" man slips unnervingly into "bad." And, in the deliberately misdirected coach, we are offered an additional image of female destiny gone awry; like the larger antiromantic narrative, it takes the heroine in circles, carrying her on and on, and always to the wrong address. Evelina's account of what follows is necessarily euphemistic. Her sexual innocence prevents her from articulating the precise danger posed by Sir Clement, and this, paradoxically, jeopardizes that innocence.[8]

> He caught hold of me, exclaiming, "For Heaven's sake, what is the matter?"
> "I—I don't know," cried I (quite out of breath). . . ."
> "You amaze me," answered he (still holding me), "I cannot imagine what you apprehend." (87)

Later on Sir Clement makes Evelina promise not to tell. As before in the alley, so now in the coach they agree to overlook his indelicacy— although even before promising, Evelina, knowing something is up, can scarcely say what. Yet while the girl in the carriage cannot pronounce "seduction," her letter manages to describe it in nonetheless vivid detail. She writes that Sir Clement had seized and was passionately kissing her hand, when she cried out in terror, "If you do not intend to murder me . . . for mercy's, for pity's sake, let me get out!" (87) Susan Staves sees this cry as further euphemism: "Her vocabulary can hardly include terms directly descriptive of sexual assault and rape" (371). To me it operates on two levels: as euphemism and, at the same time, hyperbole. Though Evelina never does identify the threat, her fear is perfectly, even extremely, conveyed. As in my first example, the account of Evelina's persecution is elided only partially, for through the polite version both the full extent of Sir Clement's villainy and the process of its disavowal can be quite readily perceived. In these two scenes involving Sir Clement, *Evelina* not only dramatizes female anger provoked and then muted; it also, returning to the scene of the crime and telling what the heroine promised not to tell, recovers that anger and the story behind it.

This second case of rescuer-turned-assailant is structurally identical to its earliest and paradigmatic instance in *Evelina*, which I take as my third example: the tragic story of Caroline Evelyn, mother of the heroine. These events involving previous generations and taking place before *Evelina* begins are crucial but complicated, and I will try briefly to summarize them here.[9] Caroline's well-born father (Evelina's grandfather) married a French barmaid (Evelina's grandmother), known to the reader as Madame Duval. Soon regretting his infatuation and on his deathbed two years later, he appealed to his faithful tutor—that perennial father-figure, Villars—to rescue Caroline from her "low-bred and illiberal" mother (4). Villars obligingly took Caroline from her mother and raised her, reluctantly letting her go only when she turned eighteen and his guardianship expired. At this point, "her mother, then married to Monsieur Duval, sent for her to Paris" (4). There Madame Duval, at her husband's behest, tried to force her inexperienced daughter to wed a cousin. Frantic to escape this fate, Caroline was once more "rescued" from the clutches of her mother, this time by the profligate Sir John Belmont. Sir John married Caroline only to deny the legality of their tie so that, in a now recognizable sequence, the promise of release was broken by new difficulties. Poor Caroline returned to Villars and died, disgraced, giving birth to Evelina. Villars (who else?) raises Evelina, in her turn the "best-beloved" in the clergyman's heart (3–5, 113–115). The obvious culprit here is Sir John, his rescue/betrayal of Caroline the original sin that generates Evelina and *Evelina* in the first place: the heroine and the heroine's quest for her father's recognition. But here the logic of impediment puts an interesting spin on the standard seduction plot. Usually marriage is the safe harbor reached by a Pamela Andrews or Lydia Bennet after weathering the storm of seduction or its threat. But this time, by some sleight of hand, marriage is not the haven it appeared to be but is (as it was for Lady Pennington) itself another danger. Sir John's deception reveals that even marriage may be a form of entrapment, and this insight will necessarily shade the meaning of the book's final union.

As I have suggested, Sir John's place in this schema is the same as Sir Clement's in the last. Like Sir Clement, he is a highborn man offering a girl escape from her lowborn mother or grandmother (Madame Duval), and his intentions turn out to be dishonorable. One implication of this paradigm is a warning against snobbery and a loyalty to maternal as opposed to paternal figures that Burney critics have largely neglected.[10] But what interests me most is the light it sheds on Villars's still earlier "rescue" of the daughter from her mother, since in this his position in the paradigm strongly resembles Sir John's and Sir Clement's. Could the kindly, aging, clerical Villars possibly belong to the category of "redeemers" with ulterior motives? Does he, too, introduce the daughter to a species of captivity? At first glance this affectionate father appears irreproachable, as critics unanimously agree—yet given that *Evelina*'s pattern of abuse depends precisely on the slide from saint to devil, even the holiest of male figures may be suspect. I am going to argue that Villars is indeed implicated by this pattern, defined by Sir John and Sir Clement, in which the man abducting a daughter from her mother proves to be a scoundrel in spite of claiming to save her. In fact the novel's first sin may be not Sir John's refusal to acknowledge his relation to either mother or daughter, but Villars's much-replicated refusal to acknowledge and respect the mother-daughter tie.[11] Above all, I would stress that to view Evelina's guardian as in some sense her jailer and her mother's jailer, to see his direction as misdirected, is effectively to recast—as downcast—the narrative that begins and ends in his arms. I want to turn now from these mini-tales of obstruction to the masterplot they indicate: the overall courtship narrative that kills Evelina's linear momentum by circulating her between Villars and (his surrogate) Orville, so that even in this largest movement of her life she is passed from one spurious redeemer to another. However exemplary they may seem, both Villars and Orville further *Evelina*'s logic of impediment by participating in local instances of hindrance such as those detailed above and, even more, by tracing out between them the regressive path of Evelina's destiny.

To elaborate on this characterization of Villars I want to return to the issue of female anger in *Evelina*, which as we have seen is closely tied to its antiromantic narrative. In fact, the novel begins with a woman's rage in two respects. The earliest letter we get in terms of the novel's fictional chronology is Caroline's dying outcry—"most cruel of men!"—against Sir John. In the context of Burney's text, however, this letter does not appear until chapter 74. Instead the novel starts with Madame Duval's explosion at Villars, conveyed to him in a letter from Lady Howard:

> Her letter is violent, sometimes abusive, and that of *you!*—*you*, to whom she is under obligations which are greater even than her faults, but to whose advice she wickedly imputes all the sufferings of her much injured daughter, the late Lady Belmont. (1)

Mediated (and later echoed) by Lady Howard, Madame Duval's fury at Villars engrosses *Evelina*'s opening page. Such a placement of female wrath serves, first, to sound it as one of the book's important motifs. In addition, by situating Madame Duval's maternal curse at the abducting surrogate father *before* the more obvious anger of the abandoned woman, it offers an unexpected etiology of seduction. One might say it starts the story of betrayal earlier, beginning not with the daughter's entrance into the world, but with her seclusion from the world by her father. It traces Sir John's cruelty and Caroline's cry back to Caroline's "illadvised" (1) upbringing by Villars, judging him complicitous in the crime against her.

Yet given that at some level the novel seems to credit Villars as father and discredit the Frenchwoman as mother, why should anyone believe her claim to the contrary? For one thing, Madame Duval's maternity is quietly but carefully authenticated by her extreme grief at Caroline's death (5), her undeniable joy at recovering Evelina, and her despair when Evelina almost faints—"Let me not lose my poor daughter a second time!" (42). Though Villars accuses her of expressing no interest in Evelina, we are specifically informed she was prevented from doing so by a despotic husband (42). It was also this husband, and not Madame Duval, who instigated plans to marry Caroline against her will (4). Similarly it is Branghton, Senior, who invents (though Madame Duval would implement) the parallel plan to unite the unwilling Evelina with the acne-aged Branghton, Junior. A close reading of these instances suggests that Madame Duval is not merely a tyrant, but also tyranny's servant and further—what her continual abuse by Captain Mirvan serves to stress—its victim. She is also an unexampled mother in one decisive regard. If a warning against seduction is critical to eighteenth-century maternal discourse, Madame Duval enters this discourse more persuasively than anyone else. Mother figures Mrs. Mirvan, Mrs. Selwyn, as well as Villars, caution Evelina against Sir Clement, and her actual mother offers a warning by example. But only Madame Duval—by scorning male approval, spurning female modesty, and roaring with indignation at her own molestation—actually practices the self-defense they preach.

Villars, on the other hand, conveys at best a mixed message, bled by qualification, and this contributes not a little to his ward's developmental bind. In tones reminiscent of courtesy writers Fordyce and Gregory, he exhorts Evelina in terms that waver indecisively:

> Though gentleness and modesty are the peculiar attributes of your sex, yet fortitude and firmness, when occasion demands them, are virtues as noble and as becoming in women as in men: the right line of conduct is the same for both sexes, though the manner in which it is pursued may somewhat vary, and be accommodated to the strength or weakness of the different travellers. (202)

Women, according to Villars, are gentle in contrast to men, but no less firm than men, at least when the occasion demands; women's right line of conduct is the same as that for men, but they pursue it differently because they are weaker. When it comes to resistance, in short, a disabling double standard is briefly questioned before being nervously reas-

serted. Further, the abstraction of Villars's advice from the sexist practices of her culture leaves Evelina dangerously unprepared to cope with
them. Her first days in London teach her that female modesty means
deference to men. She learns to squelch her dislike for Lovel, hide her
preference for Orville, and accept both these men's objectifying views
of her. Captain Mirvan, she finds, can mock his daughter with impunity—"He began some rude jests upon the bad shape of her nose, and
called her a tall ill-formed thing"—while the women "have too much
prudence" to retaliate in kind (27). And Evelina is all the more educable
in acquiescence because of the inexperience Villars has cultivated. Her
rusticity calls attention to her as a curiosity and easy target, while rendering her, for fear of committing a faux pas, all but unresisting. The
illegibility to her of high society, because it puts her continually in the
wrong, makes confidence unlikely and indignation impossible. Along
with her contemporary, Mary Wollstonecraft, Burney seems to equate
the "innocence" so prized in women with a bumbling ignorance that
only abets their exploitation.[12] Patricia Spacks tells us this equation
occurred to not a few women novelists of the eighteenth century,
"whose hidden anger at the implications of the idea finds expression in
the train of misfortunes they devise for their innocent heroines" ("Ev'ry
Woman," 30).

Not only did Villars twice nurse (in mother as in daughter) such
highly exploitable innocence, there are numerous hints he did so for
selfish reasons. His paternal feelings are, *Evelina* implies, over-tender;
indeed he measures his love for Caroline by conjugal standards: "To me
she became so dear, that her loss was little less afflicting than that which
I have since sustained of Mrs. Villars herself" (4). Likewise, regarding
Evelina he seeks a husband who appears, in this ambiguous sentence, to
be himself: "My fondest wish is now circumscribed by the desire of bestowing her on one who may be sensible of her worth, and then sinking
to eternal rest in her arms" (5). Little wonder, therefore, that Villars
explains the cloistering of his ward in terms that are defensive, apolo-
getic, and even confessional. In his letter to Lady Howard, he comes
close to admitting that the mother's demerit was trumped up to in-
dulge the father's desire: "Even had Madame Duval merited the charge
she claims, I fear my fortitude would have been unequal to the parting"
(5). "Such, Madame, is my tenderness," he pleads, "and such my weak-

ness!" (6) All this in his very first letter, followed by one that begins: "I blush to incur the imputation of selfishness. In detaining my young charge thus long with myself in the country, I consulted not solely my own inclination" (7). The blush, indicating passion under pressure; the detention, implying an application of force; the admission that he did indeed consult his own inclination while appearing to consult her interest—all of these liken the virtuous Villars to the scandalous Sir John and Sir Clement more than one might initially have thought.

They support, at least, Sir John's contention, and my own, that the "good" father is not so simply opposed to the "bad":

> It seldom happens that a man, though extolled as a saint, is really without blemish; or that another, though reviled as a devil, is really without humanity. Perhaps the time is not very distant, when I may have the honour to convince your Ladyship of this truth, in regard to Mr. Villars and myself.   (143)

Sir John never does pinpoint Villars's blemish, but he does raise a question about Villars's complexion that the text in general supports. [13] As I have tried to show, Villars's rescue/confinement of Caroline/Evelina may differ in degree but not essentially in kind from Sir John's more notorious betrayal. Both men take advantage of female dependency to satisfy themselves. Both possess a young woman (whether briefly or permanently) in a way that impairs her self-possession. Both, finally, are aroused by an enfeebling female innocence, and the roles they play in relation to this are complementary: Villars fetishizes the intactness that makes its violation by Sir John a thrill. He overprotects the chastity that, Nancy K. Miller notes, in eighteenth-century fiction "attracts rape as the sacred invites sacrilege" ("*Justine*," 217). In practical terms, he teaches the docility and imbecility that make Sir John's scheme plausible. The significance of this blurring between chaperon and ravisher, between good father and bad—linked in courtesy literature and in *Evelina* to a slippage between right suitor and wrong—cannot be underestimated. Its effect is to shift the blame for violence against women from the anomalous rogue to *paternalism per se*. It suggests that patriarchy itself is the villain.

I have been trying to argue that the similarity between "Villars" and "villain" may signify. It is a likeness that sets off a whole train of speculations about names involving "ville," popular in French novels and curiously ubiquitous in this English one. It serves, for one thing, to link "Villars" to "Orville"—adored by Evelina and universally admired by critics, who chide him for nothing worse than woodenness—and to associate "Orville" in turn with "villainy." The etymological case against Orville is clearer when we consider that, by *Cecilia*, the leading man's name has modulated to "Mortimer Del*vile*." In this second of Burney's novels, Orville's devilish successor does not defile, but does defraud the heroine before finally marrying her (nor is his first name consistent with a wholly comic outcome). The other reference in "ville" is, of course, to "city": the place Evelina seeks, like many a would-be *Bildungsheld*, to find the world and her place in it. She goes by the name of "Anville," a homonym for "*en ville*" or "in the city." What can we make of the fact that Orville is a homonym for "*hors ville*" ("outside the city") except that he is somehow opposed to her "entrance into the world?" Indeed, if we look at Evelina's "progress" in terms of her name, we see only a retreat from worldliness, a flight from urbanity: the Miss *Anville* who begs to go to London leaves the city by way of the pastoral *Belmont* and ends up decidedly *Orville*. Her marriage, then, would seem to be semantically at odds with her desire for knowledge and her impulse to enter a less sheltered space. [14]

I want to preface my discussion of Orville—in what sense he could possibly be, like Villars, a villain barricading Evelina's way—by recalling one of her early social blunders. To avoid dancing with Sir Clement, Evelina pretends to be preengaged. Sir Clement dogs and pesters her, faking indignation at his mystery rival: "I long to kick the fellow round the room!—unless, indeed,—(hesitating and looking earnestly at me,) unless, indeed,—it is a partner of your own *creating?*" (30) Tired and disconcerted, Evelina finally names Lord Orville, who profits from the confusion to engage her on the spot (for the rest of the book, as it turns out). Orville is, to be sure, portrayed in appealing contrast to his fellows, and it is easy enough to share Evelina's admiration for his almost feminine delicacy. Yet this question of Sir Clement's remains in the air, suggesting to me that the gallant hero who saves Evelina from the wicked rake may well be a convenient fiction—made up by Evelina in her effort to resolve the difficulties of courtship and useful to that narrative strain satisfied with marriage as the capstone of female development.

This comic strain is, as I have argued, contested by a less euphoric one, and here Orville and his relation to Evelina's quest are portrayed in more ambiguous terms. In fact, Lord Orville's dishonorable rival, Sir Clement (like Sir John in relation to Villars), occasionally seems less this lord's foil than his darker alter ego; at times the two men's actions or words are disturbingly continuous, complicitous, and even temporarily confused. The confusion of Clement with Orville follows the commandeering of Orville's coach by Evelina's pushy relatives. Evelina sends the coach owner a polite apology and gets back an insultingly passionate reply, signed "Orville." The pen turns out to have been Sir Clement's, but in the meantime Evelina and the reader are asked to believe that Orville is capable of a rakish turn. Evelina's first impression upon reading the letter is delight; it is only on a *second reading* (242) that she recognizes the disrespect underlying its elaborate praises. We are invited by this, I propose, both to suspect Lord Orville's chivalry and to subject chivalry itself, its encomium to women, to a second reading; Evelina's double take on this letter models, it might be said, just that mode of double reading in which we are presently engaged.

Evelina provides many examples of an ugly, gang-banging kind of male bonding. Sir Clement helps Captain Mirvan torture Madame Duval, just as Captain Mirvan helps Sir Clement get his hands on Evelina. In the alley scene I have already described, Sir Clement's cohorts stand by smirking as he carries off their prize. It is by precisely this kind of misogynist complicity that Orville, too, seems compromised. As Evelina disappears into the gaping jaws of Sir Clement's coach, for example, Lord Orville stands by and watches resignedly (85). His attempt to intervene is perfunctory (Evelina wonders at how little he insists), and one senses at work a gentlemen's agreement concerning territorial rights. Even Evelina guesses that Orville "had a suspicion of Sir Clement's design" (89), and the reader knows that Orville, man of the world, could hardly have mistaken his friend's intent. So what is intended by the curious "half smile" (85) with which he bids Evelina good night? Is Orville trying to smile encouragingly, in spite of his fears for her? Or is he trying *not* to smile, in spite of his knowingness and the vicarious pleasure this induces? How different, finally, is Orville's expression from the smirks of Clement's other cohorts under similar circumstances?

This is not the only occasion on which Orville fails—by appearing to tolerate if not condone what *Evelina* defines as immoral male behavior—to be a credible redeemer. There is also his unpardonable good humor about Lord Merton's and Mr. Coverley's racing of elderly women for sport. The episode opens with Merton and Coverley determined, out of boredom, to drive their phaetons against each other for one thousand pounds. The ladies are alarmed, prompting gentle Orville to suggest they change the bet "to something less dangerous" (269). What began as a contest in machismo (Merton versus Coverley), now becomes a contest between two modes of masculinity (Merton/Coverley versus Orville): though both aim to bolster male esteem, the first dogmatically ignores or offends women, while the second assumes an attitude of deference toward them. When Orville's proposal passes, deference triumphs, and it seems to be from sour grapes that Coverley, reverting to his own terms, compares Orville's driving to an old lady's. Evelina tells us that "this sally occasioned much laughter" (270), apparently injuring Orville, since later he half-jokes about escaping Coverley's wit (277). But clearly it is Orville who carries the day, for his ostentatiously humane suggestion—"The money should be his due, who, according to the opinion of the judges, should bring the worthiest object with whom to share it!" (274)—succeeds in enchanting Evelina.

How unprepared one is, then, for Orville's announcement on the following day that

> to his great satisfaction, the parties had been prevailed upon to lower the sum from one thousand to one hundred pounds; and that they had agreed it should be determined by a race between two old women, one of whom was to be chosen by each side, and both were to be proved more than eighty years of age, though, in other respects strong and healthy as possible. (277)

While the gist of Orville's achievement is to lower the stakes, his "great satisfaction" appears to include the whipping on of two women in what must be, for them, a life-threatening activity. Could this be Orville's answer—I'll show you who the *real* old ladies are—to Coverley's quip?

Can this be the same man who, out of respect for womankind, seemed to offer a moral alternative? Now this prince-turned-dragon laughs off Evelina's surprise, admires the quaintness of her qualms, and admits that he never expected his humane proposal to be effected. As Orville matter-of-factly takes up the New Bath Guide, the distinction between competing masculinities collapses, noble courtier falling in upon vulgar boor. Of course these modes have distinct class connotations, which *Evelina* has already dismantled by picturing Lord Merton et al. as skirt-chasers and gluttons, inattentive at the theater, ignorant of the classics, and surpassing their social inferiors only in ribaldry.[15] Here, by portraying the *chevalier par excellence* blithely content to bruise old ladies, Burney once again tarnishes the tale of the knight in shining armor.

The point is driven home by the actual race, depicted in shocking detail. At a spot Orville has helped to choose, the men watch and cheer as the frightened contestants stumble repeatedly. Grandmothers run aground, they "complained of being much bruised; for, heavy and helpless, they had not been able to save themselves, but fell with their whole weight upon the gravel" (293). At this, their backers rush up with chairs and wine, reviving the women only to set them back on track. When Coverley finds his help unavailing—"the poor creature was too much hurt to move" (294)—he suddenly becomes "quite brutal: he swore at her with unmanly rage, and seemed scarce able to refrain even from striking her" (294). Men who "help" the frailer sex, *Evelina* continually implies, usually have their own interests at heart, and when these are foiled, the force underlying their relation to women is soon enough explicit.

The race is followed by another case in point. Resuming his ongoing harassment of Evelina, Lord Merton drunkenly belies his "high-flown compliments" by resorting to violence, much to the company's distress and Evelina's terror. But the brutality of a Coverley or Merton is hardly surprising; the reader is more intrigued by the behavior of an Orville, and throughout these events Burney's hero is notably inactive. Never once during the race does he register the faintest disapproval, though Evelina imagines he looks "grave." Later he appears "thoughtful," and when Evelina is actually under attack his expression becomes, strangely enough, one of "earnestness" (294). He watches thus, biding his time until virtually everyone else has tried and failed to loosen Merton's grip, before at last disengaging her. We feel he is right to apologize for not interfering sooner, and can only remember the blamable earnestness of his gaze. Instead of sharing Evelina's "undissembled anger," Orville seems again to anticipate her molestation with mixed emotions, going almost so far as to participate in it as voyeur. [16]

At moments like these, Orville slips from a boys-will-be-boys complacency into being, himself, one of the boys. He is arguably also of the fraternity in two telling conversations about female beauty. In the first, Orville joins Lovel in an extended meditation, in her presence, on Evelina's blush. Where Lovel means to insult, Orville intends to admire, but they likewise ensure that Evelina will continue to exhibit the phenomenon in question. Sir Clement and Captain Mirvan join in, and as the exchange concludes on a self-congratulatory note—Sir Clement pronouncing Orville "a *connoisseur* in beauty," Orville terming him "an *enthusiast*" (68)—Burney's message emerges: though Orville savors Evelina instead of gulping her with Clement's gusto, he is equally guilty of appraising her as if she were a wine or a cheese.

The topic of the second conversation is still girl-watching, and Orville is droning on about nature and art and female beauty, much as he did in the earlier scene. Captain Mirvan begs to differ:

"I should be glad to know what you can see in e'er a face among them that's worth half-a-guinea for a sight."
"Half-a-guinea!" exclaimed [Orville], "I would give half I am worth for a sight of only *one*, provided I make my own choice." (96)

Though meaning to disagree, Orville actually proves himself simply a more extravagant version of Mirvan, no less willing to estimate female value in monetary terms. Accepting the Captain's commodification of women, he finds himself once more sharing metaphorical ground with someone he thought to disdain. Complaining of Lord Merton's unmatched rudeness (Clement seems gracious by comparison), Evelina has earlier remarked that the *"audible whisper . . .* is a mode of speech very distressing and disagreeable to by-standers" (94–95). This is clearly the register of both conversations above, since they force Evelina to hear herself discussed in tones neglectful of her presence. I suggest that the whisper of masculinist discourse in a woman's ear may also approximate the register I would audit in this chapter.

Usually Orville's underlying condescension to women is so genteelly phrased as to pass unremarked. It is discernible, as I have tried to show, only in relation to Sir Clement's leer and Captain Mirvan's sneer, at which point its distant kinship to these becomes apparent. Orville is repeatedly guilty by association: with Sir Clement and Lord Merton, rabid womanizers; with Captain Mirvan, unapologetic woman-hater; and with Lovel, whose failure to be the first has made him the second. [17] I want, however, to close my discussion of Orville by considering a case of more direct and independent willingness to regard women as objects for his purchase and use. [18] Whereas Clement and Merton immediately place the illegitimate Evelina in the class of molestable not marriageable women, Orville is distinguished chiefly by his more ennobled view of the heroine, even before her real aristocratic status is disclosed. As he says to Sir Clement:

> This young lady, though she seems alone, and, in some measure, unprotected, is not entirely without friends; she has been extremely well educated, and accustomed to good company; she has a natural love of virtue, and a mind that might adorn *any* station, however exalted: is such a young lady, Sir Clement, a proper object to trifle with? (328)

Several pages later he proposes. Yet Orville does not question the practice of trifling with unprotected ladies, only the choice of Evelina instead of a more "proper object." Orville reclasses Evelina, perceiving the imminent aristocrat in her, but he accepts, as unthinkingly as Sir Clement or Lord Merton, the dichotomization of women along class lines and the marking of lower-class women as fair game. Mrs. Beaumont weakly claims, upon learning that Evelina is of noble birth and affianced to a nobleman, "The young lady's rank in life, your Lordship's recommendation, or her own merit, would, any one of them, have been sufficient to have entitled her to my regard" (363). In fact the whole book has gone to show the insufficiency of Evelina's own merit, in the absence of elevated rank, to secure her from insult. Her indefinite class status means that she is treated like a goddess one minute and taken for a prostitute the next. Balancing her bastard heroine on the thin line between male reverence and derision, Burney offers an incisive analysis of her culture's unstable, contradictory, and class-bound images of women.

Burney notes, moreover, that upper-class women also suffer, their pedestals the props of a chimerical chivalry. Lord Merton, she makes clear, treats his fiancée with only slightly more veiled disregard than he does Evelina. Nor is the loftiest woman ever secure, for as Maria Edgeworth's Belinda is warned: "Even a coronet cannot protect a woman, you see, from disgrace: if she falls, she and it, and all together, are trampled under foot" (181). With a bitterness shared by most women writers of the period, Burney uses Evelina and Caroline to show that a woman's position essentially depends on whether men call her madonna or whore. Though Evelina angrily objects to just this shifting, double view of women when she discovers it in Sir Clement—"he seems disposed to think that the alteration in my companions authorises an alteration in his manners" (186)—she manages to overlook a comparable alteration in her beloved Orville. It occurs when Evelina flees an advancing officer and begs two women to protect her. Walking uncomfortably between, as she soon realizes, two prostitutes, Evelina is aghast to spy Lord Orville. "However," she relates, "to my infinite joy, he passed us without distinguishing me; though I saw that in a careless manner, his eyes surveyed the party" (219). Indeed it is Orville, not Evelina, who is disclosed by this unguarded moment. He has kept his distance as *Evelina*'s patrician villains bully women; he has held his own as the same men posture at women's expense; now, faced with underclass women, he frankly discards his chivalrous attitude for the careless one of a Merton or Clement; and if Evelina misses the point, the reader finds it difficult to do so.

Surveying these women's wares, Orville *sees* Evelina but fails to *recognize* her, and in this he further refigures the marital and paternal crimes of that arch-villain Sir John Belmont, who sees but refuses legally to recognize his wife or daughter. By continually assimilating the "right" kind of partner to the disastrously "wrong," *Evelina* echoes the fears of conduct writers such as Pennington and Chapone who warn that marriage is a "dangerous die." I want to conclude and in some sense summarize this section by observing that—in contrast to many eighteenth-century protagonists of enigmatic origins, from Marivaux's Marianne to Fielding's Joseph Andrews—Evelina herself knows who she is from the outset.[19] The issue, I have said, is getting Sir John not to see she exists but to identify her as his daughter, and the effect of rephrasing the problem in this way is to stress the dependence of women on ruling-class men to say who they are and what they may become. While Wilhelm Meister comes to recognize his true nature, the developing heroine becomes recognizable in terms of received female types. Against the fiction of individual self-making, *Evelina* poses a different, overdetermined story of deindividuation and conventionalization.

III

I have been trying to fathom the narrative level at which Villars and Orville are bound to a disreputable brotherhood, one whose predatory view of Evelina (and of women generally) stalks, snares, ambushes her formation. As we have seen, the thwarting of this formation is argued anecdotally by the accumulation of episodes in which Evelina's sense of mobility and potentiality is impaired. It is also argued in larger terms by a plot that runs against the grain of a *Bildungsroman*, shaped instead to suggest circularity, belatedness, and futility. Hardly a critic has failed to notice the resemblance between Villars and Orville, which Evelina describes and their names so strenuously imply. They are, more precisely, inversions of each other, and together their names map the circularity of Evelina's course as she moves from one father figure to another—a circularity literalized by her return to Villars and Berry Hill, hard upon her wedding, with vertiginous haste. [20]

Toward the end of the novel Evelina seems to accomplish two things: first her engagement to Orville, then her recognition by Belmont. But if her marriage, as I argue, is actually regressive, her patrimony turns out to be irrelevant, for she is already Lady Orville by the time she becomes Miss Belmont, legitimate daughter of nobility. Orville's willingness to second-guess her status drains all the urgency from Evelina's quest for her rightful title. [21] Practically speaking, Evelina's reunion with Belmont is belated and therefore useless, and it proves to be further redundant in psychological terms. Bearing her mother's face and letter, Evelina comes to Sir John for emotional as well as material restitution. Caroline's letter imagines her errant husband wracked by guilt and requires him to clear her name and receive their child. In fact, though Sir John writhes through renewed pangs of remorse, he has long since repented his desertion and adopted the girl he believes to be his daughter. As Evelina explains, "At the very time we concluded I was unnaturally rejected, my deluded father meant to show me most favour and protection" (357). All this yearning after the father to gain a pedigree and apology that are already hers; all this desire for the world only to return to rural seclusion; all this straining away from an overzealous guardian only to marry his mirror image, another man who cherishes the girlish in Evelina and chastens the adult. Surely a sense of futility is intrinsic to such a narrative, as it is to so many of the minor events that beset the women of this book.

I have already referred to the runoff of anger produced by this narrative, too great for the comic story to absorb. Female rage in *Evelina* is most theatrically expressed by Madame Duval and most subtly by Lady Howard, who turns out to be Madame Duval's unlikely ambassador and ally. It is, for example, Lady Howard who takes up the grandmother's suit against Villars, pressing him to release Evelina. "It is time that she should see something of the world" (7), she argues. And later more accusingly: "She is a little angel! I cannot wonder that you sought to monopolize her: neither ought you, at finding it impossible" (10). Though proper as Mrs. Chapone herself, Lady Howard also joins Madame Duval in urging a lawsuit against Sir John, and when Villars objects, she once again takes up her pen on behalf of murdered mother, disinherited daughter, and irate, neglected grandmother.[22] The bluestocking, Mrs. Selwyn (whose insurgent wit has been sufficiently discussed by other critics, notably Rose Marie Cutting), succeeds Lady Howard in this activity of confronting Sir John. Suffice it to say that Madame Duval is but the book's most obviously untamed shrew. Her ranting is reinforced by several less openly obstreperous figures, from Caroline and Evelina to the learned Mrs. Selwyn and respectable Lady Howard. One purpose of my reading is to situate this ranting in the context of a narrative, to give it a reason and a shape. Throughout much of *Evelina*, however, feminist anger is deflected from its target and redirected against other women. When Captain Mirvan binds Madame Duval's feet and tethers her to a tree, Evelina cuts her grandmother loose, only to be slapped across the face. The slap is partly deserved punishment for Evelina's cooperation with the prank, but it also shows the powerless reduced to brawling among themselves, one mark of those with power being their inaccessibility. Just as Madame Duval's anger at Mirvan falls on Evelina, nearest and weakest, so I have already detailed the diversion of Evelina's anger at Sir Clement onto Madame Duval and her family. Even Mrs. Selwyn, whose satire does skewer a few noblemen, takes out much of her anger on her own sex. Her feminist strategy amounts to a kind of male impersonation, which, though empowering for Mrs. Selwyn herself, reproduces men's scorn for women as a class.

Attention to the way female anger in *Evelina* turns back at women and into self-hatred (a topic I return to with Elizabeth Bennet) can help to clarify an otherwise obscure incident: the attempted suicide of Evelina's half-brother, Mr. Macartney. Dressed in black, afflicted by family problems, this latter-day Hamlet would seem odd and extraneous were it not that he serves to dramatize Evelina's inner life. Beth Kowaleski-Wallace has noted the similarity of their circumstances, explaining that, "As her double he embodies the instincts and desires not consonant with Evelina's ideal image of herself, instincts and desires she is not allowed to acknowledge explicitly to herself" ("*Evelina*," 11). Chief among these is hostility toward their father (Sir John) and, in a completion of the oedipal pattern, desire for the mother. Stabbing his father out of incestuous love (for another apparent half-sister), Macartney acts out these feelings all too unsymbolically. As Evelina's double, Macartney externalizes her anger toward her real father, Sir John, as well as father figures Villars and Orville, and invokes a mythic structure supporting my contention that the underlying ambition in *Evelina* is for the mother and not the father. The ultimate superfluity of Evelina's rapprochement with Sir John, the circularity of her passage from Villars to Orville, the barely covert patricidal anger toward these three figures, all combine to undercut the quest-for-the-father plot. But if Macartney enacts Evelina's rage toward paternal figures, he also enacts the introversion of this rage to a self-destructive degree. The episode of his suicide attempt is clearly a coded portrayal of Evelina's own death.

Macartney expresses his dejection in a fragment of poetry deploring life as a "lingering dream of grief, of pain." His ode strikes a chord in Evelina, who muses ambiguously, "These lines are harsh, but they indicate an internal wretchedness, which I own, affects me" (162). In this mood, Evelina sees his pistol and thinks immediately of suicide, and the very thought has a deathlike effect on her. "All power of action forsook me," she remembers, "and I grew almost stiff with horror" (166).

Recovering enough to tail him upstairs, the fascinated heroine watches as he takes a pistol in each hand and calls on God to forgive him. Just when he seems about to shoot, Evelina leaps forward, grabs his arm, and—as if she had taken his place—falls down "breathless and sense-less" (167). She awakens in time to wrest away his guns, leaving him wondering what angel has been sent to save him: "Do my senses deceive me! . . . do *I* live—? and do *you?*" (168). The Branghtons think not, for by the time they arrive Evelina has swooned again. "I seemed to have suffered a violent death," she writes, "either by my own rashness, or the cruelty of some murderer, as the pistols had fallen close by my side" (169). The Branghtons are so sure she is dead, they don't even bother to help her. Lest this seem an event enabling Evelina to purge a suicidal wish, reject a suicidal double, she concludes her letter on a pessimistic note: "The rashness and the misery of this ill-fated young man engross all my thoughts. If indeed, he is bent upon destroying himself, all ef-forts to save him will be fruitless" (169).

Here, perhaps, is the excessive sentimentality that Austen's *Love and Freindship* would parody in scenes strewn with unconscious female bodies. But in a novel whose heroine purportedly enters the world, such an obvious staging of her exit by suicide/murder seems worth con-sideration. My sense that it signals despair of a proto-feminist kind is reinforced by another Burney character who attempts suicide: Elinor Jodrell of *The Wanderer*, a cross-dressing advocate of women's rights, is driven mad by a lover who prefers the more traditional heroine, Juliet. Evelina's attribution of her seeming death to either her own hand "or the cruelty of some murderer" would appear to support this reading. The double verdict specifies, too, the alternation I am tracking be-tween reluctance and willingness in *Evelina* to accuse men of murdering female development.

That Evelina's engagement coincides with a form of death is written between the lines of the novel's closing pages. Villars's last letter is over-whelmingly morbid. Should misfortune mar Evelina's happiness, Vil-lars protests, he would die. In any case, he prays only to live long enough to bless her, "closing these joy-streaming eyes in her presence, and breathing my last faint sighs in her loved arms!" (387) Whether happy or unhappy, Evelina's marriage means death to Villars, his defeat and replacement by a younger man. From this he proceeds to equally fond thoughts of Evelina's own death, wishing her an end propitious as his. "And mayest thou, when thy glass is run, be sweetly, but not bitterly, mourned by some remaining darling of thy affections—some yet surviving Evelina!" (387–88). Villars does imagine her a timely death, yet his vision of a "surviving Evelina" still serves to identify her with the ill-fated Caroline. What is more, his yen for a second, still-living Evelina has this one already buried. It makes sense for Villars to mourn Evelina, since he loses her twice (first to Belmont and now to Orville). Richardson's *Clarissa*, one might reason, helped to create an appreciative audience for novels concluding in this kind of sentimentalized grief. But if *Evelina* were all it appeared to be—a girl's growing up completed by marriage—it would still typically conclude with a hopeful account of vows, perhaps a hint of progeny to come. That it closes, instead, on a queerly elegiac note should alert readers to another developmental theme.

Evelina's (and the book's) last letter frankly conflates her marriage to Orville with her return to Villars at Berry Hill, sustaining the note of requiem where epithalamion should be. I quote the entire letter, which is addressed to Villars:

> All is over, my dearest Sir; and the fate of your Evelina is decided! This morning, with fearful joy and trembling gratitude, she united herself for ever with the object of her dearest, her eternal affection. I have time for no more; the chaise now waits which is to conduct me to dear Berry Hill, and to the arms of the best of men.   (388)

The sense of finality, of things being out of her hands, of eternity and time run out; the feelings of joy mixed with fear; the fact that neither Orville or Villars is mentioned by name—these add up to an impression that Evelina is meeting her Maker instead of her lover. The very briefness of the letter suggests a shortness of breath, a running down of words, a laying down of arms. Words have been, throughout, Evelina's best defense against assaultive experience. As the novel's preeminent narrator, she wields more power then she herself knows. To a large extent, her meanings, both conscious and unconscious, have prevailed. The loquacious Sir Clement, by contrast, speaks for himself only once—in the short, rude letter that Evelina contains inside one of her own. Clearly letters give Evelina a kind of control that, away from her writing desk, she rarely has. Ultimately, they slip beyond her control, hazarding judgments, mounting oppositions, which may have more to do with the novel's intentions than they do with Evelina's own. In her opening letter, for example, Evelina means to remain a dutiful daughter, within the geographical limits Villars has set. But the appeal of trangression, the determination to see London, continually leads her pen astray.

> Pray don't suppose that I make any point of going, for I shall hardly sigh, to see them depart without me, though I shall probably never meet with such another opportunity. And, indeed, their domestic happiness will be so great,—it is natural to wish to partake of it. I believe I am bewitched! I made a resolution, when I began, that I would not be urgent; but my pen—or rather my thoughts, will not suffer me to keep it. (13)

This has been my point about *Evelina*: that its heroine's pen is bewitched and her letters, like those of women conduct writers, haunted by dissident meanings. Though Evelina aims to tell a story of growth and fulfillment, her tale is countered by another of hindrance and frustration, and marriage to Orville does not break so much as chime with the gothic rhythms of this narrative. And if marriage serves to keep Evelina from getting anywhere, it also, by ending her letters, eliminates what has been her only mode of complaint. The heroine's amusing tongue-tiedness on first meeting Orville appears to have been prophetic, for that lord no sooner claims her—"You are now," he declares, "all my own!"—than Evelina's usual spring of words runs dry: "I could make no reply, indeed I hardly spoke another word the rest of the evening; so little talkative is the fulness of contentment" (386). Leaving its heroine in happy silence, *Evelina* challenges us to recuperate its other story of female destiny bound and abandoned, but not gagged—the story embodied by Madame Duval, feet tied and dumped in a ditch, yet "sobbing, nay, almost roaring, and in the utmost agony of rage and terror" (133).

CHAPTER THREE

The Humiliation of Elizabeth Bennet

RECENT commentary on Burney offers a good example of feminist scholarship in a recuperative vein, elaborating the obscure
diarist and one-book novelist known as "Fanny" into Frances Burney—
influential author of four, thick novels and several unpublished plays,
all of them embedded in revolutionary-era debates about the raising of
girls and the rights of women. Jane Austen, on the other hand, has long
had a place in official histories of the novel, presenting a somewhat different challenge to feminist critics who would reconceive that place and
that history. For while Burney had been more or less mislaid by scholars, Austen has been and is still the object of diversely passionate
claims. Is it, I wonder, because many of us who write about Austen first
read her at an early age that arguments about the novels seem bound up
with our earliest attachments and views, that our feelings about this
writer are often so desperately possessive? "But this isn't *my* Jane Austen," we are tempted to protest. Or is it that, to critics since George
Lewes, Austen has been invaluable as a good girl with whom to berate
bad girls such as Charlotte Brontë and George Sand, so that feminist
attention to Austen's impiety produces a kind of moral vertigo? At a
time when we, like Austen's contemporaries, turn to the family for or-

der and "values" that seem under siege, it is distressing, perhaps, to find familial relations in disarray even in Austen's well-loved and well-mannered universe. What is clear, in any case, is that resistance to feminist rereadings of Austen has been ongoing and energetic, making her a significant site of those ideological battles being fought throughout the American academy and culture in the wake of the most recent women's movement. Before approaching the representations of female development in *Pride and Prejudice* and the juvenile sketches underpinning it, I want, by way of placing my own thinking about Austen, to look briefly at two contributions to the current debate.

The "conservative" view of Austen as Tory defender of traditional beliefs and practices—handed down from the Janeites and often accompanied by the sense that Austen's politics were rather intuitive than self-conscious, more a matter of unexamined class style and female complacency than critical engagement with contemporary ideas and events—continues to be defended against feminist views to the contrary. [1] Surprisingly, however, the backlash against feminist appropriations of Austen has also come from some of those within the so-called subversive school, from scholars who apparently agree that Austen assailed the sex-gender system of her day but ignore or debunk the body of feminist work to this effect. John Halperin's 1984 work, touted as "the first biography in half a century," is a notable example of this reaction. Calling on virtually the same textual evidence that feminists have used to identify Austen's attractive impatience with gender norms, her forceful critique of conventional female destinies, Halperin's considered opinion is that the writer was not a very nice person. Commenting on the letter in which she dryly attributes a neighbor's stillborn child to a fright—"I suppose she happened unawares to look at her husband"—Halperin offers:

> This is identified by some as an example of the novelist's heartlessness. It is malicious, nasty, and tasteless, certainly; Jane Austen was frequently malicious and nasty, though not often tasteless. And undoubtedly there was a streak of heartlessness in her, a pitilessness—a coldness, as has been suggested; but she was by no means the bitch-monster of E. M. Forster, H. W. Garrod, D. W. Harding, Harold Nicolson, and others. (78–79)

Disingenuously professing to defend Austen from the charges of other critics, Halperin manages in the space of two sentences to describe her as "malicious," "nasty," "tasteless," "heartless," "pitiless," "cold," and, losing adjectival control entirely, by no means a "bitch-monster."

Halperin's subsequent diagnosis of Austen—a scholarly rendering of that postmodern axiom, "all she really needs"—speaks sufficiently for itself. Apart from this, I suggest that Halperin operates within the idiom of early 1980s culture in another, less obvious way. It goes without saying that the decade preceding the 1984 publication of *The Life of Jane Austen* saw an explosion of feminist work on this writer by critics who, following the example of Virginia Woolf in *A Room of One's Own*, made the emerging British novel, and Austen in particular, central to their construction of a female literary tradition. To write a four hundred–page book on Austen in the context of proliferating feminist perspectives on her—by Nina Auerbach (1972), Susan Gubar (1975), Patricia Spacks (1975), Ellen Moers (1976), Lillian Robinson (1978), Sandra Gilbert and Susan Gubar (1979), Judith Lowder Newton (1981), and Rachel Brownstein (1982), among others—without once mentioning any of them (while frequently citing Walton Litz, Marvin Mudrick, Joan Rees, John Odmark, and many more) is willy-nilly to enter the ideological fracas about Austen if only by conspicuous, provocative omission.[2] Moreover, Halperin implicitly addresses feminist critics; if his views about Austen are understood as an allegory for his views about Austen scholarship, then Halperin's denigration of the novelist is also a warning to nasty female scholars who share her critique of stillborn marriages and scarifying husbands. His message to the likes of Gilbert and Gubar, those popularizers of female rage and champions of "bitch-monsters" Mary Crawford and Lady Catherine De Bourgh, is that feminist criticism does not become a lady.

A second, more recent and unexpected attack by a "subversive" opposed to feminist approaches comes from Julia Prewitt Brown in her 1990 review essay, "The Feminist Depreciation of Austen: A Polemical Reading," a piece that needs to be read in conjunction with Brown's 1979 book on Austen. In *Jane Austen's Novels: Social Change and Literary Form*, Brown makes what feminists would call a persuasive "women's culture" case for Austen (not unlike the case made for Harriet Beecher

Stowe by Jane Tompkins or Gillian Brown, for example). Taking her epigraph from *A Room of One's Own*, Brown suggests that Austen's novels celebrate a "feminine consciousness" of ordinary, relational, domestic life, previously unrepresented in literature and still derided as less "historical" than accounts of military violence. As a corollary to this argument, Brown characterizes marriage in Austen (reconciling "the self and the world") as the ultimate domestic relation (6), as a crucial stage of the heroine's moral growth (7), and as the key to a quasi-biological comic vision shared by Shakespeare and Austen alike (17–18). Asserting that "the continuity of life lies in the ritual of marriage" (10), Brown parts company here with feminist critics, who tend by contrast to endorse Judith Lowder Newton's well-known remark that "marriage requires [Elizabeth Bennet] to dwindle by degrees into a wife" (84).

According to Brown's review essay, feminists consequently depreciate Austen herself, complaining that "all the novels end in marriage, affirming [their author's] allegiance to what is called the established order" ("Feminist," 305). But what Brown fails to grasp is that neither those critics she names (Gilbert and Gubar, Carolyn Heilbrun, or Mary Poovey) nor those she might have (Lowder Newton, Lillian Robinson, or Karen Newman) do, in fact, condemn the writer for marrying off her heroines, however much they may see marriage as a conservative institution.[3] Rather, they insist on the inevitably contradictory nature of Austen's novels, which both reproduce conventional beliefs about marriage as the goal of female development and, at the same time, subject those beliefs to scrutiny. In my opinion, Brown herself overstates the "different" power women of Austen's class and time derived from the domestic sphere, romanticizing the period up until *Persuasion* as a pre-industrial Golden Age, when men and women of the rural gentry worked side by side and were "nearly equal" in responsibility (*Jane*, 167). With the exception of her last novel, claims Brown, Austen's work eschews "sexual stereotypes," "for she began writing before the stereotypes had firmly taken hold" (170). Feminist critics, on the other hand, while stressing Austen's defiant genius, also recognize the limiting, gendered conditions of her artistry—conditions perceived and addressed by a developing feminist discourse long before 1817. To do so is not, as Brown accuses Claudia Johnson of doing, to depreciate Austen

("Feminist," 309) but only to acknowledge her marginalization as a woman writer—whose position, though difficult, may actually grant her a useful critical distance on her community.

Braving Halperin's attempt at intimidation and questioning Brown's claim that to disapprove of Darcy as Elizabeth's end is necessarily to disapprove of the author of *Pride and Prejudice*, I want to take my place among those who would articulate the contradictory strains in Austen's work. For many readers of Austen, myself included, the story that raises Elizabeth into a wealthy and beloved wife is equaled as credible romance only by the coupling of Anne Elliot and Captain Wentworth. Yet as I suggested in the opening chapter, that story is countered in my view by another telling of her courtship as Elizabeth's humiliating decline. This antiromantic narrative—familiar by now from conduct books and *Evelina*, sharing with these women's texts a sociolect of anxiety about marriage and female development—unfolds in *Pride and Prejudice* less as a circling than as a falling off. For unlike Evelina, whose authorial consequence is always modest, Elizabeth Bennet begins at the peak of the learning curve so ambitiously imagined by Ann Murry in *Mentoria*—a book, it will be recalled, that Austen bestowed upon a favorite niece. Enabled by her father, this unique Bennet daughter sets out with a surplus of intellectual confidence and authority which, in the course of the novel, she must largely relinquish. Helping as well as hindering the female protagonist, the father in Austen is more complex than in Burney, where he seems always on the verge of villainy; yet in *Pride and Prejudice* as in *Evelina*, the heroine's deformation involves her continual circulation among paternal figures.

Against the grain of a story that Austen herself described as "too light, and bright, and sparkling," this chapter will focus, then, on a darker, downward vector: the narrative that passes Elizabeth from one father to another and, in doing so, takes her from shaping judgments to being shaped by them. *Pride and Prejudice* is not, of course, alone among Austen's novels in turning on the heroine's discovery that her reading of the world is "wrong." Catherine Morland, Marianne Dashwood, and Emma Woodhouse all fall upon hermeneutic hard times—and, say many critics, rightly so. C. S. Lewis, for example, sees these as moments of redeeming "penitence" and quasi-religious "awakening" (25–27). Mark Schorer, from whose essay "The Humiliation of Emma

Woodhouse" I take my title, remarks similarly that "the diminution of Emma in the social scene, her reduction to her proper place . . . is very beautiful" (102). I am arguing, by contrast, that the reductions of Catherine, Marianne, Emma, and Elizabeth are not unequivocally endorsed; that Austen's novels do more than simply applaud their diminution as morally necessary or "beautiful"; that the female protagonist's humiliation, as much as it advances the romantic plot, also comments ironically on this plot and on marriage as a girl's developmental goal.

To support this view, I want to look briefly at the epistolary works *Love and Freindship* (1790) and "The Three Sisters" (1792), examples of the juvenile writing to which the writer continually returned, as Q. D. Leavis has so memorably shown ("Critical"). While "The Three Sisters" is interesting for its prototypes of Mr. Collins and the three Bennet sisters, both of these sketches are useful to me in rendering explicit the critique of romantic apprenticeship I find implicit in *Pride and Prejudice*. The convenient foregrounding in these early texts of concerns about courtship and marriage, removed to a murkier distance in Austen's later works, has arguably to do with their composition in the still politically defiant climate of the early 1790s. Three critics have recently associated Austen with early feminist politics by linking her backward to eighteenth-century movements. Margaret Kirkham ties her to the rationalist tradition of Enlightenment feminism originating with Mary Astell (1688–1731); Claudia Johnson places her left-of-center on a spectrum of politically engaged novelists during the revolutionary period; and Alison Sulloway links her to a group of eighteenth-century female satirists including Frances Burney and Maria Edgeworth, among others. All three establish some relation between Austen and Mary Wollstonecraft, and Kirkham and Johnson stress the need to veil this relationship as the 1790s become increasingly reactionary. Criticism of authority was generally inhibited by the Treasonable Practices and Seditious Meetings Acts of 1795, and connection with Wollstonecraft became particularly dangerous after Godwin published his scandalizing *Memoirs of the Author of a Vindication of the Rights of Woman* in 1798 (Johnson, xxiii; Kirkham, 48–50). Such a historical schema helps, first, to locate in the context of a residual feminist discourse what I see as Austen's mistrust of girls who resign their minds to marriage and male authority; in addition, it begins to explain why this mistrust might be closer to the surface in works written before 1794.

Love and Freindship features lovers who, while "gracefully" lifting money from unsuspecting relatives, pretend to scorn any currency or nourishment but love. "Does it appear impossible to your vile and corrupted Palate, to exist on Love?" (*Minor*, 83) Edward asks indignantly. "Yes" is this story's emphatic answer, as it humorously demonstrates that lovers need to eat and that women often marry less from love than from economic desperation. Thus in Laura's delirious rhapsody on Edward's death, "Cupid's Thunderbolts" immediately give way to more prosaic items: "I see a Leg of Mutton—They told me Edward was not Dead; but they deceived me—they took him for a Cucumber—" (100). At some essential level, *Love and Freindship* hints, what a husband means to Laura is food on the table. "The Three Sisters" also points up the unsentimental truth that middle-class women, excluded from wage labor and often from inheritance, may be forced to wed for money. In this short piece, courtship is reduced to negotiating Mary Stanhope's price for living with a man she openly despises. The first line's rhetoric of romance—"I am the happiest creature in the World, for I have received an offer of marriage from Mr. Watts" (*Minor*, 57)—is dramatically exploded by the ensuing haggle over money, carriages, and servants. In *Pride and Prejudice*, too, a vocabulary of feeling conflicts with actions driven by material need, for the story of Elizabeth's sentimental education is countered by the story of Charlotte's simple exigency— and Elizabeth's own, which Lillian Robinson has noted is actually more dire (187–88). As I will be emphasizing, in *Pride and Prejudice* class and monetary motives for marrying are not supplanted by emotional ones but only submerged by them. Brown mentions that the late eighteenth-century emergence of "affective individualism," first described by Lawrence Stone, gave the women of Austen's time unprecedented latitude in choosing a husband ("Feminist," 306). Yet I would argue that Austen remained suspicious not only of excessively sentimental rhetoric but of all attempts to deny the material contingencies of marriage and to romanticize it as a simple matter of female interest and choice.

I do not mean to suggest that Elizabeth's and Darcy's betrothal lacks all emotional integrity, only that its bliss is qualified by Austen's shrewdly complex understanding of marriage as an economic and social institution. Girls may marry because they are poor and also, Austen intimates, because they are bored.[4] Once again, *Love and Freindship* thematizes this in usefully exaggerated terms. While the heroines of Austen's mature novels live incestuously among "3 or 4 Families in a Country Village," poor Laura of *Love and Freindship* has exactly one neighbor. In the quiet Vale of Uske, a knock on the door is a shattering occasion, causing endless speculation among a company dying for event. Laura knows that this knock is her only chance to flee the Vale of Uske, and she says of the Stranger, "I felt that on him the happiness or Misery of my future Life must depend" (78–80). It is precisely such circumstances of female isolation, boredom, and constraint that make the prospect of Frank Churchill so refreshing to Emma Woodhouse and Mr. Bingley's arrival in town so momentous to the Bennet girls. The tedium of their days is brought home to these sisters when it rains: "Even Elizabeth might have found some trial of her patience in weather, which totally suspended the improvement of her acquaintance with Mr. Wickham; and nothing less than a dance on Tuesday, could have made such a Friday, Saturday, Sunday and Monday, endurable to Kitty and Lydia" (88). Hinging her plots on a strange man's knock at the door, Austen submits that a woman's escape from lonely monotony is just so precariously hinged.

That women turn to marriage hoping to see more of the world, to increase their personal mobility, is likewise suggested in "The Three Sisters" by Mary Stanhope's fixation with Mr. Watts's carriage. Though her passion seems to be for blue with silver spots, Mary quarrels with her fiancé as much about her use of the coach as its color, and Mr. Watts's enthusiasm for "Women's always Staying at home" (59) almost makes her refuse him. That Mary gets brown with a silver border plus a prohibition against going "to Town or any other public place for these three Years" (67) indicates that husbands may not, after all, guarantee the wished-for freedom. *Love and Freindship* is finally skeptical toward husbands as well. While promising to be about "the determined Perseverance of disagreable [sic] Lovers" (77), the tale is actually inversely cruel, for its lovers are not disagreeable—neither do they persevere. Sophia's husband is immediately imprisoned, and Laura's vanishes in pursuit. Accidentally reunited with her spouse, Laura begs him to explain his absence, but Edward's sudden expiration leaves this question unanswered, so adding desertion to Austen's list of the hazards of married life. *Pride and Prejudice* has its share of disagreeably persevering lovers in Mr. Collins and, initially, Mr. Darcy; like *Love and Freindship* and scores of women's conduct books it also—in Wickham, Mr. Bennet, and Mr. Bingley—warns of lovers whose affections do not last. Here I would observe that both of these negative categories include not only the unappealing husbands of undiscerning women, not only men previously rejected by the more perceptive heroine, but also the suitors that she and her elder sister eventually accept.

If Austen shows that the meanness of women's estate forces them to wed insufficient men, this may go some way toward explaining her notoriously abbreviated proposals and rushed endings. In both "The Three Sisters" and *Love and Freindship*, Austen's burlesque of proposals, marriage, and neat, comic closure is predictably broad. "The Three Sisters" lampoons Watts's offer to transfer his proposal from Mary to Sophy, laughs darkly at Mary's reluctance to accept him—"Well then (said Mary in a peevish Accent) I *will* have you if I *must*" (64)—and leaves the happy couple wrangling their way down the aisle. In *Love and Freindship* Edward meets, proposes to, and weds Laura all in an instant—after which he departs from the scene. This text closes its account of two disastrous marriages with the requisite multiplication of unions, all of them so improbable or improper as to strain this convention to the breaking point. The marriage of Augusta and Graham unites two vaguely unpleasant, entirely minor, and previously unacquainted characters; Sir Edward, gothic heir to Walpole's Manfred and forerunner of Austen's General Tilney, finally clarifies his greed and incestuous desire by taking for himself the lovely heiress he intended for his son; lastly, male cousins Philander and Gustavus, flouting heterosexual expectations altogether, crown their theatrical collaboration by removing "to Covent Garden, where they still Exhibit under the assumed names of *Lewis and Quick*" (109). Halperin accuses Austen's conclusions of being invariably "unsubtle, undramatic, and ineffective," and he finds the end of *Pride and Prejudice* typically botched:

> To be told in cool third-person commentary, without dialogue or any
> direct access to the minds and thoughts of either character, of the

final reconciliation of Elizabeth and Darcy and their agreement to
marry . . . is an anticlimax of awful proportions, and it is a mistake
Jane Austen makes in all of her books.   (78)

Yet the calculated irreverence of the endings I have just considered, the
frank view of marriage and husbands I have just explored, not to mention *Northanger Abbey*'s explicit mockery of novels that resolve into "perfect felicity" (250), all argue that the cool haste of these last moments is
far from mistaken. It is, in my view, as pointed and dramatically effective as the grimness of Marianne Dashwood's marrying an older man
she has never much liked, the doubtfulness of Edmund Bertram waking up to find he loves Fanny, or the awkwardness of turkey-thievery
delivering Mr. Knightley to Emma.[5]

Austen's *juvenilia* are useful, then, for their grossly ironic treatment
of heterosexual romance. Further, like the conduct materials considered
in chapter 1, they may help to recover some alternative narratives about
girls becoming women, which in Austen's later novels appear only under erasure: unavailable or lost to the female protagonist and, at some
textual level, lamented. *Love and Freindship*, for example, tells of a love
and friendship between two women that actually displaces the traditional courtship plot. Is this, perhaps, the female homosocial story
whose underlying presence in *Emma* has disconcerted readers from Edmund Wilson onward? Is it, moreover, the story only weakly gestured
toward by *Pride and Prejudice* when it makes Mrs. Bingley and Mrs.
Darcy neighbors? I would argue that Austen's early, epistolary works
point, in addition, to the story of a girl who grows up writing; this is
the story, retold in *Pride and Prejudice* as a history of rescinded authority,
that I hope to recuperate in the following pages. Along with Lady Pennington's letters to her daughters and other courtesy books in letters,
along with *Evelina* and other epistolary novels, much of Austen's *juvenilia* catches women in the act of writing and comments implicitly on
the novelist's own vocation. Patricia Spacks has noted that Austen's
Lady Susan (c. 1794) differs from previous epistolary novels in which
characters "*feel* rather than *do*" (93). Lady Susan uses letters instead to
make things happen: in the hands of this manipulative character "writing
becomes a form of agency" (91). I would say, similarly, that in *Love and
Freindship* Sophia's anonymous letter-within-Laura's-letter is an active
intervention (94–95): like Austen's own unsigned manuscripts, it deft-

ly orchestrates the demise of one courtship and the triumph of another. Is it just a coincidence that, shortly after her authorial feat, Sophia gets caught "majestically" robbing the paternal desk (95–96)? The contiguous episodes dramatize, I believe, Austen's recognition both that writing gives women performative power and that it constitutes an illicit raid on the father's library. This association of scribbling women with (stolen) authority has, however, more ominous implications as I turn now to *Pride and Prejudice*, which opens with Elizabeth in her father's library but proceeds to trace her expulsion from that paradise.

II

Elizabeth Bennet is introduced as the daughter of a reclusive and apparently ineffectual father; beside the rigid figure of *Northanger Abbey*'s General Tilney, Mr. Bennet may seem flimsy by comparison. But the general (despite his new gadgets) is an old-fashioned patriarch whose authoritarian style was all but outmoded by the end of the eighteenth century. Mr. Bennet is not actually a bad father—just a modern one. Smooth-browed advocate of instruction over discipline, user of reason instead of force, he typifies the benevolent father proposed by John Locke in his often reprinted tract, *Some Thoughts Concerning Education* (1693). As Jay Fliegelman explains, however, Locke's concern in this text "is not with circumscribing paternal authority, but with rendering it more effective by making it noncoercive" (13).[6] Apparently benign to the point of irresponsibility, Mr. Bennet may seem to wield nothing sharper than his sarcasm, but what he actually wields is the covert power of the Lockean patriarch, which is all the more effective for its subtlety. This aloof, unseen power of Mr. Bennet's suggests to me, for several reasons, the peculiar power of an author. As evidence of his literary disposition, Mr. Bennet takes refuge from the world in his library, prefers the inner to the outer life, chooses books over people. He asks two things only: the free use of his understanding and his room (112), precisely those things Virginia Woolf associates with the privilege of the male writer and privation of the female. Above all, among women whose solace is news, Mr. Bennet keeps the upper hand by withholding information—that is, by creating suspense.

In the opening scene, for example, Mr. Bennet refuses to visit the new bachelor in town, deliberately frustrating Mrs. Bennet's expectation and desire. In fact, "he had always intended to visit him, though to the last always assuring his wife that he should not go; and till the evening after the visit was paid, she had no knowledge of it" (6). Like any writer, Mr. Bennet relishes the power to contain his reader's pleasure and then, with his dénouement, to relieve and enrapture her. But the suspense is not over, for Elizabeth's father continues to be as stingy with physical description as some fathers are with pocket money. He controls his family by being not tightfisted but tight-lipped, and in this he resembles Austen herself. George Lewes first noted the remarkable paucity of concrete details in Austen, her reluctance to tell us what people, their clothes, houses, or gardens look like (O'Neill, 8). If female readers flocked to Richardson for Pamela's meticulous descriptions of what she packed in her trunk (Watt, 153), we may imagine their frustration at Austen's reticence about such matters. So Mr. Bennet only follows Austen when, secretive about Bingley's person and estate, he keeps the ladies in the dark. Their curiosity is finally gratified by another, less plain-styled father, Sir William Lucas, whose report they receive "second-hand" from Lady Lucas (9). For much as women talk in this novel, the flow of important words, of what counts as "intelligence," is regulated largely by men; in this verbal economy, women get the trickle-down of news.

The scene following Mr. Collins's proposal to Elizabeth offers another instance of this, as Mr. Bennet again contrives to keep his female audience hanging. In a stern prologue he pretends to support his wife—insisting that Lizzie marry her clerical cousin—only to undermine Mrs. Bennet in a surprise conclusion: "An unhappy alternative is before you, Elizabeth. From this day you must be a stranger to one of your parents. —Your mother will never see you again if you do *not* marry Mr. Collins, and I will never see you again if you *do*" (112). Not only this particular coup but the entire episode demonstrates the efficacy of paternal words. Throughout his proposal, much to Elizabeth's distress and the reader's amusement, Mr. Collins completely ignores her many impassioned refusals. He discounts what she says as "merely words of course" (108), for even his dim, self-mired mind correctly perceives that a lady's word carries no definitive weight. Mr. Collins accuses Elizabeth of wishing to increase his love "by suspense, according to the usual practice of elegant females" (108), yet creating suspense is exactly what Elizabeth, rhetorically disadvantaged, cannot do. She has no choice but "to apply to her father, whose negative might be uttered in such a manner as must be decisive" (109). Mr. Bennet's power resides, as I say, in his authorial prerogative, his right to have the last word.

Though Mr. Bennet uses this right to ridicule and disappoint his wife, he uses it in an opposite fashion to praise, protect, and apparently enable his daughter. Like so many heroines in women's fiction, Elizabeth has a special relationship to her father. She is immediately distinguished, both as a family member and as a character, by his preference for her and hers for him. Entail aside, she is in many respects his heir, for Mr. Bennet bequeaths to Elizabeth his ironic distance from the world, his habit of studying and appraising those around him, his role of social critic. Colleagues in this role, father and daughter scan Mr. Collins's letter together, dismissing man and letter with a few, skeptical words. Mr. Bennet enables Elizabeth, in short, by sharing with her an authorial mandate that is Austen's own: the need and ability to frame a moral discourse and to judge characters accordingly. Through her father, Elizabeth gains provisional access to certain authorial powers. But Mr. Bennet also shares with her, illogically enough, his disdain for women. He respects Elizabeth only insofar as she is unlike other girls, so that bonding with him means breaking with her mother or even reneging on femaleness altogether. In this sense Elizabeth is less a daughter than a surrogate son: like a son, by giving up the mother and giving in to the father, she reaps the spoils of maleness. Freud's charting of female development supplies an alternative view. In this scheme, girls turn, disillusioned, from the mother to the father out of penis envy. To complete their oedipal task, however, they must cease to identify with the powerful father, come to accept their own "castration," and learn to desire a baby as a substitute for the phallus.[7] In these terms the cocky Elizabeth of the book's first half is charmingly arrested in the early phase of male-identification, victim of what Freud would call a "masculinity complex." And in either case—whether one sees her as an honorary boy who has completed his oedipal task or as a backward, wayward girl who refuses to complete hers—Elizabeth's discursive power arises from an alliance and identification with her father. As the scene with Mr. Collins shows, the force of her words is highly contingent, any authority she has merely borrowed. Like a woman writing under a male pseudonym, Elizabeth's credibility depends on the father's signature.

I want also to reiterate that, however empowering, Mr. Bennet is fundamentally ambivalent toward Elizabeth. "They have none of them much to recommend them," he says of his daughters in chapter 1. "They are all silly and ignorant like other girls; but Lizzy has something more of quickness than her sisters" (5). Insisting that all his daughters are silly, that none have much to recommend them, Mr. Bennet blithely classes Elizabeth with "other girls" even as he appears to distinguish her from them. Already in the opening scene a tension exists between Elizabeth's "masculine" alacrity and the slow-witted "femininity" threatening to claim her. Mr. Bennet's double vision of her suggests right away the basic ambiguity of Austen's father-daughter relationship, which is coded both diachronically in the Mr. Bennet-Mr. Darcy sequence and synchronically in Mr. Bennet's duplicity regarding Elizabeth. For in Austen the male bonding between father and daughter is set up to collapse. Sooner or later, what Adrienne Rich calls "compulsory heterosexuality"—a conspiracy of economic need and the ideology of romance—forces Elizabeth out of the library, into the ballroom, and up to the altar. The father's business in this ritual is, in every sense, to give the daughter away. If Mr. Bennet is supportive up to a point, her marriage obliges him to objectify Elizabeth and hand her over. At this juncture, he not only withdraws his protection and empowerment but also gives away her true "castrated" gender, revealing her incapacity for action in a phallocentric society.[8] This ceremony— posing father as giver, daughter as gift—could be said to underlie and ultimately to belie the relation of fathers to daughters in *Pride and Prejudice.*

To put this another way, consider Mr. Bennet's failure to protect Lydia from ruinous male designs, a failure the novel explicitly condemns. It is possible, I think, to see the father's profligacy with Lydia as an extreme instance of a general, cheerful readiness to bestow his daughters upon anyone who knocks at the door.[9] "I will send a few lines by you," he tells his wife, "to assure [Bingley] of my hearty consent to his marrying which ever he chuses of the girls" (4). By exposing a pattern built in to the marital plot, Lydia's overblown story functions in relation to the rest of the novel (and to other Austen novels) just as the *juvenilia* do: Mr. Bennet's abandonment of his silliest daughter to Wickham reveals the basic paradigm underlying his milder estrangement from Elizabeth and the literal distance between father and heroine in *Northanger Abbey* and *Mansfield Park*.[10] Elizabeth's gradual falling out with her father and the loss of authorial status this entails are, therefore, intrinsic to the marriage toward which the novel tends. It is this account of courtship as, by its very structure, injurious to female authority that *Pride and Prejudice* poses—plaintively, I think—against its own fable of moral and social elevation.

In his discussion of marriage and the incest taboo, Lévi-Strauss famously proposed that the exchange of women among kin groups serves, like the exchange of money or words, to negotiate relationships among men. He explained that women function as a kind of currency, their circulation binding and organizing male society (61), and I am suggesting that *Pride and Prejudice* may offer a similar anthropology. Here, too, marriage betrays the tie between father and daughter in favor of ties among men with agendas of their own, involving both male sexuality and male class ambitions. To begin with the first, I appeal to Georges Bataille regarding the (bestowing) father's libidinal investment in the marriage ceremony:

> Marriage is a matter less for the partners than for the man who gives the woman away, the man whether father or brother who might have freely enjoyed the woman, daughter or sister, yet who bestows her on someone else. This gift is perhaps a substitute for the sexual act. (218)

According to Bataille, marriage substitutes for the incestuous heterosexual act a homoerotic exchange in which the father gives his own flesh, as it were, to another man. Dropping the daughter from the sexual equation except as a mediating term, this substitution italicizes male sexuality at the expense of female sexuality. Revising Bataille, one might say that marriage is at once an expression/renunciation of the father's desire for the daughter and the renunciation of the daughter's right to a sexual agenda of her own. As anthropologist Gayle Rubin observes in "The Traffic in Women," the systematic exchange of women imprisons female desire in a "debt nexus":

If a girl is promised in infancy, her refusal to participate as an adult would disrupt the flow of debts and promises. It would be in the interests of such a system if the woman in question did not have too many ideas of her own about whom she might want to sleep with. (182)

What does this have to do with Austen, who has been accused, by Charlotte Brontë among others, of eliding passion altogether? Granted that what Bataille describes as Mr. Bennet's fantasy is symbolically enacted by his role in Elizabeth's marriage. But if Regency mores prohibited the expression of Elizabeth's desire, isn't Darcy's sexuality equally imprisoned by his shyness and rigid formality? Isn't it his coldness that hurts Elizabeth's feelings and makes her accuse this gentleman of pride? I want to suggest that the class and gender logic of Darcy's engagement to Elizabeth actually turns upon his heatedness, that it points implicitly to the transgressive force of his desire and consequent irrelevance of hers. As Ian Watt has explained in relation to *Pamela* and premodern English fiction in general, "Mr. B. can properly follow his fancy and marry beneath his station because it is undeniable and irremediable fact that men are subject to the sexual passion; but for a woman to do so would amount to an admission that she had lost her immunity from sexual feeling" (164). Marrying below oneself confesses to sexual feelings drastic enough to surmount social boundaries, and that wealthy male characters can do this more readily than female is one example of the way class privilege is variously inflected by gender. The dynamic that motivates Mr. B. is the same that encourages Darcy, in spite of "his sense of her inferiority—of its being a degradation—of the family obstacles" (189), to offer Elizabeth marriage not once but twice, forcing the conclusion that between his initial hesitation and ultimate determination lies a tacit passion of considerable violence. Going further than Watt, I would say that Darcy's proposals buttress what Adrienne Rich identifies as an enduring myth: that a man's sexual urge, having the precedence and undeniability of a natural force, cannot be checked by culture or held responsible for its actions ("Compulsory," 46–47). Mr. Bennet in handing Elizabeth over, and Mr. Darcy in claiming her, make a joint statement about the primacy of male and the effaceability of female desire.

The Humiliation of Elizabeth Bennet

The fathers' other interest in the daughter's circulation concerns, as I say, class ambitions. Mr. Bennet's obvious interest in the Elizabeth-Darcy match is similar to Elizabeth's own. He may laugh at Mrs. Bennet's schemes, but the fact remains that he, too, will benefit from a noble connection. And despite his philosophic detachment, Mr. Bennet is not without a streak of pragmatism—after all, he has always intended to visit Mr. Bingley. Capable of being impressed by wealth and rank, he is frankly delighted that Darcy has used his money and influence to straighten out the Lydia-Wickham affair. "So much the better," he exults. "It will save me a world of trouble and economy" (377). Sounding even, for a moment, strangely like Mr. Collins, Elizabeth's father consents to her marriage with little of his habitual irony. "I have given him my consent," he tells her. "He is the kind of man, indeed, to whom I should never dare refuse any thing, which he condescended to ask" (376). Though Mr. Darcy's class interests may seem to rule against a tie to the Bennets, they too are subtly at work here. Eighteenth-century Cinderella matches not only brought titles to the middle class but also, by distributing merchant profits, put oft-needed cash into the coffers of the well-born. Only with *Persuasion*'s Sir Walter Elliot does Austen fully represent the material as well as moral impoverishment of her landed contemporaries; yet by *Sense and Sensibility* she has already given us one Willoughby who, unsure of his aristocratic heritage, leaves Marianne for a certain Miss Grey with fifty thousand pounds. Of course, in *Pride and Prejudice* capital flows the other way, but even here a decline in aristocratic welfare is nevertheless suggested by the sickly Miss De Bourgh. It may well be the enfeeblement of his own class that encourages Darcy to look below him for a wife with greater stamina. As a figure for the ambitious bourgeoisie, Elizabeth pumps richer, more robust blood into the collapsing veins of the nobility, even as she boosts the social standing of her relatives in trade. Most important, however—to the patriarchs of both classes—she eases tensions between them. By neutralizing class antagonisms, she promotes the political stability essential to industrial prosperity and the fortunes of middle-class and noble men alike. What does it mean, *Pride and Prejudice* encourages one to ask, for female development and destiny to be thoroughly entangled in patriarchal enmities and interests so far beyond the purview of any one girl?

I turn now to the handing of Elizabeth from Mr. Bennet to Mr. Darcy, which is prefigured by a scene on the Lucases' dance floor. At this point Sir William Lucas stands in for Mr. Bennet, lamely jockeying for power with the disdainful Mr. Darcy. Sir William begins to despair, when suddenly he is "struck with the notion of doing a very gallant thing": laying claim to Elizabeth, he offers her up to Darcy as "a very desirable partner" (26). Sir William intuitively understands that gift-giving can be an "idiom of competition," for as Gayle Rubin explains, there is power in creating indebtedness (172). One imagines the three of them—Elizabeth is between the two men, her hand held aloft by Lucas, he eager to deposit it and Darcy "not unwilling to receive it" (26). The fathers' device here is synecdoche, reducing the girl to a hand extended in friendship or hostility, the means of fraternal intercourse. Abruptly, however, Elizabeth withdraws herself from the debt nexus and indeed, throughout much of the novel, resists the conventional grammar of exchange. She would not only extract herself as object but, sabotaging the fathers' syntax, insert herself as subject. Needless to say, this makes for one of the stormier courtships in nineteenth-century fiction. As I have noted, it was Lévi-Strauss who first saw marriage as a triangulated moment, as a woman exchanged between two men. Gayle Rubin went on to identify this kind of traffic, its organization of a sex-gender system, as the basis for female subordination. But the immediate model for my placing such an exchange at the heart of *Pride and Prejudice* is provided by Eve Sedgwick, who has brilliantly examined the way men bond across the bodies of women in a range of English texts. Her mapping of "male homosocial desire" posits, however, an essentially passive female term and a configuration that is stable and uncontested. Even women who embark with goals of their own vanish mysteriously as subjects once drawn into this sexual Bermuda triangle. My point has been that Elizabeth does not readily accept such a merely pivotal role. The book stretches out because she puts up a fight before acceding (and never entirely) to the fathers' homosocial plot. The site of her resistance, as well as her compromise, is language.[11]

This brings me to Mr. Darcy—a father by virtue of his age, class, and a paternalism extending to friends and dependents alike. A man given to long letters and polysyllables, a man with an excellent library

and even hand, Darcy may also be seen as an aspiring authorial figure. If
Mr. Bennet sets out to create suspense, Mr. Darcy hankers to resolve it.
They are literary as well as sexual rivals, and Elizabeth is the prize—or
would be, were this surrogate son, father's heir, not herself a contender
for authorial status. In these terms, Elizabeth's and Darcy's matching of
wits, more than flirtation, is a struggle for control of the text. There are
two heated and defining moments in this struggle: Elizabeth's refusal
of Darcy's first proposal and the morning after when he delivers his letter. The first begins with Elizabeth alone at the Collins's house in Kent,
studying Jane's letters. Suddenly Darcy bursts in and blurts out a proposal; the chapter closes by resuming Elizabeth's internal dialogue,
"the tumult of her mind" after Darcy's departure (188–94). But where
has the reader been throughout this chapter if not in the heroine's for-
midable mind? By all rights this should be Darcy's scene, his say, while
in fact Austen transcribes relatively few of his actual words. His ama-
tory discourse is quickly taken over by a narrator who represents the
scene and renders even Darcy's language wholly from Elizabeth's point
of view: "His sense of her inferiority . . . [was] dwelt on with a warmth
which . . . was very unlikely to recommend his suit" (189). The text of
Darcy's proposal is completely glossed and glossed over by Elizabeth's
response to it. Of her refusal, on the other hand, Austen includes every
unmediated word, a direct quotation four times as long as that permitted Darcy, and this sets the pattern for what follows. Each time Darcy
opens his mouth, he is superseded by a speech of greater length and
vehemence. She answers his question—why is he so rudely rejected?—
with a tougher question of her own.

> I might as well enquire . . . why with so evident a design of offend-
> ing and insulting me, you chose to tell me that you liked me against
> your will, against your reason, and even against your character? Was
> not this some excuse for incivility, if I *was* uncivil? (190)

Conceding nothing, she accuses him at some length of everything: of
breaking Jane's heart and unmaking Wickham's fortune, of earning and
continually confirming her own dislike. She betters his scorn for her
family by scorning him. "I have every reason in the world to think ill of
you" (191), she declares. Her language, her feelings, and her judg-

ments overwhelm his and put them to shame. Driving poor Darcy to platitude, apology, and hasty retreat, they leave Elizabeth the easy winner of this first rhetorical round.

The following day, however, Elizabeth is obsessed by Darcy: "It was impossible to think of any thing else" (195). As the man crowds out all other thoughts, so the letter he delivers soon crowds out all other words, monopolizing the narrative for the next seven pages. Longer than the entire preceding chapter, it completely dispels Elizabeth's inspired performance of the day before. If Darcy was not "master enough" of himself then, he regains his mastery now. In a play for literary hegemony (to be author and critic both), he recovers his story and manages its interpretation. The letter establishes, for example, that Darcy's judgment of Jane was entirely impartial:

> That I was desirous of believing her indifferent is certain,—but I will venture to say that my investigations and decisions are not usually influenced by my hopes and fears.—I did not believe her to be indifferent because I wished it;—I believed it on impartial conviction. (197)

As for Wickham, the letter documents Darcy's early suspicions and the events that follow, proving him right. It demonstrates, too, Darcy's fatherly influence upon others, the moral sway he holds over Bingley and Georgiana: his friend has "a stronger dependence on [Darcy's] judgment than on his own" (199); his sister, fearing big brother's disapproval, decides not to elope after all. Only after Darcy's unabridged text does the narrator describe Elizabeth's reaction to it. She reads "with an eagerness which hardly left her power of comprehension, and from impatience of knowing what the next sentence might bring, was incapable of attending to the sense of the one before her eyes" (204). Darcy's letter saps her power to comprehend, disables her attention. She is addressed as reader—recall with what certainty she dispatched a letter from her previous suitor—only to be indisposed in this role. At first Elizabeth protests: "This must be false! This cannot be! This must be the grossest falsehood!" (204) She rushes through the letter and resolves to put it away forever, but the text, unrelenting, demands to be taken out, to be read and read again. Against the broad chest of Darcy's logic, Elizabeth pounds the ineffectual fists of her own. She puts the paper firmly down, then "weighed every circumstance with what she meant to be impartiality—deliberated on the probability of each state-ment—but with little success" (205). Resolutions, procrastinations, do nothing to stop the inexorable drive of Darcy's narrative to its fore-gone conclusion. In what Roland Barthes might call its "processive haste" (12), the text sweeps away Elizabeth's objections and has its way with her.

In his second sentence, the writer denies "any intention of paining" (196). He apologizes for wounding and yet proceeds, all too knowingly, to wound. There is indeed a disturbing insistence on the letter's hurt-fulness, a certain pleasurable recurrence to the violence of its effect. "Here again I shall give you pain" (200), Darcy announces more than once. But at last his will to inflict coincides with Elizabeth's to be af-flicted, and they meet in their enthusiasm for her humiliation:

> "How despicably have I acted!" she cried.—"I, who have prided my-self on my discernment!—I, who have valued myself on my abilities! who have often disdained the generous candour of my sister, and gratified my vanity, in useless or blameable distrust.—How humili-ating is this discovery!—Yet, how just a humiliation!" (208)

Vindicating Darcy's judgment and debasing Elizabeth's, the letter leaves her "depressed beyond any thing she had ever known before" (209). This is the point, the dead center, on which I believe the whole book turns. Darcy's botched proposal marks the nadir of his career after which, launched by his letter, he rises up, verging even on apotheosis. In the remaining chapters he is a veritable deus ex machina, magically setting everything straight. While Mr. Bennet fumbles, it is Darcy who arranges for three lucky couples to be, each, the happiest couple in the world; like the authorial persona of *Northanger Abbey*, it is he who herds us all to "perfect felicity." Darcy's letter proves his textual prow-ess. At this point he succeeds Mr. Bennet as controlling literary figure and displaces Elizabeth as her father's scion. From now on the pen, as Anne Elliot might say, is in his hands.

Soon after receiving Darcy's letter, Elizabeth meets up with Kitty and Lydia. Officer-crazy as ever, Lydia gushes on about Brighton and her plans to join the regiment there for its summer encampment. This first reference to Brighton unfolds into an unexpectedly earnest seduction plot—latent perhaps in Lydia's very character, throwback to earlier, too sentimental heroines—that might be more at home in a novel by Richardson or Burney. That such a seemingly anomalous plot should surface now and dominate for more than seven chapters is not accidental. For one thing, the Lydia-Wickham fiasco serves to reveal both Bennet's inadequacy and Darcy's capacity. Elizabeth first doubts her father regarding his decision to let Lydia go to Brighton, and she blames him bitterly for the subsequent scandal. For Darcy, by contrast, the calamity is a chance to display his nobility of heart and purse, his wish to rectify and his power to do so. The Lydia plot thus accomplishes Elizabeth's separation from her father as well as her reattachment to another: a changing of the paternal guard. By showcasing Darcy, the upstart story that appears to delay and even to replace Elizabeth's and Darcy's courtship actually works to advance it.

But there is another reason that Lydia's seduction moves into the foreground at this moment. It happens to occupy the curious gap between Elizabeth's first, private softening and her final, public surrender to Darcy. This leads me to suspect that Elizabeth's narrative is displaced for the length of these chapters onto her sister's, that Lydia's seduction codes an emotional drama—of coercion, capitulation, and lamentation—missing from but underlying Elizabeth's story proper. Far from being an unrelated plot, Lydia's may be its ruder, telltale twin. Of course Lydia is a foil for Elizabeth, one sister's folly held up to the other's wisdom, yet there remains a sense in which they, or their fates, are similar. When Lydia calls Mary King "a nasty little freckled thing," Elizabeth admits that "however incapable of such coarseness of *expression* herself, the coarseness of the *sentiment* was little other than her own breast had formerly harbored" (220). Taking seriously this point that Lydia and Elizabeth may differ more in style than substance, I find that Lydia's interpolated tale does not so much distract from the central courtship as distill its darkest meaning. While the overread version of Elizabeth's *Bildung* marks her gaining of self-knowledge and security, the eruption into Elizabeth's midst of Lydia's more sordid history points to a counternarrative of seduction and surrender.

III

At the end of volume 2, chapter 13, Elizabeth "could think only of her letter" (209); no wonder that by the next chapter, "Mr. Darcy's letter, she was in a fair way of soon knowing by heart" (212). The inverted syntax here, unusual for Austen, indicates a new order in which Mr. Darcy and his text are placed before Elizabeth, would-be subject. At the same time, the awkwardness of this order seems to mark it as a wrenching from what is pleasing and right. The state of the heroine's mind is also new: "When she remembered the style of his address, she was still full of indignation; but when she considered how unjustly she had condemned and upbraided him, her anger was turned against herself" (212). In an introversion of rage that may remind us of Evelina, Elizabeth's initial judgment of Darcy is now recanted as unjust, its accusation redirected against herself. When the novel opens, Elizabeth is proud of her ability to know and evaluate, yet by its closing chapters she claims only to be high-spirited. Regretting her refusal of Darcy, the new Elizabeth longs to be schooled by his better judgment: "By her ease and liveliness, his mind might have been softened, his manners improved, and from his judgment, information, and knowledge of the world, she must have received benefit of greater importance" (312). It should not be surprising to find that in an Austen novel judgment, information, and knowledge rate higher than ease and liveliness. None of Jane Bennet's neutrality for Austen—the former are her primary professional virtues and essential to her moral lexicon.[12] What may surprise and sadden us, however, and what the novel surely registers with a touch of irony, is that a heroine who began so competent to judge should end up so critically disabled, so reliant for judgment on somebody else. Not that Elizabeth lapses into sheer Lydiacy. Yet the final pages suggest nonetheless that her eye is less bold, her tongue less sharp, the angularity—setting her off from her more comfortably curvaceous sex—less acute.

According to one critical truism, *Pride and Prejudice* manages a kind of bilateral disarmament: Elizabeth gives up her prejudice, while Darcy relinquishes his pride.[13] I am arguing, however, that Darcy woos away not Elizabeth's "prejudice," but her judgment entire. For while Darcy defends the impartiality of his views, Elizabeth confesses to the partiality of hers; while his representation of the world is taken to be objective, raised to the level of universality, hers (like that of women generally) is condemned for being subjective and dismissed as mere "prejudice." But what does Austen's record actually show? Elizabeth was certainly wrong about Wickham, but was she really that wrong about Darcy? He may warm up a bit, and his integrity is rightly affirmed, but he is hardly less arrogant than Elizabeth at first supposed. Her comment to Fitzwilliam is ever exact: "I do not know any body who seems more to enjoy the power of doing what he likes than Mr. Darcy" (183). And what about Darcy's own accuracy? His judgment of Jane is just as mistaken—and, though he denies it, as partial—as Elizabeth's view of Wickham. Yet Darcy's credibility remains intact. Finally admitting to having misinterpreted Jane, Darcy explains that he was corrected not by Elizabeth but by his own subsequent observations (371), and on this basis he readvises the ever-pliant Bingley. Whereas Lizzie's mistake discredits her judgment for good, Mr. Darcy's, far from disqualifying him, gives him an opportunity to judge again. What happens in *Pride and Prejudice*, then, is not simply that an a priori prejudiced character at last sees the error of her ways. Rather, a character introduced as reliable, whose clarity of vision is evidently the author's own, is re-presented—in the context of her marriageability—as prejudiced. In my reading, the psychological drama of a heroine "awakening" to her true identity is brought into conflict with the social drama of an outspoken girl entering a world whose voices drown out her own.

If Elizabeth does not overcome her "prejudice," neither does Darcy abandon his pride. Early in the book Elizabeth declares, "I could easily forgive *his* pride, if he had not mortified *mine*" (20). But by the last volume she suggests just the opposite:

> They owed the restoration of Lydia, her character, every thing to him. Oh! how heartily did she grieve over every ungracious sensation she had ever encouraged, every saucy speech she had ever directed towards him. For herself she was humbled; but she was proud of him. (327)

There is a rueful women's joke about how "it was one of those love-hate relationships: by the end of it we both loved him and both hated me."

At the outset, Elizabeth and Darcy are each proud, each skeptical of the other, yet finally they reach what is in some sense the conjugal consensus of this joke: in the end both are skeptical of her, both proud of him. But wait. Doesn't Darcy make a pretty speech to his bride confessing, "By you, I was properly humbled" (369)? Here it is useful to see how the novel itself defines "pride" and how this definition relates to Mr. Darcy. The bookish Mary (another figure for Austen, if a self-mocking one) distinguishes "pride" from "vanity": "Pride relates more to our opinion of ourselves, vanity to what we would have others think of us" (20). As for Darcy, Charlotte Lucas contends that his pride is excusable: "One cannot wonder that so very fine a young man, with family, fortune, every thing in his favor, should think highly of himself. If I may so express it, he has a *right* to be proud" (20). A younger Lucas puts it more bluntly: "If I were as rich as Mr. Darcy, I should not care how proud I was. I would keep a pack of foxhounds and drink a bottle of wine every day" (20). The practical Lucases have a point. Darcy's richness gives him if not the "right" then the ability, in Mary's formulation, to be proud. A man in Darcy's social position need not consider any opinion but his own; he is proud because he does not have to be vain. In this sense, pride is less a psychological attribute than a social one—it comes with the territory and is therefore, if anything, heightened by Darcy's enhanced status in *Pride and Prejudice*'s last act.

Vanity, by contrast, is the adaptive strategy of those who depend on the kindness of strangers. In these terms, pride and vanity are arguably gender as well as class specific, as Rachel Brownstein intimates in her comparison of eighteenth-century heroines and heroes. "What the neighbors say can ruin a girl's life, and run like water off a duck's back off a boy's" (83), Brownstein explains. Darcy is therefore free to ignore the neighborhood's negative gossip, while female reputation is so fragile that Elizabeth can be severely shaken by a quake of talk whose epicenter is Lydia. "Under such misfortune as this," she says of Lydia's elopement, "one cannot see too little of one's neighbors" (293). Dependent on what the neighbors say for their status as proper ladies, reliant on male admiration and marriage for their economic survival, middle-class women are vain because they cannot afford to be proud. The story I am tracing of Elizabeth's decline involves not only the interrogation of her judgment but her fall from a "male" impersonation of pride into the vanity of other girls. John Berger might put it that the heroine shifts from proudly "acting" on her own behalf to merely "appearing" in the eyes of others; from seeing the world herself to seeing only herself *being seen* by the world (46).

To begin with, Elizabeth resists maternal efforts to school her in self-display. Warned by Mrs. Bennet that if she walks to Netherfield she "will not be fit *to be seen*," Elizabeth firmly activates her mother's passive voice. "I shall be very fit *to see* Jane—which is all I want," she replies (32; my emphases). Three chapters later, Miss Bingley and Mr. Darcy stroll along discussing Elizabeth's portrait, recasting their guest as an appearance for acquisition and exhibition. At that moment, they encounter the object of their speculation/specularity. As if refusing to sit for her portrait, Elizabeth quickly inverts the visual economy by assuming the position of artist who studies and composes them: "No, no; stay where you are.—You are charmingly group'd, and appear to uncommon advantage. The picturesque would be spoilt by admitting a fourth. Good bye" (53). Running "gaily off," she still defies any attempt to capture and frame her. A volume and a half later, Elizabeth approaches Pemberley with a similarly assertive eye. She wants particularly to see the area without being seen by Darcy: "But surely I may enter his county with impunity, and rob it of a few petrified spars without his perceiving me" (239). Driving through the park she gazes long and delightedly over the grounds. After "examining the nearer aspect of the house" (245), she enters the building and surveys the dining-parlor with appreciation, admiring the good taste of the furniture. With increasing excitement, she stares out of every window, commands the view from each room (246). She does not merely look, but looks with a desire to possess—from thinking to rob Darcy's county "of a few petrified spars," she now imagines herself mistress of his estate. Challenging the usual gender of the aggressive gaze, she positively leers. [14]

In the picture gallery, Elizabeth's desire to behold Mr. Darcy's portrait seems part of the visual assault she has mounted thus far. "At last it arrested her—and she beheld a striking resemblance of Mr. Darcy, with such a smile over the face, as she remembered to have sometimes seen, when he looked at her" (250). Like Darcy's letter, his picture is terribly compelling. Though she sets out to track it down, it arrests her and,

before she can leave the gallery, draws her back to it again. Most remarkably, it reorganizes the pattern and sexual politics of seeing—for
even as Elizabeth looks at the painting, it reminds her of Darcy looking
at her. She marvels at the vast proportions of his influence "as a brother,
a landlord, a master."

> And as she stood before the canvas, on which he was represented, and
> *fixed his eyes upon herself, she thought of his regard* with a deeper senti-
> ment of gratitude than it had ever raised before.   (251; my empha-
> sis)

Elizabeth, visual libertine, is suddenly shy and conventionally vain.
Now her act of looking unexpectedly fixes his eyes on her; now her gaze
sees only how she looks to him. It is clear from this passage that Elizabeth's deepening gratitude, the change of heart that propels her into
marriage, coincides with a novel concern for Darcy's "regard," a heightened awareness of herself as the object of his gaze and estimation. But
surely this bit of description, dramatically reversing what people usually do in front of a painting, is self-consciously strange; for the woman
positioned as spectator to fix the eyes of the image upon herself cannot
but strike us as perverse. As with Darcy's letter, which seizes the female
reader and turns her into the object of its force and her own hatred, here
is another striking inversion—one that by flipping the idiom sets up
the moment as a problem, making the reader pause and consider. The
result, I would say, is once more to phrase Elizabeth's humiliating loss
of pride as an awkward disordering, to defamiliarize the clichés of
female development.

Of course, one continues to admire Elizabeth. She may care for Darcy's regard, but she is never so utterly enslaved by it as Miss Bingley.
She may hesitate to laugh at Darcy, but she does show Georgiana that a
wife may take (some) liberties. She is admirable because she is not Charlotte, because she is not Lydia. I want nevertheless to insist that Elizabeth is a better friend to Charlotte and closer sister to Lydia—that one
version of her story runs more parallel to theirs—than previous readings have indicated. The three women live in the same town, share the
same gossip, and attend the same balls. Why, as some critics have
claimed, should Elizabeth alone be above the social decree?[15] There
are, in Elizabeth's marriage, elements of both crass practicality and

coercion. Elizabeth is appalled by Charlotte's pragmatism, yet in her own preference for Darcy over Wickham she shows herself beguiled by the entrepreneurial marriage plot. [16] And though clearly embarrassed by the family connection to Lydia, Elizabeth, too, is implicated by the formal intersection of their stories: in the course of the novel she loses not her virginity but her authority. For while the heroine marries a decent man and a large estate, Austen seems concerned to show that she pays a certain price. If Mr. Bennet embodies the post-Enlightenment, modified patriarch, Mr. Darcy harks back to an earlier type and time, before fathers were curbed by Lockean principles, before aristocrats began to feel the crunch. Recall how ambiguously his power looms before Elizabeth: "How much of pleasure or pain it was in his power to bestow!—How much of good or evil must be done by him!" (251). Darcy disempowers Elizabeth if only because of their unequal positions in the social schema—because he is a Darcy and she is a Bennet, because he is a man and she is his wife.

Pride and Prejudice presents a girl growing up to make choices, even as it portrays her struggling in the grasp of a complex mechanism whose interests are not hers. It does this, I have said, less in resignation than in protest, or at least in keeping with the contradictory structures of feeling—the simultaneous optimism and "heartache" about female development—common to the novels and conduct books by women of the period. The interests competing with Elizabeth's arise, I have suggested, from those male homosocial relations underlying the institution of marriage: the transactions between various fathers made over Elizabeth's head and apart from, if not quite against, her will.

I would like to close by offering some further support for this view. By the end of the book, Mr. Bennet's paternal role has been assumed by Elizabeth's uncle, Mr. Gardiner. Though "gentlemanlike," Mr. Gardiner lives by trade "within view of his own warehouses" (139) and represents, more than Mr. Bennet, the rising middle class. No wonder Elizabeth fears that Darcy will rebuff him, given that nobleman's past intolerance for her vulgar relations. She is quite unprepared for Darcy's civility to Gardiner and for the apparent power of fishing to overcome class differences. Perhaps their shared fondness for Elizabeth, their lengthy haggle over Lydia, as well as their equal passion for trout serve to reinforce the shared social/economic advantages of Darcy's and Gardiner's alliance. They become, in any case, suggestively close; indeed, the very last paragraph of the novel informs us that

> with the Gardiners, they were always on the most intimate terms. Darcy, as well as Elizabeth, really loved them; and they were both ever sensible of the warmest gratitude towards the persons who, by bringing her into Derbyshire, had been the means of uniting them.   (388)

At first this seems an oddly insignificant note on which to end. On second glance it appears to confirm the suspicion I have had—that just as the Gardiners have been the means of uniting Darcy and Elizabeth, so Elizabeth has been useful as the means of uniting Mr. Darcy and Mr. Gardiner. *Pride and Prejudice* attains a satisfying unity not only between a man and a woman but also between two men, an intercourse not merely personal but social, a marriage of two classes no less than a marriage of true minds.

CHAPTER FOUR

Jane Eyre's Fall from Grace

PART of *Jane Eyre's* myth, and perhaps appeal, is that it offended some of its contemporary readers. Published in 1847, its immense popular success was qualified by a few high-toned denunciations, of which Elizabeth Rigby's 1848 review is the most frequently cited.[1] Repudiating the book as "an anti-Christian composition" (451), Rigby had especially harsh words for its protagonist:

> The impression she leaves on our mind is that of a decidedly vulgar-minded woman—one whom we should not care for as an acquaintance, whom we should not seek as a friend, whom we should not desire for a relation, and whom we should scrupulously avoid for a governess. (452)

It is easy enough to dismiss Rigby as a bad or irrelevant reader because, inevitably, we fail to share her particular sense of outrage. If, however, one is interested in Brontë's text not as a timeless work of genius but as one complicit with historically specific views and vocabularies, then Rigby is the best reader. By reproaching Jane in class terms (as "vulgar"), even while identifying a central confusion about Jane's class status (does the genteel reader count her an acquaintance? friend? relative?

employee?), Rigby's review helps to stress *Jane Eyre*'s participation in those discursive struggles around class as well as gender that were so vehement in the 1840s. To me it suggests, more specifically, that the tension in Brontë's novel between conflicting narratives of female development be viewed in relation to ongoing class conflict between "vulgar" and "genteel" interests.

Rigby was also unnerved by Rochester's rough charm. "Mr. Rochester is a man who deliberately and secretly seeks to violate the laws both of God and man. And yet," she moralized, "we will be bound half our lady readers are enchanted with him" (450). Her anxiety about Rochester's illicit appeal may suggest an analysis of *Jane Eyre* in terms of the unstable Victorian discourse about sexuality—at once affronted and fascinated by bigamy—and many recent critics have taken this cue. In such a context, *Jane Eyre* has been seen as anomalously modern, inspiring comparisons to D. H. Lawrence and to Freud. John Maynard, for example, appealed to Charlotte Brontë in 1984 for "a vision of sexual experience that can rival that of any of her successors in the twentieth century for depth of psychological insight and fidelity to the protean and complex nature of sexuality itself" (6). Other critics read off from the novels case histories of the author's own sexuality, as in Helene Moglen's illuminating biography (published the same year as Maynard's book), one of numerous "psychosexual" studies.[2] And even those works that do not probe the sexual text per se have tended to explore *Jane Eyre*'s powerful articulation of interiority, the buried life that Brontë remarked was missing from Austen. Robert Heilman's often reprinted 1958 essay on Brontë's "new Gothic"—her adaptation of the gothic to give "dramatic form to impulses and feelings . . . their depth or mysteriousness or intensity or ambiguity" (458)—is a good example of this; so is Karen Chase's important book on Brontë's representations of "personality" over against reigning Victorian psychological theories, which also appeared in 1984. Five years earlier, Sandra Gilbert and Susan Gubar had argued persuasively that *Jane Eyre*'s rendering of female anger, not sexuality, caused critics such as Rigby to chide—but their paradigm, too, while implying a social context enraging to women, remained a predominantly psychological one.

I want to suggest that Rigby's anxiety was not only about the personal and passional, that it was also about the framing of female development by larger, external structures of gender and class, both under scrutiny and attack when *Jane Eyre* was written in 1847. The following year was, needless to say, one of singular political upheaval and rhetorical output. Revolutions broke out in France, Italy, Austria, Germany and, following the great potato famine of 1846–47, seemed imminent in Ireland. *The Communist Manifesto* appeared in Paris in June. In America, the clash between abolitionists and an increasingly vocal opposition began shaping up along distinctly sectional lines. At the same time, a group of women led by Elizabeth Cady Stanton convened in Seneca Falls, New York. Closer to home, in England the 1848 presentation of the third People's Charter marked the culmination of a decade of Chartist agitation for wider enfranchisement. These political demands coincided with demands more directly economic and industrial—for trade unions, improved work conditions, and shorter days—forcefully witnessed by the Plug Strikes of 1842. Recalling the Luddite "Riots" of 1811–13, this systematic sabotaging of factory boilers disrupted textile production in the Manchester area for several months and wrecked the peaceful sleep of property owners for a good deal longer. If the years 1780–1832 saw, as E. P. Thompson has demonstrated at length, the making of the English working class, by the writing of *Jane Eyre* it had been made and was dramatically present not only to itself but to the members of all classes.

In a now familiar sequence, Chartist and trade union campaigns, Anti-Corn Law League efforts in the name of free trade, and widespread abolitionist protests produced, as a particularly compelling afterthought, a movement on behalf of women. The 1840 International Anti-Slavery Convention in London has been seen as pivotal. British men, astonished by the presence of women among the American delegates, secluded the ladies behind a curtain where they could listen but not speak. The indignation of Elizabeth Cady Stanton and Lucretia Mott led, so the story goes, to the historic meeting at Seneca Falls eight years later. While this convention signaled the formal beginning of an organized women's movement, its polemical underpinnings had been put in place during Brontë's lifetime: by the publications and speeches of women such as Frances Wright (1795–1852), Sarah Grimké (1792–1873), Sojourner Truth (1795–1883), Margaret Fuller (1810–1850),

and many others. Women's experience with Chartism, as with aboli-
tionism, was formative in two senses. Their inclusion (women voted at
general meetings, formed associations of their own, and were recognized in the first and third charters' petition for universal suffrage)
schooled them in political practice and made available to them a rhetoric of entitlement. Their exclusion (the first and third charters were revised to specify *male* suffrage) suggested they extend this rhetoric to
themselves and take up the cause of their own rights. Following the
American lead, British women began in the 1840s to make their concerns a matter of public debate. Their first concern was, of course, the
vote. In its advocacy, Mrs. Henry Reid's *A Plea for Women* was published
in 1843, and Anne Knight's leaflet, the first of a great wave, around
1847. Harriet Martineau, Brontë's esteemed friend, was also active at
this time—as were Harriet Taylor and Taylor's second husband, author
of the most renowned manifesto of the period, John Stuart Mill.

These distinct but not unrelated events relied upon and contributed
to a diversity of claims about the rights of workers and women. A York-
shire writer apprenticing in the 1840s, Brontë grew up on these
claims—I take them as a key discursive context for her work—and her
letters suggest she viewed them with equal measures of interest and
ambivalence. In 1848 she reacted to the spread of insurrection by suggesting that "revolutions put back the world in all that is good, check
civilization, bring the dregs of society to its surface" (Gaskell, 341).
But despite the antirevolutionary fervor of this last phrase, she continues in a more divided vein: "With the French and Irish I have no
sympathy. With the Germans and Italians I think the case is different;
as different as the love of freedom is from the lust for license."[3] The
rhetorical gesture here—setting off "the love of freedom" from "the lust
for license"—only apparently resolves what remains, in my view, a
deeply contradictory view of popular revolt. In 1850 Brontë expressed
her approval of Sir Walter Scott's "Suggestions on Female Education,"
noting that men's views of learned women were changing for the better:
"In these days, women may be thoughtful and well read without being
universally stigmatised as 'Blues' and 'Pedants'" (Gaskell, 405). Yet the
following year she was of two minds in regard to Harriet Taylor's piece
on the "Emancipation of Women" (wrongly attributed by Brontë to J.

S. Mill), which appeared in the *Westminster Review*. She found the article deficient in "self-sacrificing love and disinterested devotion," even as she praised its rational views on women and paid work:

> He speaks admirable sense through a great portion of his article—especially when he says, that if there be a natural unfitness in women for men's employment, there is no need to make laws on the subject; leave all careers open; let them try; those who ought to succeed, will succeed, or, at least, will have a fair chance. . . . In short, J. S. Mill's head is, I dare say, very good, but I feel disposed to scorn his heart. (Gaskell, 458–59)

Brontë's response to an article entitled "Woman's Mission," published in 1850, was similarly mixed. Agreeing that women had, themselves, to improve their lot, she goes on to lament the rootedness of injustice in social structures—then, finding herself on unexpectedly radical ground, veers off mid-sentence into resignation:

> Certainly there are evils which our own efforts will best reach; but as certainly there are other evils—deep-rooted in the foundations of the social system—which no efforts of ours can touch: of which we cannot complain; of which it is advisable not too often to think. (Gaskell, 422)

These are hardly the cadences of conviction, and I will be arguing that Brontë did indeed think and often dared complain about wrongs she perceived to be systemic. Certainly she did so in *Shirley*, her second published novel, which appeared in 1849 and looked back to an actual incident of Luddite rebellion: the attack on William Cartwright's mill at Rawfolds in April 1812. Although *Shirley*, I agree with E. P. Thompson, finally discredits the Luddites' organized violence, portraying their leaders as opportunists and drunks, it also condemns the mill owner's love for machines and money at the expense of his workers.[4] More than this, it compares working-class hunger in a time of war, bad harvests, and unemployment caused by mechanization, to the emotional hunger of a bored and isolated middle-class woman. While neither starvation is satisfactorily fed, nor is there more than a brief mutual sympathy between the two groups, *Shirley* nevertheless endeavors to represent, to put into historical context, to analogize and even tenuously to ally the complaints of workers and women. Though less explicit, *Jane Eyre* also pays extreme—if, as in *Shirley* and the letters, ambivalent—attention to the constraints of class and gender both. In fact, it brings these together in the developmental trials of a small, plain girl without money, bereft of family. Its drama, I would stress, is external as well as internal, its ken not only the overwrought psyche, the heated imagination, but also the prosaic and material, the practical concerns of a girl growing up to be a governess. Its mode is history as much as fantasy, its referent England as much as Angria, and the story's "happy" and reclusive ending can only partly hide *Jane Eyre*'s continuity with other ongoing forms of social protest. Here, then, is Rigby's usefulness: as a contemporary reader she saw with great clarity this novel's contribution to a timely lexicon of defiance.

> There is throughout it a murmuring against the comforts of the rich and against the privations of the poor . . . there is a proud and perpetual assertion of the rights of man. . . . We do not hesitate to say that the tone of mind and thought which has overthrown authority and violated every code human and divine abroad, and fostered Chartism and rebellion at home, is the same which has also written *Jane Eyre*. (451–52)

Rigby's further distaste for Jane's unemployable vulgarity, her implication that *Jane Eyre* is not only politically threatening but morally unsavory responds, I think, to the manifestation of Chartist sentiments in a specifically *female* protagonist. The governess who petitions for her rights, by challenging class privilege, simultaneously assails the Victorian ideal of docile femininity.

There have been, to be sure, readers since Rigby aware that *Jane Eyre* is a dangerous book. Its feminism has been discussed at length. Virginia Woolf, oddly and famously, both criticized and incorporated it into *A Room of One's Own*; more than one contributor to the *Brontë Society Transactions* has, since Woolf, remarked it; and Carol Ohmann agreed with Margaret Blom in the early 1970s about its limitations.[5] But the book that has weighed most heavily in recent discussions of *Jane Eyre* is undoubtedly *The Madwoman in the Attic: The Woman Writer and the Nineteenth-Century Literary Imagination* (1979), whose foregrounding of the eponymous Bertha Mason (and the rise of feminist criticism in general) has attuned a host of critics to strains of feminism in Brontë. Gilbert and Gubar's dazzling discussion of female confinement, claustrophobia, rage, and rebellion ignores, however, the way issues of gender in *Jane Eyre* are crucially bound up with those of class. Terry Eagleton has, on the other hand, usefully investigated class tensions in *Jane Eyre* between the landed and industrial sectors of the ruling class, yet without more than passing attention to the categories of sexual difference that inform these tensions (*Myths*).

My project, like Rigby's and Eagleton's, is to stress the "Chartism" of *Jane Eyre*—the way it interrogates (though it may not finally threaten) the structures of class, the way it is part of a moment when coherence about class was failing—and to see this as inseparable from its feminism. What is at issue for me in this text, what is rattling in its attic and recurrently at large, is a woman who is also a worker. I want to take for the book's emblematic figure not the debauched, highborn Bertha Mason, suffering from sensual extravagance and inherited insanity but her plebeian caretaker: the under-glossed Grace Poole, whose lousy job has driven her to drink. To recuperate a fiction of development that ties Jane less to Bertha than to the working-class Grace is not to elide what some feminist critics have rightly insisted is the making of a bourgeois and imperialist as well as female subject.[6] I would argue, however, that the formation of Mrs. Rochester, like that of Lady Orville and Mrs. Darcy, is continually interrupted and essentially destabilized by a second, subversive narrative, one that in this case involves the heroine's identification with other working women. Though written over by subsequent chapters, this radical narrative originates in the very first, Gateshead section of *Jane Eyre*—in what might tentatively be called its "primal scene"—and persists, submerged and contested, throughout the novel.[7]

II

Jane Eyre opens with Jane's sense of "physical inferiority" to the robust Reed children, as if her subordination to them were natural and therefore right. It soon appears, however, that John Reed's superior size results not from nature but from nurture—more precisely, overnurture: "He gorged himself habitually at table, which made him bilious, and

gave him a dim and bleared eye and flabby cheeks" (7). As John is "habitually" well fed, so Jane is "habitually obedient to John" (8). One of
the novel's first concerns is to illustrate hierarchical social practices,
habits of privilege and deference. Jane is banished from the abundant
table, the bright fireside, and from the exercise of power because she is
poor; her devaluation on this account is compounded by being a girl
who is, moreover, plain. Even bleary-eyed John can see it is property
and primogeniture that give him the right to bully. "You are a dependent," he tells Jane.

> You have no money; your father left you none; you ought to beg, and
> not live here with gentlemen's children like us, and eat the same
> meals we do, and wear clothes at our mamma's expense. Now, I'll
> teach you to rummage my book-shelves: for they *are* mine; all the
> house belongs to me, or will do in a few years. (8)

Hurling a book at Jane, he proceeds to employ the violence that maintains, even as it expresses, his advantage.

The famous red-room scene is, I think, an echoing occasion of violence. This scene has been memorably interpreted by Elaine Showalter
as Jane's initiation into a lurid female sexuality: "With its deadly and
bloody connotations, its Freudian wealth of secret compartments,
wardrobes, drawers, and jewel chest, the red-room has strong associations with the adult female body" (115). I want to stress, however, that
this "largest and stateliest" (10) of chambers, with its chair "like a pale
throne" (11), also resonates with the authority of the elite adult male.
This is the room in which Mr. Reed died, the vacated seat of his power.
"Remote from the nursery and kitchens," it rebuffs the young, working, and female; even Mrs. Reed comes only "at far intervals" (11). The
mirror on its wall makes Jane, imprisoned there, seem small and
strange to herself. Most horrifying of all is her suspicion that the throne
has not really been abdicated, that the patriarchal spirit still lingers
there. Jane has always blamed her unhappiness on Mrs. Reed, believing
that Mr. Reed (though she cannot remember him) would surely have
befriended her. But now that she considers his actual presence, the
effect is unexpectedly dreadful. "This idea," Jane explains, "consolatory
in theory, I felt would be terrible if realized" (13). Thinking suddenly
that she perceives the restless, avuncular ghost, Jane is indeed suffo-

cated by fear and, unpitied by Mrs. Reed, passes out. Here it is possible to accuse Jane, as Freud accused Dora, of a "reversal of affect"; John Maynard contends that Jane's fear of Mr. Reed is in fact overpowering, incestuous love—"too strong emotions in the Electra attraction of father and daughter" (103). But if Jane is taken at her word, the meaning of this scene seems clear. I would say that it stages the return of the ruling-class male in a way that violently dispels the myth of his benevolence. It also symbolically replays the previous scene, in which the father's power was, in the bloated person of his son, uncannily refigured. By resisting this power, Jane has been doubly guilty of insubordination—as a girl and as a dependent: the red-room punishes Jane less, I think, for her female sexuality than for questioning what she boldly identifies as her "slavery."[8] A recurring trope, as many critics have observed, the red-room implies two things about what Jane is up against throughout the novel. First, that John Reed represents a magisterial power larger, more elusive, and more threatening than any particular privileged boy. Second, that this power, even when apparently quiescent, is apt to be sensationally resilient and reiterative.

The opening chapters make a point, therefore, of rattling the chains of gender and class that bind Brontë's heroine. At the same time, they introduce a degree of uncertainty about her class status. Jane's parentage, for one thing, is mixed. Her mother, Mr. Reed's sister, was a disobedient daughter of the middle class who married scandalously below her. Her father, a penniless clergyman (perhaps of peasant stock, like Brontë's own clerical father), lived and worked with "the poor of a large manufacturing town" (21). While visiting among these poor, he contracted the typhus that soon killed both him and his wife. Their grave, as later described, "formed part of the pavement of a huge churchyard surrounding the grim, soot-black old cathedral of an overgrown manufacturing town" (334); in life, death, and burial, then, Jane's parents bear witness to the stress of filth and crowding on working people in new industrial towns. But though her father was poor, his clerical education would have set him apart from his flock; and though her mother was middle-class, her persistent downward mobility flew in the face of bourgeois values. If these two met and married in the space between classes, they were also, each of them, socially ambiguous, and this ambiguity is part of their legacy to Jane. Terry Eagleton, it will be recalled, says the pull in *Jane Eyre* is between new mercantile powers (the Reeds) and old aristocratic ones (the Rochesters). While crediting the former with a spirit of rebellion, Eagleton explains that—as merchants buy up land, landowners industrialize, and both unite against threats from below—the interests of these two ruling classes inevitably converge. It seems to me he defines the forces of dissent in *Jane Eyre* as being, from the start, provisional and easily assimilated to the conservative. Small wonder, then, that Eagleton finds "bourgeois initiative and genteel settlement" mythically unified in the end (*Myths*, 32), since the tension he identifies is set up to collapse. To my mind, Jane's socially ambiguous position corresponds to a different tension, less readily resolved and potentially more disruptive to existing class arrangements: between the propertied classes (Reeds and Rochesters) and the working poor.

Jane's social status is further destabilized by the fact that she is, like Evelina and *Villette*'s Lucy Snowe, an orphan, disengaged from the social structure and adrift. At Gateshead and Thornfield both, she is neither family nor servant, but floating uncomfortably between. In relation to the middle and working classes alike, she occupies a set Gayatri Spivak calls "counter-family" (267). More specifically, as Mary Poovey has shown, in her role as governess Jane points at once to the middle-class, maternal ideal and to the denigrated, lower-class woman who works for wages (*Uneven*, 131). She is torn, Helena Michie agrees, between the two, classed bodies that Jane represents in her sketches of Blanche and herself: the privileged beauty and the girl whose poor features are implicit in her poverty (50). Problematizing Jane's station, Brontë motivates and divides her developmental fiction by asking: What family/class does Jane belong to? Will hers be the apprenticeship of a middle- or working-class girl? On what terms will she come to reengage the social structure? The dilemma introduced by this first section is, to put these questions another way: Who is Jane's mother—the bourgeois Mrs. Reed or Bessie, the nurse?[9]

Jane inclines to Bessie, to the servant's folk stories and glimmers of sympathy. Over Christmas Jane is hidden upstairs, listening to the jangle of bourgeois gaieties below, but instead of yearning toward the genteel company, she would rather spend a quiet evening with Bessie. Bessie, however, has other pleasures: she, too, abandons Jane for "the lively regions of the kitchen and the housekeeper's room, generally bearing the candle along with her" (23). And so for much of this first section Jane looks wistfully toward the light and warmth of the servant community but has no more place there than she does among the Reeds. There are several other instances of the child's thwarted desire for Bessie's society. Desolate at the departure of Mr. Lloyd, the kind apothecary who visits after the red-room ordeal, Jane hears Bessie say to the housemaid, "Sarah, come sleep with me in the nursery; I daren't for my life be alone with that poor child to-night" (16). Knowing herself the object of their pity and fear, Jane is left outside their consolatory scheme. She catches, sadly and enviously I sense, at fragments of their pillowed whisperings: "'Something passed her, all dressed in white, and vanished'—'A great black dog behind him'—'Three loud raps on the chamber door'—'A light in the churchyard over his grave'" (16). Nervously fascinated by Jane's rebellion, but spooked as she was by its preternatural repercussions, Bessie and Sarah comfort each other to sleep, while Jane remains, unaccompanied, in "ghastly wakefulness." Soon after, Jane overhears another intimacy between lower-class women, again concerning yet, finally, excluding her. The maid Abbot tells Bessie the story of Jane's orphaning. Contrasting her to the beautiful and fortunate Miss Georgiana, the servants are tempted to pity Jane but cannot bring themselves to claim "such a little toad as that" (21). The conversation closes by shifting away from Jane to her pretty, pampered cousin; sympathy for the poor orphan is displaced by class deference and a retreat to the kitchen. "Bessie, I could fancy a Welsh rabbit for supper," Abbot concludes. "With a roast onion," Bessie replies. "Come, we'll go down" (22). These are prosaic moments—no more, it may seem, than dashes of local color thrown in by the older, hindsighted narrator. But they also suggest to me the strained attention of a young, desiring Jane. It is her wishful presence, her position adjacent to but outside such companionable exchanges, that is indicated by the terse report: "They went" (22). Jane's initial relation to working as well as leisured society is one of lonely spy or eavesdropper, frequently the object but rarely the subject of conversation, a role Brontë goes on to explore more fully and painfully in *Villette* (1853).[10]

In truth, what keeps Jane from the camaraderie of servants she carefully, even jealously, describes is her own ambivalence toward the status of servant. Scolded by Abbot for daring to strike her "young master," Jane is indignant: "Master! How is he my master? Am I a servant?" (9) Asked if she would rather live with some poorer relations, Jane imagines "ragged clothes, scanty food, fireless grates, rude manners, and debasing vices" (20). Shading their poverty into vice, she buys into Mrs. Reed's view that the poor are a "beggarly set" and chooses to be abused rather than debased. Both cases of snobbery, however, are actually deconstructed, repudiating this pejorative apprehension of the working classes. In the first case, Abbot's sharp reply to Jane's question is unexpectedly definitive: "No; you are less than a servant, for you do nothing for your keep" (9). This is a notion pervasive in Brontë: that the parasitic middle-class woman (*Villette*'s Ginevra Fanshawe or even Polly Home, for example) is in some moral sense *less* than her social inferior, the self-sufficient working woman. Jane's later preference for being Rochester's plain, paid governess rather than be "dressed like a doll" (236) at his expense is in keeping with this perception. For gender, Brontë recognizes, can put a spin on masculine class schemata and, consequently, class strategies. Eagleton is to some extent correct that Brontë's protagonists, *déracinées*, are "free to be injured and exploited, but free also to progress, to move through the class structure" (*Myths*, 26). Yet Brontë is acutely aware that the struggle up from hard times gets a girl no higher than governess or, at best, school mistress. From there she obtains class leverage only by marrying, and certainly Brontë wonders if marriage can be genuinely improving for women. The realization that bourgeois initiative is simply less rewarding for a female protagonist (and this is what Eagleton overlooks) inevitably gives Brontë and other women writers some useful distance on the narrative of upward mobility. In the second case, the child's shrinking from poverty is voiced-over by the authoritative adult. "Poverty for me was synonymous with degradation," the narrator recalls, placing this opinion in the distant past. Children, the grown-up Jane explains, "have not much idea of industrious, working, respectable poverty." Casually rebuking drawing-room prejudice, the older Jane appropriates "respectability" for the hardworking poor. Wiser now, she recognizes that she was not as a child "heroic enough to purchase liberty at the price of caste" (20). Suddenly, in a moment that is key to my reading, kinship with the poor is seen as liberation, middle-classness mocked as a craven attachment to caste.

And here I arrive at my central proposition: that over and against the child's class confusion, her fear of as well as desire for the servant, Brontë's opening chapters set in motion an emancipatory, homosocial narrative of female development in relation to working women who are no less respectable for being poor. This does not mean growing up to become Bessie, whose dread of the poorhouse and dreams of *Pamela* keep her caste-bound in a peculiarly gendered way. Jane's object is rather to claim and reconceive Bessie's place—the place of the working woman, later refigured by Adèle/Céline, Grace Poole, and by Rochester's servant, Mary—as a "heroic," morally righteous, and potentially revolutionary one. The point, in other words, is not to stay submissively at the bottom rather than seeking the top of the social ladder, but to shake the ladder itself by identifying oneself in extrinsic terms. I am saying that the initial, though soon countermanded, project of Jane's formation may be, as Rigby suspected, a loosely Chartist as well as feminist one: by developing a class consciousness, to name herself outside the master-servant paradigm, to grow up without the romantic plot of social mobility through marriage.

This project is, in fact, ultimately advanced by the fierce, unhappy child at Gateshead. By chapter 4, Jane's separation from the well-cushioned Reed children has intensified. While her cousins gambol in the drawing room, she is relegated, like Bessie, to the nursery. Here Bessie employs her as "a sort of under-nursery maid, to tidy the room, dust the chairs, &c." (25), apprenticing her in the ways of serving, as a mother would her daughter. This apprenticeship is consistent with Jane's developing self-perception, as several images imply. The doll she enfolds, warming it as if warming herself, is no glossy figurine like Miss Georgiana, but "shabby as a miniature scarecrow" (24); the bird she feeds, as if feeding herself, is "a little hungry robin" (25), and Jane knows how dear its bread. Eliza and Georgiana, meanwhile, are preparing for a different social station altogether. Eliza indulges her youthful penchant for selling, hoarding, and usury (tomboyish hobbies that get her only, in the end, to a nunnery). Georgiana, as true to her class but truer to her gender, studies the art of marketing herself and displaying male wealth. By contrast, then, Jane's nonbourgeois status becomes increasingly clear. But Jane does not merely resign herself to being déclassée; she manages, instead, to use her debased position at Gateshead as a kind of moral fulcrum. She is able to identify Eliza's wealth and Georgiana's beauty as nothing more than greed and vanity. Her feat is to remake the Reeds' rejection of her, their denigration of her sullen poverty, into her own rejection of them and their managerial values. "If they did not love me," she realizes, "in fact, as little did I love them" (12). Likewise, when Mrs. Reed warns her children against associating with Jane, Jane cries out in return, "They are not fit to associate with me" (22). Having answered John blow for blow, his sisters sneer for sneer, Jane's counterattack climaxes with her stunning renunciation of Mrs. Reed:

> I declare I do not love you: I dislike you the worst of anybody in the world except John Reed; and this book about the liar, you may give to your girl, Georgiana, for it is she who tells lies, and not I. . . . I am glad you are no relation of mine: I will never call you aunt again as long as I live. (30–31)

These are brave words for an orphan child, and Jane's immediate euphoria soon gives way to remorse. From the depths of her misery, however, she is finally, as this section draws to a close, lifted up into family by Bessie. What follows is a scene, provisional as it may be, of recognition and reunion, in which Jane and Bessie embrace more frankly than ever before. The nurse reports her own mother's maternal concern on Jane's behalf—"she would not like a little one of her own to be in your place" (33)—so that Jane is now like a sister as well as a daughter to Bessie. A new side of the seemingly conservative nurse emerges as Bessie rewards Jane for defying the masters, and the chapter concludes with the reader's first glimpse of Jane in tender relation. "Bessie told me some of her most enchanting stories, and sang me some of her sweetest songs. Even for me," she discovers, "life had its gleams of sunshine" (34). By the end of chapter 4, breaking with the Reeds and allying herself with Bessie, Jane has broken out of an order that consistently devalues her. The result—as Sarah Stickney Ellis predicted for her community of slaves, her shipwrecked mariners, her women united together against a common enemy—is sudden expansion and empowerment: "the strangest sense of freedom, of triumph . . . as if an invisible bond had burst" (*Jane Eyre*, 31).

III

If Gateshead stages Jane's revolt, Lowood functions punitively—in effect, as another red-room. It also introduces a more conventional narrative of female development involving, as in *Evelina* and *Pride and Prejudice*, the acquisition of humility, aspiration after respectability through Cinderella-style romance, and the restraint of gender and class rage. The manner of Jane's installation at Lowood, described primarily in the passive voice, communicates her sense of being once again manipulated by adult hands: she is taken out of Bessie's arms, whirled away, carried into an inn, returned to the coach, and finally lifted out. The red-room's bloody tint is evoked by the inn's red gallery, where Jane feels "very strange, and mortally apprehensive" (36) of kidnappers; above all, when she finally passes through the walls of Lowood, the door is carefully shut and locked behind her. The presiding spirit of this reconfinement is the horrible clergyman, Mr. Brocklehurst, who exhorts the students to be satisfied by hunger, content with injustice, and grateful for abuse. He encourages them (as Jane remarks bitterly over a mess of inedible porridge) to give thanks for what they have not got (39). More than this, Brocklehurst projects onto their undernourished, underclass female bodies his own ruling-class male desires, and in this he intimates the exploitative sexual dynamic that Steven Marcus sees as a central concern of the Victorian novel and that also, I suggest, cannot but inform Rochester's later courtship of Jane.[11] Requiring the girls to "direct their faces to the wall" (55), he scrutinizes their "reverse" at length before ordering their "top-knots" cut off (56). The scene enacts both Brocklehurst's sadistic fantasies and, ironically, a moral rhetoric in which the immodesty of working women is seen to legitimate his right to discipline and punish them. Lowood, in short, reinforces class and gender hierarchies through dominative practices masquerading as charity and piety, and the narrator's reassurance that, with Brocklehurst's departure, the school "became in time a truly useful and noble institution" (72–73) does little to soften the preceding depiction of its cruelty and hypocrisy.

If Brocklehurst, though urging obedience, only elaborates the radical Gateshead narrative insofar as his parent injustice (like Mrs. Reed's) rationalizes rebellion, then the sympathetic Helen Burns begins to represent his repressive educational goals in more attractive and credible terms. Helen is a student of Johnsonian stoicism who—echoing Mrs. Reed: "Jane, I don't like cavillers or questioners" (5)—advises Jane, "You ask rather too many questions" (44). However much these two maternal figures differ (the one robust and unscrupulous, the other consumptive and good), both attempt to discourage the girl critic. To a child whose mode is interrogative—her first words, "What does Bessie say I have done?" (5)—both preach a message of quietism. Helen, a motherless charity child like Jane, is humble and uncomplaining in the face of a particular typing of marginal women. Beaten and ridiculed for having dirty nails, untidy drawers, and blotted exercises, she fully accepts the stigmatizing description of herself as "slatternly." Whether Helen is in fact as sloppy as she thinks, Miss Scatcherd's decrial of her as a "dirty, disagreeable girl" (46) reflects and reinforces several cultural myths. First, that working people live more in the body than the mind, closer to the earth and more like animals; second, that women are responsible for order in the domestic sphere, for an immaculate home and the spiritual hygiene it connotes; and third, that lower-class women—being slovenly in their habits, "dirty" in a way that implies they are whores—fall, by very definition, short of the feminine ideal.

Thus Helen's image of herself as unkempt functions as a precise rationale for Mr. Brocklehurst's contemptuous view of poor women. Yet Brontë is also, at this point, concerned to dispute such a view.[12] Helen is virtually a saint and so little attached to the flesh that she lasts a scant thirty pages. Brontë also interjects Jane's argument (Helen could not clean her nails because the water pitcher was frozen) that cold and hunger, poverty and not the poor, are to blame for squalid conditions. To some extent the Lowood section repudiates both the prejudice against Helen and her acquiescence in it. The example of Helen's brief life serves arguably to steer Jane away from the shoals of submission, the elder's complaisance provoking only the younger's mutiny. "The fury of which she was incapable," Jane admits, "had been burning in my soul all day" (64). So saying, she rips the sign "Slattern" from Helen's passive body—disconnecting, as it were, this signifier from its signified.

Helen Burns offers Brontë's heroine the possibility, then, of a familiar developmental mode, resigned to conventional class and gender destinies; climbing into Helen's deathbed, quizzing her about heaven, sleeping in her arms, it is as if Jane tries Helen on for size. Yet though she studies and admires her dying friend, Jane still hesitates to accept such a fate, and by morning the heroine-as-angel/whore is dead, while Jane awakens to another pagan day.

Miss Temple, however, makes a stronger case for the conservative narrative. Jane's "organ of Veneration" swells at the very well-dressed sight of her: not the pharisaic finery of the ladies Brocklehurst, but just enough quiet elegance to indicate that here stands a proper specimen of the bourgeois female (40–41). As her name suggests, Miss Temple is a living shrine to this type, and Jane quickly comes to worship there (Gilbert and Gubar, 344). She masters French, drawing, and eventually climbs up from the bottom of the lowest class, through the ranks of middle girls, until she is "the first girl of the first class" (73) and then a teacher, like Miss Temple herself. The meaning of this movement up through the "classes" is, it seems clear, more than simply educational. Leaning away from working-class resentment toward a sense of bourgeois entitlement, *Jane Eyre* now begins in earnest to redefine female formation not as the achievement of class consciousness but, complacently, as social mobility. Bessie, reappearing after eight years, finds the once rebel slave plain as ever, but accomplished, genteel, and evidently "quite a lady" (80). She also informs Jane that the beggarly Eyres are really "as much gentry as the Reeds are" (80). Bessie herself, by contrast, is "attired like a well-dressed servant" (78), and Jane does not even immediately recognize her beloved nurse. Of Miss Temple, on the other hand, the maturing heroine says: "She has stood me in stead of mother, governess, and, latterly, companion" (73). By the end of the Lowood chapters, the refined superintendent has apparently all but dislodged her humble rival from the maternal place in Jane's heart.

What kind of mother is Miss Temple and in what does she apprentice *Jane Eyre*'s protagonist? In many ways Jane's experience at Lowood is improving—her mind is challenged, possibilities multiplied—just as Miss Temple is an improvement over the Reeds and Brocklehursts. Finally, however, Miss Temple is in league with the Reed/Brocklehurstian project, and insofar as Jane emulates the one, she willfully subordinates herself to the others. Miss Temple may, for example, occasionally order up an extra lunch of bread and cheese or treat her favorite pupils to a large seedcake taken from her private stock. But as Helen tells Jane, Miss Temple "has to answer to Mr. Brocklehurst for all she does. Mr. Brocklehurst buys all our food and all our clothes" (43). And while Miss Temple confesses to her charities, she does *not* answer to Mr. Brocklehurst's sermon on the salutary effects of hunger. Marble-silent, she teaches Jane strict self-repression as well as complicity in the oppression of others. There are, in addition, limits to Miss Temple's philanthropy, which manages only "to supply deficiencies for this once" (63), while privation remains the rule. Putting a kinder face on institutions such as Lowood, the proper lady allays suffering without seriously rebuffing it. She may even, by keeping discontent at a governable level, make it easier for the Brocklehursts to operate—just as the domestic sphere generally, offering refuge and consolation, saps resistance to oppressive conditions. The aristocratic heroine of *Shirley*, in a sudden fit of generosity to rebelling workers, invokes precisely this logic:

> What I want to do is to *prevent* mischief. I cannot forget, either day or night, that these imbittered feelings of the poor against the rich have been generated in suffering. . . . To allay this suffering, and thereby lessen this hate, let me, out of my abundance, give abundantly. (269)

Miss Temple's attitude toward Helen is also compromising. Though she cares for Helen and admonishes her gently, she nevertheless shares the received belief that Helen is basically disordered. In short, the superintendent softens the cruelty of gender and class relations, without fundamentally dissenting from them. By relating herself to Miss Temple Jane does gain some personal power, but is no less implicated in the master-servant paradigm. Aspiring to middle-class womanhood, she is still haunted by the ruling-class male, and now she concurs in the maintenance of class hierarchies.

So Jane's formation over and against conventional caste is hardly served by her years as an inmate at Lowood. Yet even as the trajectory of social improvement takes over, the early plot of gender-class rebellion continues, as I have said, to rival and disrupt it. On the eve of Jane's departure for Thornfield there are several indications that the defection from rebellion is incomplete, that Miss Temple's domesticating effect is beginning to wane. First, the able administrator marries and is last seen entering a carriage with a man "almost worthy" of her (73).[13] This, Brontë suspects, is the fate of the middle-class woman: to be abruptly removed from her former usefulness, to enter a diminished space and function quite probably in a reduced capacity. Represented as such, it clarifies for the reader, while suggesting to Jane, the limitations of Miss Temple as a developmental model. With her mentor's departure, Jane makes a surprising discovery: "My mind had put off all it had borrowed of Miss Temple," she realizes. "Now I was left in my natural element, and beginning to feel the stirring of old emotions" (73). Second, if Miss Temple exits during this last Lowood chapter, Bessie, though initially unrecognized, does reappear. That her daughter is named "Jane" raises again the possibility of Jane Eyre's affiliation with working people. That this daughter is conspicuously absent, and that Bessie is distanced by Jane's new demeanor, would argue the connection is tenuous at present. Jane escapes Lowood torn, then, between two subject formations—her manners polished by Miss Temple, Chartism dozing in her heart. She resolves to leave in a fevered petition for liberty (prefiguring the famous roof-top speech), no sooner framed than withdrawn and re-cast in humbler terms: "Grant me at least a new servitude!" (74) This modest wish might seem to preclude the Chartist plot entertained at Gateshead, yet I would argue that the very word "servitude," like "slavery," signals Jane's perception that Lowood has somehow indentured her. Far from suggesting resignation, by naming a degraded condition it promises unrest and reserves the possibility of protest.

IV

As if to emphasize Jane's still transient status, the curtain rises not on Rochester's manor house, but on "a room in the 'George Inn' at Millcote" (81). Once at Thornfield, she is welcomed by the housekeeper, Mrs. Fairfax, who immediately sets herself off from the rest of Rochester's staff. However lonely the winter, the kindly old lady explains, one dare not fraternize with Leah, John, or his wife, Mary. "They are only servants," she tells Jane, "and one can't converse with them on terms of equality: one must keep them at due distance, for fear of losing one's authority" (84). The motherly manager is no less observant of lines drawn above. Though related by marriage to Rochester's mother, she would "never presume on the connection" (87). Mrs. Fairfax cannot tell Jane about Rochester's personal qualities because to her his social ones suffice: he is a gentleman and a landowner, period. Consequently, as it turns out, she is willing to help guard his violent secrets. Mrs. Fairfax thus delimits for herself and models for Jane a position of extreme class conservatism, of scrupulous regard for the semiotics of station, a position referring as much to residual notions of birthright as to the bourgeois ideology of self-making. If the former works less to contradict than to complement the latter—both are invested in hierarchy, tolerant of patriarchal abuses, and condescending to the working class—so the feudal Mrs. Fairfax only urges Jane along the road to middle-class respectability discredited by Mrs. Reed but recuperated as normative by Miss Temple.

The new appeal of this mode for Jane is evident as she revises the Gateshead pattern of eavesdropping and spying on servants, so that now what is glamorous and desirable coincides with wealth. With the arrival of Rochester's aristocratic guests, Jane and Adèle, her bastard charge, position themselves to overhear the sound of beautiful ladies settling and arraying themselves. As the narrator recounts:

> Then light steps ascended the stairs; and there was a tripping through the gallery, and soft cheerful laughs, and opening and closing doors, and for a time, a hush.
> 'Elles changent de toilettes,' said Adèle; who, listening attentively, had followed every movement. (146)

Later, as the ladies emerge from their rooms and flock through the gallery, Jane hovers in the shadows admiring their dresses, "lustrous through the dark," and listening to their "sweet subdued vivacity." The report continues:

> They then descended the staircase almost as noiselessly as a bright mist rolls down a hill. Their collective appearance had left on me an impression of high-born elegance such as I had never before received.
> I found Adèle peeping through the schoolroom-door, which she held ajar. 'What beautiful ladies!' cried she in English. (147)

Jane Eyre's Fall from Grace

In each of these cases, caught listening and looking, admiring and yearning, the guilty Jane quickly projects her feelings and actions onto Adèle, much as Lucy Snowe does onto little Polly Home. But by the time Adèle expostulates "in English," Jane has begun to acknowledge and accept this newly reverent relation to "high-born elegance," and soon she openly joins the poor Parisian child in wishing after the fashionable guests. Banished alike from the drawing room, they eavesdrop together from the top of the stairs. It is as if the Christmas festivities at Gateshead were being replayed—only now Jane's desiring attention has turned, as it were, from Bessie to the Reeds.

This self-abasement before monied beauty appears, at first, to define Jane's sense of herself in relation to her raven-haired rival, Blanche. Using her paints, Jane reproduces Mrs. Fairfax's view of Blanche's noble proportions, then sketches her own meager form (141). The juxtaposed portraits—contrasting paint to crayon, ivory to paper, the well-wrought to the carelessly made—seem to argue the inferiority of poor governess to lady of rank at a fundamental, physical level. Blanche, in her mistreatment of Jane and her diatribe against governesses as a "class" (155), reinforces this view very much as John Reed did. Surprisingly, however, here too the heroine manages defiantly to claim her lower social status as a morally superior one, for Jane no sooner insists on being undeserving because plebeian than she rephrases this with considerable class pride:

> Not that I humbled myself by a slavish notion of inferiority: on the contrary, I just said—"You have nothing to do with the master of Thornfield, further than to receive the salary he gives you. . . . He is not of your order: keep to your caste, and be too self-respecting to lavish the love of the whole heart, soul, and strength, where such a gift is not wanted and would be despised." (142)

With the angry recurrence of "slavish," the early narrative of rebellion and self-respect as a working woman reemerges, so that while Rochester pays Jane's wages, he cannot be said to own her soul; indeed, it is she, not he who has riches to "lavish."

In fact, Jane at Thornfield remains an unstable, ambiguous figure, still oscillating between two stories of growing up, both of which are represented by her pupil and double, Adèle Varens. Of mixed and stigmatized parentage, Adèle makes explicit the illegitimacy so often associated with Jane. The irregular mating of Adèle's mother and father was, as with Jane's, short lived, leaving its issue alone; as Jane starved and shivered at Lowood before finding a home at Thornfield, so Adèle was "destitute" before Rochester plucked her dispassionately from "the slime and mud of Paris" (127). Jane describes her student as "a lively child, who had been spoilt and indulged, and therefore was sometimes wayward." Under Jane's tutelage, however, "she soon forgot her little freaks, and became obedient and teachable" (95). Insofar as Jane's role as Adèle's governess involves the regulation of gender and class "waywardness"—the Brocklehurstian chastisement of a poor girl's "little freaks"—the domesticated child dramatizes Jane's own capitulation to Lowood's educational process. At the same time, however, by keeping an eye on Adèle, Jane keeps before her a faded but provoking image of her own vulnerable and intractable pre-Lowood self. There is, indeed, a notable occasion—en route to Millcote, where Rochester would dress and bejewel Jane as a sultan would his favorite slave—on which Adèle resumes Jane's old role of caviller or questioner. Giddy with his conquest, the gentleman spins out a fantasy of complete possession: he will take Jane to the moon and bury her in a cave for his pleasure alone. "You will starve her," accuses Adèle. "I shall gather manna for her morning and night," replies Rochester, a man who has never known hunger. "What will she do for a fire?" Adèle demands. "Fire rises out of the lunar mountains," the poet explains dreamily. "I'll carry her up to a peak and lay her down on the edge of a crater." "Peu confortable!" retorts the little materialist. "She is far better as she is" (234), the girl concludes, and dismisses her guardian as "un vrai menteur" (235). No wonder Rochester wanted to leave such a child at home, whose blunt observations needle him much as Jane once needled Mrs. Reed. And no wonder Jane sues to keep this little critic, who expresses (subsequent pages show) her very own thoughts.

Adèle's essential argument here—that Rochester's sexual pleasure may be Jane's deception and discomfort—is implicit in her very history as the daughter of Céline, a Parisian "opera-girl" and one of Rochester's several discarded mistresses. The first song Adèle lisps for Jane is about an abandoned woman (89). The first poem she recites is La Fontaine's "La Ligue des Rats," in which the collective efforts of mice fail to save a

particular mouse from a ravenous cat (90). Through the pathetic character of Adèle and her refiguration of Céline, Brontë hints at what
seems to me a recurrent fear in this book—the working woman's fear of
the predatory gentleman. Feminist critics have tended to see the "bigamy" issue in *Jane Eyre* as merely a red herring. According to this view,
Jane doesn't really want to be Rochester's child-bride any more than she
wants to be his mistress; the revelation of Bertha's existence only encourages Jane to act on apprehensions she has had all along. But this
reading for gender neglects the class aspect of Jane's female predica-
ment. Marriage is Georgiana Reed's and Miss Temple's middle-class
story, one that, however confining, offers at least a degree of social status and protection. It is not, at this juncture, the plot that imperils
Brontë's heroine. For though Jane's accomplishments resemble Miss
Temple's, her dependent, sexually vulnerable condition is closer to
Adèle's/Céline's. As Mrs. Fairfax reminds her, "Gentlemen in [Mr.
Rochester's] station are not accustomed to marry their governesses"
(233). I would point out that a "mad" wife gives Rochester an excuse to
do what men of his station *are* accustomed to do: to have not two wives
but, rather, one wife and a mistress whose defamed status leaves her
wholly at his mercy. It must, in short, be recognized that the governess's fate as mistress is even more socially disabling and personally
degrading than that as wife; that the "marriage" and "mistress" plots
are complementary versions of the same story; and that it is the
second—what might be called, à la Steven Marcus, the "*other* Victorian" plot—by which Jane is threatened here.

If the figures of Adèle and Céline help to bring out Jane's particular
sexual vulnerability as a working woman, the figure of Grace Poole—
also, Jane imagines, an abandoned mistress—invokes the earlier radical narrative by defining Jane's response to this vulnerability as an enraged and insurrectionary one. Jane hears the woman she calls "Grace
Poole" laugh crazily at the close of her celebrated feminist-on-the-roof
speech, which Virginia Woolf cited and many others have admired for
its angry eloquence. Jane's proposal in this polemic of a story for women
beyond puddings and stockings has earned it a distinguished place in
the annals of "high feminist criticism."[14] Yet often as this scene has
been discussed, Cora Kaplan has only recently called attention to what
is perhaps its most revolutionary moment:

It is in vain to say that human beings ought to be satisfied with tran-
quillity; they must have action; and they will make it if they cannot
find it. Millions are condemned to a stiller doom than mine, and
millions are in silent revolt against their lot. Nobody knows how
many rebellions besides political rebellions ferment in the masses of
life which people earth. Women are supposed to be very calm generally: but women feel just as men feel.   (96)

Underlining the words *human beings*, *millions*, and *masses*, Kaplan argues that here Brontë begins to reinvent the generic "men," daring to
make it genuinely democratic. Further, in its association of "masses"
and "women," this passage represents "a significant moment of incoherence, where the congruence between the subordination of women
and the radical view of class oppression becomes, for a few sentences,
irresistible" ("Pandora's" 173).

While agreeing with Kaplan that *Jane Eyre* keeps the masses but
inconsistently in sight, I am asserting that Brontë links Jane's situation as a woman to her plight as a worker for more than a few sentences. My reading would bear out but extend Kaplan's sense that
Brontë's class politics are "incoherent," straining against even as they
reproduce dominant ideologies. For the insane laughter that closes
this scene serves not, I think, to warn that "the association of feminism and class struggle leads to madness" ("Pandora's," 173). On the
contrary, I would argue that it combines and concretely manifests
these struggles in the figure of the serving woman, Grace Poole, who
will be a continually disruptive presence at Thornfield. I take as axiomatic the coincidence, so thoroughly demonstrated by Gilbert and
Gubar, of Jane's own fury with the "madwoman's" many acts of violence. I want to put special stress, however, on the fact that, for most
of her residence at Thornfield, Jane thinks of this woman not as
"Bertha" but as "Grace." Though Grace is in many ways continuous
with Bertha (they are both in some sense Other), in class terms the
mistress and her caretaker are, instead, opposed. Mrs. Rochester, for
example, is feared by the servants for "her violent and unreasonable
temper . . . absurd, contradictory, exacting orders" (269), and in this
she is more her husband's double than Jane's. The abused wife is, at
once, the abusive employer. The relation between the phlegmatic servant and raging arsonist may be thought of in another way as well.

The image of the worker whose bland, obliging front conceals a desire to burn down the house seems a fairly transparent expression of middle-class fears and, for that matter, working-class hopes; Grace represents both of these affectional options for Jane.[15] I would offer, then, the madwoman "Grace Poole" as a figure capable of gathering into her all the unseen or scarcely seen lower-class women in this book and acting out their collective revenge. In her role as nurse she refers to Bessie; in her hypothetical past as Rochester's mistress she refers to Céline; and in her riotous outbreaks she refers to the young, disinherited Jane. I want, moreover, by emphasizing Grace over Bertha to link her incendiary recurrence not only back to Bessie but also out to contemporary mass movements on behalf of women and of workers—to see her eruption into the text as the reemergence with a vengeance of that alternative formation introduced by the novel's first scene.

I would like to look more closely at one such eruption: when "Grace" stabs the effete Mason, and Rochester enlists Jane's service in nursing him. Earlier in the day Jane had inauspiciously sworn, "I'd give my life to serve you" (179). Now in the dead of night Rochester has her fetch a sponge and salts, clean clothes, a cloak, a phial and glass—running up and down the stairs each time until (like the poor servant, Sam) her "calves must have ached with the exercise" (171). Jane sounds plaintive when she tells us her "untiring master" had still another errand for her (187). But all of this pales beside Jane's most grueling duty: the vigil she keeps with Mason, two hours of nursing that seem like a week.

> I must keep to my post, however. I must watch this ghastly countenance. . . . I must dip my hand again and again in the basin of blood and water, and wipe away the trickling gore. I must see the light of the unsnuffed candle wane on my employment. (184)

When his guests were alarmed by the midnight commotion, Mr. Rochester told them not to worry—it was only a servant having a nightmare. Unwittingly, Jane's master told the truth, for the distasteful and repetitious labor that ensues is, precisely, a servant's nightmare. The scene represents with some exactitude the social relationship central to my reading of Brontë's novel: between the ruling classes, one of whose prerogatives is to have their bodies tended in sickness and in health, and the serving women on whom the greatest burden of this care falls.

What does it mean to discover this relationship at the heart of what turns out to be Jane's and Rochester's first night together, complete with pastoral aubade? Jane shudders to think that, throughout her ordeal, the woman she still calls Grace Poole is in the very next room. I would say, rather, that Grace is in the *same* room, or that for this interval Jane *is* Grace, while the servant's wild rage, though hidden, snarls and groans only a wall away. The night that identifies Jane with Grace is thus both monitory and exemplary: its thankless labor reveals to Jane the substructure of her class as well as gender relation to Rochester, even as the madwoman's proximity of violence urges her to resist this relation.

V

The morning after her engagement to Rochester, Jane's first action is to empty her purse to "a beggar-woman and her little boy—pale, ragged objects both" (226). Though Jane means to share her joy, the exchange functions in fact to separate the woman who gives from the woman who begs. The charity-school girl gives money to charity—what better way of marking her new status? But when Jane's romance turns out to be hoax, her refusal of what I have called the "other Victorian" plot produces a sudden, dramatic shift in her relation to this beggar-woman. Whereas before Jane was concerned to distance herself from the poor, now she becomes one of them in a way that involves her and the reader in a sympathetic exploration of their condition and, at least potentially, in a bitter critique of class and gender inequities. Wandering the countryside in desperate search of food and work, the heroine has fallen from the pedestal of an almost-lady, past her old, ambiguous post as governess, past even the situation of servant or proletarian to the most feared and degraded place of all, that of the vagabond—a class including, in the damning estimation of Victorian social commentator Henry Mayhew: "the pickpockets—the beggars—the prostitutes—the street-sellers—the street-performers—the cabmen—the coachmen—the watermen—the sailors and such like."[16] Gazing up at it from below as it were Jane recovers her early respect for humble work in home or factory—recognizing, from this new perspective, the necessity and respectability of such work to those who have it, the misery and indignity of not having even this, and the harshness of a society in which willing workers are turned away. While *Shirley* alludes to the dire effects of mechanization in the woolen industry, the hunger and rage of unemployed men, the vagabond section of *Jane Eyre* enters into their crisis with all the complex sensibility of a main character. Further, while working women are virtually invisible in *Shirley*, these chapters of *Jane Eyre* suggest that what is hard for men is harder for women. Jane's homelessness is made all the more trying by her constant fear of "some sportsman or poacher" (284), and jobs for women, she finds, are especially difficult to come by. Hearing that Mr. Oliver doesn't employ women in his needle-factory, she asks, "What do the women do?" and is told evasively, "Some does one thing, and some another. Poor folk mun get on as they can" (287).

Having fled Thornfield Jane therefore has another chance to contest received beliefs about the working and nonworking poor, and to identify her formation with their revolution. Yet while the young Jane was prepared to question and to challenge, now she reaches toward only to back away from such disconcerting skepticism. The girl who once declared, "I must resist those who punish me unjustly" (50), now swallows her anger at mistreatment and forgives injustice with Helen's own complacency. After being turned away hungry from a shop, she considers, only to dismiss, her right to work and to eat:

> I blamed none of those who repulsed me. I felt it was what was to be expected, and what could not be helped. . . . To be sure what I begged was employment: but whose business was it to provide me with employment? . . . And as to the woman who would not take my handkerchief in exchange for her bread, why, she was right; if the offer appeared to her sinister, or the exchange unprofitable. (289)

Here the account breaks off suddenly—"Let me condense now. I am sick of the subject" (289)—thereby refusing the possible protest of "to be sure what I begged was employment" and suppressing any irony toward an economy in which profit is all. So if Jane's wandering raises old questions about identity and loyalty to the class and gender systems, by the time she arrives at Moor House they have already been put at a distance. Her conversation with the Rivers' servant, Hannah, is in keeping with this reactionary trend. Although Jane defends the dignity and rights of the underclass—"You ought not to consider poverty a crime" (301), she scolds—the heroine is primarily concerned to assert her status as a lady, unused to begging or even to manual labor. Identifying the rough-faced Hannah as "an honest and faithful servant" (301), Jane places herself among the book-learned bourgeoisie in opposition to her working-class interlocutor. While this passage has its ambiguous moments, it ultimately eschews the possibility of equality in favor of normative hierarchies.

And so with the Moor House section, Jane's ambivalence toward caste yields, in the end, to accommodation. Much of her ambivalence centers on the village school, with its humble students and their cottager or farmer families. Here as schoolmistress, Jane comes close to extending the servant mother-daughter dyad of the Gateshead section into a consciousness of the larger, working-class community. As she and her best pupils grow to like and admire each other, as she begins to pass "many a pleasant evening hour in their own homes" (322), she develops a new sense of being defined and valued in positive relation to others, of being buoyed up by love, sustained by family. "To live amidst general regard," Jane explains, "though it be but the regard of working-people, is 'like sitting in sunshine, calm and sweet:' serene inward feelings bud and bloom under the ray" (322). The metaphor of sunshine and sensations of sweetness, peace, and grace link this moment to one of Jane's few previous experiences of kinship: when Bessie's "sweetest songs" followed an afternoon of "peace and harmony" and felt to little Jane like "gleams of sunshine." Against the much-discussed Edenic imagery surrounding Jane and Rochester's courtship, it is important to pose these images of blissful solidarity with working people, and to cite Jane's last stand against class prejudice:

> These coarsely-clad little peasants are of flesh and blood as good as the scions of gentlest genealogy; and the germs of native excellence, refinement, intelligence, kind feeling, are as likely to exist in their hearts as in those of the best-born. (316)

Yet even as Jane reasons thus, she cannot help feeling degraded by her new position: "I doubted I had taken a step which sank instead of raising me in the scale of social existence" (316). Ironically, it is the man who set her up in the school, St. John Rivers, who encourages her in this view. He gives her the job stressing "how trivial—how cramping" (312) it is and assuming it will never satisfy her. By piecing together Jane's past, it is he who discovers her as an heiress, causing her to leave her post as schoolmistress and the community it provided. It is also, of course, St. John who initially takes Jane in, and Hannah says he defends the poor. Yet he rescues Jane only because she seems "a peculiar case" (296), as if the run-of-the-mill beggar might very well die on his doorstep. As a Christian, St. John claims to appreciate the lowest work and the humblest people, but he reveals his real biases by mocking Jane's cleaning down of Moor House and baking of cakes as demeaning "housemaid's work" (345). St. John is, in short, a churchman in the Brocklehurstian mold, anxious to raise himself up by keeping others down. His Christian rhetoric barely disguises his hierarchical views, and as a missionary he exports these around the world. As Jane puts it:

> He is a good and a great man: but he forgets, pitilessly, the feelings and claims of little people, in pursuing his own large views. It is better, therefore, for the insignificant to keep out of his way; lest, in his progress, he should trample them down. Here he comes! I will leave you, Diana. (366)

St. John manages to trample Jane nevertheless, making her another Miss Temple to his bullying Brocklehurst. He introduces her to wealth and genteel family and would consolidate her rank by marrying her. Like Miss Temple, if Jane is thereby elevated above her students, she is still subordinate to the ruling-class male, and now he enlists her in his imperialist project.

VI

Whether they basically approve (Rich, Gilbert and Gubar) or disapprove (Spivak, Boumelha), feminist critics have usually seen Jane's development into a middle-class female subject as a success, the end of *Jane Eyre* as a cautiously "comic" one, and certainly it reaches a less ambiguous conclusion than any of Brontë's other novels. Yet Gilbert and Gubar, while calling "Jane's progress" an "emblem of hope" (371), agree with Robert Martin that Ferndean is marked by an "autumnal quality" (369), and I would like, as in previous chapters, to elaborate on those aspects of the text that press against the happy ending. Some (male) commentators have linked their discomfort with the end to Rochester's symbolic castration, but I wonder—might some (female) readers' lingering unease spring less from their regret that Rochester is now less of a man than from their fear that he may, like Uncle Reed, remain too much of one? In making this case, I mean to distinguish between the heroine's own unprotesting happiness (or is it that she protests her happiness too loudly?) and those textual details that darkly suggest Ferndean may be nothing more than a still newer servitude. This is not, however, to see the conclusion as a simply defeatist one. For if the final pages are subdued, by naming (as Jane once did) a degraded condition, they may continue nevertheless to argue on behalf of the secretly rebellious masses.

In terms of gender, I am tempted, first of all, to see even the fallen Rochester as far more continuous with the trampling St. John Rivers than Jane's passion for her master might suggest. We recall that she hears his voice in the middle of a frenzy wrought up by Rivers. Jane herself invokes the parallel, noting that "I was almost as hard beset by [St. John] now as I had been once before, in a different way, by another. I was a fool both times" (368). Rochester calls his lover to Ferndean, almost Bertha's prison-house, except that its damp walls would soon have killed her, and Rochester denies "a tendency to indirect assassination" (264). Is this deadly site an improvement over St. John's India, where Jane knows she would not last three months? Other similarities connect the two suitors. Both men play shepherd to Jane's little lost sheep—Rochester is fond of this metaphor, and Rivers invokes it vocationally; both men play professor to Jane's naive student, the unequal dyad that carries so much erotic weight in Brontë. [17] I suggest, in short, that if *Shirley* expresses ambivalence about marriage by splitting the heroine into an eager and a balking bride (Caroline versus Shirley), *Jane Eyre* may express a similar ambivalence by splitting the hero into a loving and a murderous husband. (Jane to St. John: "If I were to marry you, you would kill me. You are killing me now" [363].) In both Brontë novels, as in *Evelina* and *Pride and Prejudice*, the darker double, hovering too close, threatens to deconstruct the fair one. Taking this further, I find myself imagining a kind of alliterative conjugation from Uncle Reed to Rivers to Rochester, each with his canine familiar—for the red-room, I have said, may prophesy subsequent reincarnations. Thus Rochester, like Reed, first appears in a supernatural haze, as if he had come galloping out of one of Bessie's nightmarish tales. [18]

It is sobering, moreover, to look at Rochester's crippling in terms of its effect not on him, but on Jane. True, it gives her the physical advantage and the importance of being relied upon. "I was then his vision, as I am still his right hand" (397), the bride of ten years boasts. But as Eagleton notes, becoming Rochester's "prop and guide" is an ambiguous achievement (*Myths*, 30). In fact, this role as interminable caretaker bears an uncanny resemblance to the maternal role women conventionally play in relation to men, and servants in relation to masters. It binds Jane in service to Rochester just as she feared being bound by Rivers—"as a useful tool" (366). As her husband's very eyes and hand, she is indeed "chained for life to a man," just as she was briefly chained to Mason, and Grace to the man-sized Bertha. There is also additional evidence of Jane's domestication in the fate of that littlest double, Adèle. Jane gets permission from Rochester to visit her stepdaughter at boarding school:

> She looked pale and thin: she said she was not happy. I found the rules of the establishment were too strict, its course of study too severe, for a child of her age: I took her home with me. I meant to become her governess once more: but I soon found this impracticable; my time and cares were now required by another—my husband needed them all.   (396)

Adèle is placed in a "more indulgent" school where in time she becomes "docile, good-tempered, and well-principled." The reader hears nothing of her marriage and can only guess what this means for the daughter of Céline. Insofar as Adèle stands for Jane's oppositional child-self, it is ominous that she is banished from Ferndean, returned to a punitive Lowood, and at last reduced to grateful docility. [19]

In terms of class, the end of *Jane Eyre* finds Jane with all the privileges of an upper-bourgeois wife; now she is Miss Temple indeed. It is possible to read this, as Boumelha and Spivak do, as *Jane Eyre*'s greatest and only good: *Bildung* defined as social mobility, bourgeois female subjectivity gained at the working-class and native woman's expense. Certainly there is much, as we have seen, to support this narrative, which is increasingly predominant in the novel's final two sections. Jane's first act after her wedding, for example, is to hand the servant, John, a five-pound note saying, "Mr. Rochester told me to give you and Mary this" (395). It is a gesture that serves to crystallize the economic/power relations present at the book's close. As with the beggar-woman, Jane demonstrates here that she has the power to bestow whereas John and Mary can only thankfully receive, that she has access to capital whereas they have only their own labor. Class is not, moreover, this transaction's sole category. Regardless of Jane's inheritance, it is Rochester who originates this donation; Mrs. Rochester— like a lunatic or idiot, without property or any other legal rights of her own—only carries out his order. And Rochester's male privilege is repeated at the working-class level as well, where John controls the money that accrues to Mary. Yet Brontë does not, arguably, put the rebel slave entirely to rest. If class servitude were figured by John and Mary alone, one might guess that the story had simply naturalized their labor as intrinsic to the Rochesters' status. Jane, however, reintroduces herself to Rochester at Ferndean by assuming Mary's place and bringing her master some water. "I stretched out to take a glass of water from a hireling, and it was given me by you" (385), he says, marveling at her return. Might this imply that a residual bit of the heroic remains with the hireling, requiring us still to see and resent her subordination? Might it suggest that Jane, or at least *Jane Eyre*, has not completely fallen from Grace?[20]

What further saves this ending from complete resignation are the certain hints of irony. Surely there is an ironizing impulse in the too pat, absurdly idealized description of what happens to Diana and Mary Rivers:

> My Edward and I, then, are happy: and the more so because those we most love are happy likewise. Diana and Mary Rivers are both married: alternately, once every year, they come to see us, and we go to see them. Diana's husband is a captain in the navy; a gallant officer and a good man. Mary's is a clergyman: a college friend of her brother's; and, from his attainments and principles, worthy of the connection. Both the Captain Fitzjames and Mr. Wharton love their wives, and are loved by them. (398)

Husbands are no longer "almost worthy" in this implausibly perfected vision, but then its hyperbole and singsong symmetry seem calculated to discredit it, even to cast doubt on its first premise: "My Edward and I, then, are happy." (Here Brontë's strategy resembles Austen's, especially in the last sardonic pages of *Northanger Abbey* and *Sense and Sensibility*.) For if *Jane Eyre*, as I have said, is split between rival narratives—between the two class positions evoked by the miscegenated child and ambiguous governess—then these result, by the final scene, in two opposing images of the mature heroine: the happy, rich, and conventionally respectable lady *and* the overworked, always potentially irate nurse. While the story of gentrification and heterosexual romance ostensibly prevails, it is interrogated to the end by the subtler, homosocial story of Jane's continuing service, binding her to those she earlier calls the "millions . . . in silent revolt against their lot" (96). If Jane loses sight of the radical plot introduced at Gateshead, the novel, I would argue, does not. Mrs. Rochester may neglect Adèle, abandoning her previous wayward self, yet the novel makes a point of remembering the fate of those who are poor and female, thus reviving indignation. The narrator may likewise forget her once intimate connection to Bessie, yet the novel's very telling depends upon the knack for narrative that Jane acquired at Bessie's knee.

As I move into this study's final chapter, I would reiterate two things. By attending to class differences, by being itself divided by these differences, Brontë's novel obliges its readers to differentiate female development in terms of class and, for that matter, sexuality, nationality, race, etc.—challenging us to account for multiple and often conflicting female formations. By cutting across the classic, vertical story of marrying up the social ladder with a horizontal story of community among working women, it urges us also to imagine a developmental turn away from individualism, in the direction of a dissenting collectivity.

CHAPTER FIVE

The Mill on the Floss, the Critics, and the Bildungsroman

CRITICS of *The Mill on the Floss*, no less than Maggie herself, have been troubled by the questionable appeal of Stephen Guest. Alongside the more famous debate between those who favor the pictorial charms of *Adam Bede* and those who prefer the philosophical challenges of *Middlemarch*, readers of Eliot have continued to ask: Is the handsome heir to Guest and Co. really, as Leslie Stephen would have it, "a mere hair-dresser's block"? F. R. Leavis's contribution in *The Great Tradition* (1948) was arguably not only to recuperate the later novels and Eliot's reputation in general but also to raise the stakes in discussions of Maggie's lover by claiming that Eliot herself, identifying with her heroine, "shares to the full the sense of Stephen's irresistibleness" (44). Eliot's own blind weakness for Stephen constitutes, according to Leavis, a lapse from "the impersonality of genius" into an embarrassing mode of "personal need" (32). Gordon Haight, on the other hand, in his 1961 introduction to the Riverside Edition, spent several pages defending Stephen. Noting Eliot's interest in the theory of evolution, he characterized Philip and Stephen as rivals in a Darwinian process of sexual selection and observed that "in simple biological terms Stephen is a better mate" (xiii). As Haight's formulation implies, the continual question of Stephen is in many ways the question of finding a mate for Maggie.[1] A similar phrasing of Maggie's dilemma—and the dilemma of *The Mill on the Floss*—as a matter of heterosexual options was implicit, I think, in John Hagan's careful 1972 overview of Eliot criticism. Hagan sorted Eliot critics into two opposing camps: those who value Maggie's self-denial, associated with her loyalty to Tom and her father (Bernard J. Paris, Reva Stump, George Levine) and those who value her self-assertion, associated with her attraction to Stephen and Philip (William R. Steinhoff and Jerome Thale). Resuming Hagan's metacritical project some twenty years later, I would say that his reading not only codified but was itself the culmination of that pre-1970s critical strand tending to cast *The Mill on the Floss*'s narrative alternatives in terms of competing male claims.[2]

Yet there were also critics of the fifties and sixties who, rather than judge the sufficiency of this man or that to satisfy Maggie, interpreted her fate in ways that exceeded such a framework. In his 1968 book on the early novels, U. C. Knoepflmacher paused over the "enlightened," pro-Stephen view (that Maggie should just have gone with the flow) only to moot the controversy altogether by asserting that "Stephen is merely a convenient device" (214). Arguing that "Maggie is condemned, regardless of her choice" (213), he speculated on the relation between her downfall and issues of gender identity.[3] Barbara Hardy's reading of Maggie, though written nine years earlier, went further still to circumvent the Stephen-Tom continuum. The tragedies of Eliot's heroines begin, she proposed, in their disabilities as women, particularly their lack of education (47–53). Since Hardy and Knoepflmacher, the emergence in the seventies of feminist criticism—an intervention that will be one of this chapter's recurrent concerns—has produced a wealth of elaborations on these early gender analyses of Maggie's plight. Whereas Hagan saw both of Maggie's male-defined objects as "good," her tragedy arising from their incompatibility (57), feminist critics have in general insisted that both goals available to Maggie are "bad"; variations on the same catastrophe, the endings implied by lover and by brother may each, in and of itself, entail Maggie's self-denial. Though Stephen and Tom still have their partisans, critics of many feminist stripes have taken for granted the overdetermination of Maggie's doom, reshaping the critical debate accordingly. If they agree on

Maggie's inevitable defeat (and its comment on conditions for Victorian women), they are divided about whether she goes to her destiny kicking or quiescent.

In the context of an early seventies feminism concerned to expose and protest female victimization, one strain of readings stressed Maggie's systematic disempowerment and resignation to her plight. Elizabeth Ermarth, in "Maggie Tulliver's Long Suicide" (1974), suggested that Maggie internalizes "crippling norms" and "grows up fatally weak" (587). Three years later, in *A Literature of Their Own*, Elaine Showalter concurred, calling Maggie a "heroine of renunciation" in contrast to the rebellious Jane Eyre (112). Another early feminist critic, in an impulse again typical of the seventies, gave this reading for female self-sacrifice a different political twist. Patricia Spacks (*The Female Imagination*, 1975) also identified Maggie with what seem to be choices against herself but explained that, in terms of Eliot's distinctly "female" Victorian morality, the acceptance of worldly defeat may constitute a spiritual victory (44–46).[4] Marianne Hirsch's more recent consideration of *The Mill on the Floss* as a female *Bildungsroman* is arguably in this tradition as well. Like Ermarth and Showalter, Hirsch laments Maggie's disadvantage in the social sphere; like Spacks, however, she is also interested in tracing another, compensatory path of spiritual success. Once again, by shifting into a recuperated "female" register (in this case a developmental model valuing inner over outer growth, return to origins over separation from family), Hirsch is tempted to redeem Maggie's fate. What looks like a disastrous *Bildung* by male standards may actually look something like success within a renovated paradigm (37). Of course this kind of revision is crucial, and Hirsch makes an appealing case. Yet to conclude that Maggie's untimely death completes what is "nevertheless a development of a total individual, spiritual, moral, intellectual, emotional, even sexual" (37) is to downplay what Hirsch admits is the continual difficulty of Maggie's story and to ignore the anger and resistance packed around this difficulty. Focusing either on failure or on a redefined success, the ground-breaking readings I have outlined above seem limited, finally, by their inattention to *The Mill on the Floss*'s portion of radical discontent. Here Nina Auerbach's depiction of Maggie's "demonism" provides a valuable antidote. In "The Power of Hunger: Demonism and

Maggie Tulliver" (1975), Auerbach catalogued not Maggie's weakness but rather her power to terrorize: Maggie kills rabbits, spills wine, crushes cake, mutilates dolls, drops books, dashes card houses, and hangs on Tom in "a strangling fashion." This forceful rendition of the gothic extremity present in *The Mill on the Floss* strikes me as a necessary corrective to more palliating versions. Oddly, however, Auerbach's essay links Maggie to witches, pagan goddesses, vampires, and other types of the monstrous female without examining the social meaning and operation of these types, and the result is almost to reify Maggie-the-witch as evil.[5] Only by placing Maggie's witchery in the context of "St. Ogg's" circa 1825 can seemingly simple and arbitrary evil be recognized as systematic defiance and, moreover, a key site of protest in Eliot's text.

Just as feminist scholarship in general needs to maintain a doubled view of women as agents as well as victims, it seems to me the most useful responses to *The Mill on the Floss* combine the two perspectives I have described. As the 1970s gave way to the 1980s, feminist critics began to explore the complex tension between resignation and defiance in Eliot's work. They did this in part by looking less at Maggie as a character and more at authorial strategies: George Eliot's manipulation of "masculine" plots and discourse. Sandra Gilbert and Susan Gubar (1979), Nancy Miller (1981), and Mary Jacobus (1981), to take three prominent examples, all decline to romanticize Maggie's fate but look elsewhere in the text for struggle and ire. My own argument proceeds from these, and specifically from the view that the thwarting of Maggie's *Bildung* can coexist with oppositional effects. I want to reaccent the way Maggie is dominated at every turn—denying, however, that all disobedience is curbed or that subordination can be rescued for a new ethical scheme. Sharing the interest of many of the studies above in *The Mill on the Floss* as a fiction of female development, I would situate the text's polemic in precisely the story of Maggie's embattled formation, which both invokes and, I believe, finally distances itself from the *Bildungsroman* based on Goethe's *Wilhelm Meister*. Returning to the generic concerns of the first chapter, I want to move from the perception that Maggie has trouble growing up to argue that George Eliot's text takes on and has trouble with Goethe's version of growing up, in a way that begins to call it into question. Inquiring into the uncomfortable fit between the conventional *Bildungsroman* and *The Mill on the Floss*, I will eventually be asking not only what this says about the novel but also what it might further reveal about the generic category. Taking up where chapter 1 left off, I will be resuming that genealogy of the genre with a few of those critics subsequent to Susanne Howe, exploring somewhat further the ideological implications of her legacy. Extending the investment throughout this book in feminist interventions into literary studies, I will be, more specifically, returning to the early 1970s in order to situate some popular notions about the *Bildungsroman* in relation to the dawning of American feminist criticism. Finally, I will be offering an alternative way of reading for formation, insisting less on the progress of an alienated individual than on her or his constitution by manifold social relationships—once again, attending less to the single-minded development of one character than to the tangle of conflicting notions about development and the dueling narratives that result.

For if the novel as a genre is notoriously about the individual in society—according to Ian Watt's history, arising alongside and enabled by Cartesian, capitalist, and Calvinist conceptions of the individual— then the *Bildungsroman*, as Dilthey and Howe among others have defined it, brings this deep structure of the novel to the surface. Or if, as Fredric Jameson rephrases Watt's account, the nineteenth-century novel does not reflect individual selves born of new philosophies and practices but rather works itself to produce a "mirage" of isolate subjectivity (153), then the classic *Bildungsroman* would seem to do this work especially well. Thus Hartmut Steinecke, referring narrowly to those German novels in the wake of Goethe's *Wilhelm Meister's Apprenticeship* (1795), called the *Bildungsroman* the "individual novel" as opposed to the social novel.[6] It will be recalled that when Jerome Buckley extended the term to a British tradition from *David Copperfield* to *A Portrait of the Artist as a Young Man*, he too emphasized the special, artistic child set off from "his" inimical environment. David Miles's contention that the *Bildungsroman* since Goethe has become increasingly psychological (as the picaresque hero begins to look in his heart and write) suggests, indeed, a heightening of this genre's preoccupation with the solitary, ever more introverted self. As chapter 1 observed, these views of the *Bildungsroman* are structured by and structure assumptions not only about the (male) protagonist's autonomy but also about his progressive movement through the world. A crude picture of the genre shows an especially rugged or especially sensitive young man, at leisure to mull over some life choices, not so much connected to people or the landscape as encountering or passing through them as "options" or "experiences" en route to a better place. Travel, I have said, is key, for though the story pulls toward settling the youth—its telos is repose—what it actually recounts is his relentless advance.[7]

Several qualifications of this traditional mapping of the genre are in order. Goethe's optimism notwithstanding, few of his successors' novels progress toward happy, assimilative endings. But if the Bildungsroman is less hopeful and less integrative than Wilhelm Meister (it does not always, as Hegel claimed, bring its hero to embrace bourgeois society),[8] it still generally assumes that some kind of movement is possible. This movement is not necessarily a literal journeying, say, from country to city; it may involve mental travel to a higher moral or emotional ground. It may bring the hero to terms or to blows with society. Often, as Buckley and Miles agree, it brings him to art. But in all cases it takes for granted that the Bildungsheld has room to maneuver and somewhere to go. Finally, I would note that these two imperatives—individualism and mobility—are closely related. Their coincidence is explicit in Buckley's account, the hero journeying to the city in order to separate from his family. Of course all development narratives, including the classic German text, can be seen to strain against the composite model I have recounted. But it is fair to say that The Mill on the Floss, while alluding to the model (one that, unlike my other novelists, Eliot knew intimately), also resists it with special vehemence.[9] In their introduction to The Voyage In, Elizabeth Abel, Marianne Hirsch, and Elizabeth Langland point out the insufficiency of the Bildungsroman, as it is usually construed, to describe works by women and featuring female protagonists. Yet this volume is mostly interested in identifying "distinctively female versions of the Bildungsroman" (5); as in Hirsch's essay on The Mill on the Floss (anthologized there), its emphasis is on recuperating an exclusively female form. My own, by contrast, is on Eliot's engagement and struggle with the dominant paradigm. I read The Mill on the Floss less as a wholly alternative structure than as an ironization and interrogation of the old.[10] My primary purpose is to locate the continual collisions between gender and received genre in *The Mill on the Floss*, to examine the stress points, blockages, and jammings, because these seem to me the infuriated places productive of critique.

II

The isolating mobility of the *Bildungsroman* "proper" is strongly evoked by the adventures of Tom Tulliver. As Judith Lowder Newton has remarked, "Tom is already in motion when we first encounter him" (139). He is first seen bowling along in a gig, which soon deposits him into the arms of an eager family. His first words, spoken "with masculine reticence as to the tender emotions," suggest a kind of anticonversation: "Hallo! Yap—what! are you there?" (30) To whom, we might ask, is this actually addressed? Is "hallo!" meant for Yap (the dog) or simply shouted out into the void? Is "what!" a cry of recognition or, as the last phrase implies, a question? And again, is this recognition-immediately-doubted still directed to Yap? or has Tom suddenly noticed Maggie and Mrs. Tulliver? Perhaps he intends a metaphysical "you"—as if to ask, "Is there anyone listening?" Possibly the subject of this fragment is really "yap," or language estranged from intelligibility. More than a boy's amusing shyness, displacing his real love for sister and mother onto dog, the speech conveys an almost existential doubt about whether an interlocutor exists and whether meaningful exchange can occur. This is not an uncertainty shared by the text as a whole; indeed, I will ultimately be arguing that *The Mill on the Floss* encourages its readers both formally and thematically to see characters in interlocutory terms. What Tom's stammering hello suggests, rather, is the difficulty of dialogue for him. The subsequent action reiterates this difficulty. When Maggie grabs her brother around the neck, Tom absents himself by looking and traveling in his mind's eye "towards the croft and the lambs and the river, where he promised himself that he would begin to fish the first thing to-morrow morning" (30). In fact, Tom hardly ever allows Maggie (or any Other) to be *present* to him until their penultimate crisis, face to face in the flood. Only then does he utter a genuine cry of recognition—"Magsie!" (455)—finally controverting the elided recognition above, in which "Yap" followed by a dash seems to indicate the place where Maggie and a chance at connection are suppressed.

Tom's desire for autonomy and its relation to mobility are illustrated time and again. He maintains (the illusion of) his freedom from extended kin ties by absconding whenever the uncles and aunts appear (40). And the one time Tom decides to risk their visit for the sake of "the pudden," he braces his ego by asserting his independence of Maggie in the famous jam puff scene (41–43). Here Tom's studied division of the pastry into "mine" and "yours," the resolute descent of his "hovering knife," seems to figure the severing from Maggie that this scene literally accomplishes. Carefully orchestrated to find fault with his sister whether she gives him more or less puff, it ends like so many of their encounters with Tom running off in anger. It is also an example of how Tom's resisted family ties are mediated by food, by Uncle Deane's peppermints and Mrs. Tulliver's cakes and puddens, as if hearkening back to a pre-oedipal feeding. The violent bisection of the puff attempts to undo the children's earlier communion over cake, when Maggie "put out her mouth for the cake and bit a piece: and then Tom bit a piece, just for company, and they ate together and rubbed each other's cheeks and brows and noses together" (35–36).

When Tom abandons Maggie, he typically turns to Lucy, Luke, or Bob Jakin, "an inferior, who could always be treated with authority" (43), not to console but rather to consolidate his separateness. Anxious to lead Lucy, fire Luke, or patronize Bob, Tom defends his solitary state by demonstrating his (gender and class) superiority. This will, of course, be accomplished more lastingly by the genteel education and apprenticeship in trade that, seemingly mismatched, together raise him farther above Maggie, Bob, and even his own father. As in most *Bildungsromane*, the mobility underwriting Tom's sovereignty is finally *social* mobility. But what distinguishes *The Mill on the Floss* from *Wilhelm Meister*, *David Copperfield*, and even Ann Murry's *Mentoria* is its repudiation of precisely this story of self-advancement—its critical if not satirical view of Tom's lonely climb from averted adolescent to competitive businessman, its evident concern to dramatize the moral and narrative deficiency of Tom's story. This deficiency is especially clear at the trajectory's highest point, the moment of "arrival" that should bring semantic and formal satisfaction. For when Tom's laborious apprenticeship is at last completed by an offer to join his uncle's firm, it is still not enough. He also wants to recover and manage the mill, both to avenge his father and because, as he explains, "I want to have plenty of work. There's nothing else I care about much." Here the narrator remarks, "There was something rather sad in that speech from a young man of three-and-twenty" (348). Uncle Deane assures Tom he will one day have a wife to care about, but Tom's interest in Lucy never goes anywhere. For the male protagonist, marriage is not a goal so much as a reward for having reached his goal; it symbolizes his gratification. But unlike Dickens's social-climbing Pip, Tom never manages to reframe his great expectations, does not reroute his course in time for a chance at romantic "happiness," and he reaches a moral turning point only moments before his death. By killing instead of wedding Tom, Eliot's text refuses, narratively, to validate his formation and to invest it with significant content.[11]

Of course, *The Mill on the Floss* undercuts Tom's *Bildungsroman* principally by shoving it off to the side, unwilling to make it the center or norm. Jerome Buckley and Charlotte Goodman have tried to conserve Tom's primacy by arguing that *The Mill on the Floss* is a "double" *Bildungsroman*. Buckley cites George Eliot's own statement to publisher John Blackwood, describing her novel as "the history of two closely related lives." Though readers may prefer Maggie, Buckley says, "we must not ignore the declared duality of purpose" (97). Goodman also asserts that *The Mill on the Floss* places "virtually equal emphasis on both a male and a female protagonist" (30). This seems to me a somewhat misleading claim. Whatever Eliot's professed intention, from the very first moment one's attention, like the narrator's, is devoted to Maggie. Readers enter the Tulliver household because Maggie leads them there, and it is her interior life, more lovingly detailed than Tom's, that catches them up and carries them through. She refigures, in short, enough of Wilhelm or Pip to be recognizable in some conventional sense as the character whose formation ought to be primarily at issue. But though Maggie may be the more conspicuous protagonist, it is equally true that any comfortable centrality is thrown off by Tom. Her narrative deposes but does not, however, wholly displace his. Nor are the two balanced in some stable symmetry or amiable doubleness. They tend, rather, to pull each other off balance, to conflict with and contest one another.

Perhaps the tension is a generic one. Taking Fredric Jameson's point that "genre theory must always in one way or another project a model of the coexistence or tension between several generic modes or strands" (141), one may provisionally regard the distance between brother and sister as the space between genres. If Tom indicates the work's nominal status as *Bildungsroman*, Maggie's problem—and the problematic of the novel—is her inability to enter the designated mode. The novel is structured by her vain attempts to participate in the genre I have attributed to Tom and by her inevitable lapses back into another, something resembling the gothic and recalling *Evelina*; in spite of her aspirations to *Bildung*, Maggie is continually returned to a place of terror, reenclosed in a familiar prison. [12] In Jameson's reading of Manzoni's *I Promessi Sposi*, the separation of lovers occasions a very similar tension, splitting the work into

> two very distinct narrative lines which can be read as two different generic modes. The plight of Lucia, for instance, gives [Manzoni] the material for a Gothic novel, in which the feminine victim eludes one trap only to fall into a more agonizing one. . . . Meanwhile, Renzo wanders through the *grosse Welt* of history and of the displacement of vast armed populations. . . . His own episodic experiences, formally something like a *roman d'aventures* . . . thus provide a quite different narrative register from that, inward and psychologizing, of the Lucia narrative. (143)

Jameson describes but does not take notice of the evident gender specificity of these two registers. As in *The Mill on the Floss*, Manzoni's female character is seized by an agonizing, claustrophobic circularity, while the male adventures his way through a more spacious landscape. Insisting on the manifestly gendered aspect of these divergent plot lines is the first step toward making sense of such a seeming generic discontinuity and its organization of *The Mill on the Floss*.

I would argue that, although Tom's is the coveted mode, the elusiveness of this mode for Maggie serves to call it into question. The problem it poses for her makes the form itself finally problematic. In a sense, her continual tugging at the *Bildungsroman* works eventually to loosen its moorings. Furthermore, the rivalry between sibling narratives has a decentering effect that puts *The Mill on the Floss* itself at odds with the usual novel of formation. Buckley and Goodman are right to notice that Eliot's *Bildungsheld* is, if not doubled, then at least decentered. What they fail to appreciate is how this decentering contests the very terms of the *Bildungsroman*, to which a single, central character has been seen as fundamental.[13] Not only Tom's particular story, but the genre as a whole and its implied values are unsettled by this configuration. Apparently the centered subject was not so thoroughly or enthusiastically constructed by the nineteenth-century novel as Jameson implies. The critique he locates in our current period of late capitalism (124–125) may have antecedents in the work of women such as George Eliot for whom, from the start, the centered subject wavered suspiciously like a mirage.[14]

Maggie's wishes to learn Latin and earn money by plain sewing typify her futile efforts to make Tom's *Bildung* her own. Among these efforts, her flight to the gypsies is particularly revealing, and its disappointed outcome is key to my argument. This episode *begins* as a rejection of Tom and his middle-class values, as Maggie recklessly embraces the whole string of overlapping pejoratives marking her as "bad": darkness/dirtiness/demonism/gypsyness. In this sense, joining the gypsies is continuous with pushing "little pink-and-white Lucy into the cow-trodden mud" (91) and urging the fair-skinned Tom to "stain his face brown" (94). Repudiating the "clean" and "fair" while asserting the disreputable, reviling genteel sensibilities (much as the blackened Lucy does when she appears in aunt Pullet's parlor), it represents a strategy of impenitence. Yet claiming a nomadic people, like the act of running away itself, also expresses Maggie's longing for Tom's easy mobility. And though she begins in opposition to Tom, Maggie soon comes to imagine her relation to the gypsies in Tom's own condescending terms. She tells herself they will "pay her much respect on account of her superior knowledge" (94). At the camp, the once defiantly messy girl begins to wish her gypsy friends were less dirty and plans to introduce washing basins along with books (97). Having briefly challenged bourgeois notions of dirty and clean, Maggie now reverts to the old valuations. But the moral agenda Maggie brings to the gypsies is less about feminine virtue reflected in aunt Pullet's glossy floors than it is about teaching, improving, and "civilizing." Her eagerness to explain who Columbus was—"a very wonderful man, who found out half the world" (98)— makes explicit the colonial mission Maggie has assigned herself, and it is an eminently masculine one. [15] In fact, this second phase of Maggie's venture is a kind of cross-dressing as Columbus. Her running away to the gypsies is, the narrator remarks, a larger-scale version of what Tom would have done under similar circumstances (93). Likewise, the Columbian dream of crossing oceans to rule a "barbarian" nation is a larger-scale version and logical extension of Tom's more modest capitalist career. Here then is Maggie's bid to generate a *Bildungsroman* for herself and even to beat Tom at his own genre.

Maggie's conquesting *Bildungsroman* takes, however, a sudden gothic swerve, leading her through terror back to where she began. By the time a gypsy escorts her home, "no nightmare had ever seemed to her more horrible. . . . Not Leonore, in that preternatural midnight excursion with her phantom lover, was more terrified than poor Maggie" (102). And Maggie's "rescue" by her father only returns her to the constraining community she so desperately fled in the first place; her wanderings produce not escape but reimprisonment, and in this they anticipate her later flight with that phantom lover, Stephen Guest. Yet if the colonial version of the *Bildungsroman* proves inaccessible to Maggie, her disenchantment does make this story-type somewhat less appealing. On the one hand, Eliot's text is itself complicit with the tale of thieves and primitives in need of reform. On the other, however, Maggie's foolish misconceptions about the gypsies, her laughable arrogance about schooling and governing them, also lampoon this particular narrative of self-definition through domination, including Tom's domestic variety.

Ousted from the footloose "male" mode, Maggie lapses back into the claustrophobic "female" mode—the gothic register associated with aunt Pullet in the chapter immediately before Maggie departs for gypsydom. This scene, the unveiling of aunt Pullet's new bonnet, offers not only (what the bonnet implies) a peek at female sexuality, but also an ominous glimpse of the usual plotting of female destiny. The drawn-out solemnity of the disclosure, reverently witnessed by Mrs. Tulliver and the two fearful girls, makes it indeed a kind of ritual initiation into the ways of womanhood. [16] It is marked off as such by the perilous climb up polished stairs, Maggie and Lucy trailing after the older women, leaving Tom behind (79). Needless to say, this is not the steady march to masculine selfhood, but a slippery antiexpedition to femaleness, which threatens to be crippling. Once upstairs, in search of the touted bonnet, aunt Pullet leads her sister and nieces through a Chinese puzzle of locked rooms and wardrobes. Far from an invigorating mobility, this is an approach to greater and greater stillness, passing by "the corpses of furniture in white shrouds" (80) in a movement away from movement. Even the unshrouded furniture postures its passivity, legs in the air. Think of Paul Morel, striding at the end of *Sons and Lovers* "towards the faintly humming, glowing town"; by contrast, Maggie is led inward to compartments of increasing darkness and disuse. Think of *The Prelude*, its ecstatic protagonist looking out from Alpine heights, or David Copperfield more quietly stirred by his view of a Swiss valley; here Eliot depicts the plumbing of a house for its dimmest and narrowest perspective.

So Maggie and Lucy, excluded from a boy's roving, self-enlarging genre, are ushered into a diminishing space. Adult femininity, here as in a gothic novel, seems to require live burial in the smallest closets of a large house. More terrible still, however, is the banality of the object finally uncovered: "The sight of the bonnet at last was an anticlimax to Maggie, who would have preferred something more strikingly preternatural" (80). What aunt Pullet reveals is the trick of female destiny, that there is no rabbit in the hat—only the hat. Aunt Pullet's bonnet is ineluctably ordinary, nonmagical, empty. Like Jane Austen in *Northanger Abbey*, Eliot seems to revise the gothic in anticipation of Freud's perception that the scariest place and worst villain are not only the most remote, but also the most familiar. In these domesticated gothic novels, the cruelest torments are the boredom and triviality of a woman's routine; the tightest bonds—could they be the strings of her bonnet? There is also a sense in which the bonnet refers to the fashionable Dodson female herself. Turning "slowly around, like a draper's lay-figure," (81), aunt Pullet seems indeed a shell of clothing with very little inside. Like her clothes, she is primarily ornamental, signifying her husband's wealth and taste. And in this objectification aunt Pullet resembles her favorite sister, Bessie, who falls apart when she loses her things. "Elizabeth Dodson" is literally written into her tablecloths, so that when these are dispersed she herself is hopelessly scattered. Maggie, in short, quite correctly intuits that there is "some painful mystery about her aunt's bonnet" (82). Though uncomprehending, she is not too young to catch the allusion of this headgear to the claustrophobia, inconsequentiality, and desperate consumerism of Victorian women's lives.

In all the ways I have described, the bonnet scene suggests a gothicized formation in keeping with the long suicide view of Maggie's fate and in stark contrast to Tom's aggressive forays into the world. Yet, while marking Maggie's exclusion from the masculinized *Bildungsroman*, it may also communicate a restless desire for it and ultimately, I would argue once again, serve to criticize by parodying the official genre. Take, for example, this musing on the bonnet by the two sisters:

> "Ah," [aunt Pullet] said at last, "I may never wear it twice, sister; who knows?"
> "Don't talk o' that, sister," answered Mrs Tulliver. "I hope you'll have your health this summer."
> "Ah! but there may come a death in the family, as there did soon after I had my green satin bonnet. Cousin Abbott may go, and we can't think o' wearing crape less nor half a year for him." (81)

Aunt Pullet's moan seems at first, to us and Mrs. Tulliver, like a woeful and even wishful prediction of her own death. Yet as it turns out, Aunt Pullet is not thinking about herself at all, but about some other family member—preferably cousin Abbott. Remembering cousin Abbott's wealth, one realizes that aunt Pullet's fantasy, far from suicidal, is in fact distinctly homicidal. Judging by the lethal effect of her previous, green satin bonnet, she is optimistic about her new one. "Cousin Abbott may go," she says hopefully. So aunt Pullet in the last analysis stands for more than female victimization and more than resignation to a gothic fate; here she reveals an inflated and enjoyed sense of power over others reminiscent of Tom, and even her hypochondria is really a form of competitiveness akin to his. Aunt Pullet takes a quantitative approach to illness, enumerating the various medicines she ingests, hoarding up her physic-bottles, and calculating the shelves they fill. She measures her status in the community in numbers of visits to the doctor. In the same sad, self-dramatizing vein, aunt Pullet competes in quantities of tears: poor Bessy "couldn't cry so much as her sister Pullet did, and had often felt her deficiency at funerals" (82). The desire to surpass extends to clothes as well. According to a sartorial logic by which more is again assumed to be better, aunt Pullet's shoulders are wide as a doorway, her sleeves balloonlike, her bonnet "architectural" (51). Naturally, hers is "the best bonnet at Garum Church, let the next best be whose it would" (81).

Thus while aunt Pullet likes to think of herself as wasting away she also contrives to take up as much space as possible, at least in the terms available to her. If she cannot participate directly in Tom's economic rivalries or physical aggressions, still she finds comparable ways to push herself forward in order, like him, to tyrannize the rest. Aunt Pullet simply expresses her ambitions in acceptably female terms, challenging everyone else to be sicker or more over-dressed than she. The story she stages for Maggie is not only a gothic foil to the *Bildungsroman*; it is also an aping, humiliated rendition of it. Yet I would argue that aunt Pullet's efforts in the direction of a *Bildungsroman* do not legitimate so much as travesty the genre. The impulse she shares with Tom to scramble into selfhood over and beyond other people is shown to be petty, illogical, and even self-destructive. Like Maggie in her attempt to colonize the gypsies, aunt Pullet engages and then manages to caricature the *Bildungsroman*. Her futile pursuit of this mode defamiliarizes and eventually mocks it, so that envy slides into critique.

III

Having looked at *The Mill on the Floss* in relation to the *Bildungsroman*, I turn now to the generic category itself, especially as schematized and popularized by Jerome Buckley's *Season of Youth: The Bildungsroman from Dickens to Golding*. Published in 1974, *Season of Youth* was the first book-length study of the English *Bildungsroman* since Susanne Howe's initial mapping of the German genre onto English terrain in 1930 (Hans Wagner's 1951 book, in German, excepted). [17] Buckley's focus on canonical novels and his highly excerptable formulation have, moreover, made the book influential perhaps beyond its merits; its interest for me lies less in its scholarly than in its ideological significance as a text invariably cited in subsequent teaching and writing about the English genre. According to Buckley, this form originated with Wordsworth, who in *The Prelude* "first gave prolonged and serious attention to each stage of the imagination, to boyhood, maturity, and the darker space between" (2). Though different in tone, Buckley continues, Byron's *Don Juan* "likewise follows a young man in his progress from boyhood to the threshold of a poised maturity" (7). Carlyle's 1824 translation of *Wilhelm Meister* provided the first novelistic model, and the genre developed from there through such major works as *David Copperfield* and *Sons and Lovers*. As noted earlier, Buckley stresses the form's autobiographical cast, arguing that the English *Bildungsroman* is therefore typically a *Künstlerroman*: "what Joyce's title promises, *A Portrait of the Artist as a Young Man*" (14).

It would be easy enough to take Buckley to task for continually equating "youth" with "boyhood," but the editors of *The Voyage In* have already sufficiently shown that Buckley's phases of development (formal education, leaving home, making one's way in the city, etc.) are inapplicable to most female protagonists (7–9). My concern here is with some of the other implications of the approach I take Buckley to represent and what they meant in the particular social context of 1974. Buckley comments on "the awkwardness of the German term [*Bildungsroman*] as applied to English literature" (vii); yet, like late 1960s essays by Tennyson and Jost, his book holds onto the clumsy foreignism and what I have already shown to be its considerable ideological baggage. What, one might wonder, was at stake in privileging the German denomination at this particular moment? Like all generic categories, the *Bildungsroman* is bound up with a process of canon formation, called upon to identify a tradition of texts. Jeffrey Sammons observes that the early twentieth-century delineation of the *Bildungsroman* by Dilthey "placed Goethe and Romanticism firmly at the core of the [German] canon" (240). The concept worked then to foreground a certain thematics—Goethe's "scheme of the salvation of the striving individual in an ultimately benign universe" (241)—and also to define and promote a distinctively German literature at a time of surging nationalist sentiment. Thomas Mann among others, Sammons explains, was instrumental in setting up "the inherent German tradition of the *Bildungsroman* as a defense against the infiltration of the social and political novel" (241). Sammons argues that the *Bildungsroman* is thus a "phantom genre," more responsive to modern ideological needs than to any objective body of texts.

What canon was being asserted, what infiltration defended against in the early 1970s? The canon represented by *Season of Youth* is, not coincidentally, also derived from the Romantics and again includes Goethe. As I suggested in chapter 1, Buckley's emphasis on "portrait of the artist" novels seems to indicate that what he and others get from Romanticism and bring to the examination of later works is primarily an infatuation with alienated genius; their *Bildungsheld* is by definition a child whose lyric tendencies are at odds with a prosaic community (17). Clearly, Buckley not only invoked the emphatic individualism of the *Bildungsroman* described earlier in this chapter but also helped to construct it along these lines. He makes passing mention, in relation to the American 1930s, of "the Studs Lonigan trilogy of James T. Farrell with its new insistence on the social and economic determinants of character" (265). For the most part, however, the protagonist's constitution by social and economic factors is precisely what Buckley's canon and approach function to obscure. His conclusion—that the *Bildungsheld* from Wilhelm Meister to Stephen Dedalus "brings his own inner resources of sensitivity to confront a hostile and insensitive environment" (282)—reveals the book's attraction to heroes developing not in, but in spite of their social contexts, not shaped by cultural pressures so much as bravely withstanding and transcending them. Favoring works that dramatize a triumph of the artistic temperament, its paradigm can better explain David Copperfield's successful literary/moral apprenticeship than the bridling of Emma Woodhouse's imagination by marriage. Preferring firm, independent protagonists, stable and unequivocally central, it can only make sense of *The Mill on the Floss* by hitching Maggie's moral stamina to Tom's commercial success, as if sister and brother were the inseparable halves of a single, battle worthy character. Accordingly, in a chapter on later novels, *Season* chooses Woolf's *Jacob's Room* (though troubled by its elusive hero) over the more diffuse *To the Lighthouse*, which Buckley says "turned away from the content as well as the form of the Bildungsroman" (265). And finally, it happily leaves Woolf altogether for the Angry Young Men of the fifties, in whose "fictions reappear many motifs of the conventional Bildungsroman" (267).

To the Lighthouse is a revealing example of the kind of text that fails to register as a novel of development within the schema crystallized by *Season of Youth*. For Lily Briscoe, its putative *Bildungsheld*, is never permitted to dominate the narrative, which continues to shift away from her even as she approaches her climactic vision. [18] Lily and her vision are always inextricable from the social relationships that define the woman artist—from parent figures Mr. and Mrs. Ramsay or from Mr. Tansley, figure for the male critic. In formal terms, moreover, Lily is quite literally displaced from the center of the text by the specter of "Time Passing": Prue Ramsay, done in by childbirth; Andrew Ramsay blown up in France; Mrs. Ramsay, wearied to death by marriage and maternity; Mrs. McNab and Mrs. Bast, scrubbing against the forces of decay. And perhaps this is not Lily's story after all, so much as an array of rival fictions about gendered development variously represented by Lily, Minta, Prue, Andrew, James, Cam, and the Ramsay parents themselves. Yet the effect of Buckley's canon was to ward off the infiltration of just such texts in which history and society, not the masterful individual, are central; texts in which development is not one, clear thing, but many, unsure, contested and changing things. I want to argue that it did this at precisely the moment when feminist criticism was beginning to discover new works and reread old ones with Woolf's contextual and polyphonic model very much in mind.

So my point is not to offer the easy poststructuralist critique of Buckley's modernist view of the "self" as stable, integrated, etc., but to look at this view in relation to articles such as "Maggie Tulliver's Long Suicide" by Elizabeth Ermarth, which also appeared in 1974. This was the year the twentieth-century women's movement began to rock the academy. In literary criticism, Mary Ellmann's precocious *Thinking about Women* (1968) had already been around for six years, Kate Millett's *Sexual Politics* (1970) for four. The previous year had seen, for example, the publication of Carolyn Heilbrun's *Toward a Recognition of Androgyny* and, in *Ms.* magazine, Adrienne Rich's "Jane Eyre: The Temptations of a Motherless Woman." Clearly the storm of feminist criticism that broke in the following years—with Patricia Spacks's *The Female Imagination* in 1975, Ellen Moers's *Literary Women* in 1976, Elaine Showalter's *A Literature of Their Own* in 1977, and Barbara Smith's "Toward a Black Feminist Criticism," also in 1977—was visible on the horizon in 1974. Not that Buckley consciously sought to head off feminist criticism when he refused to look at Maggie Tulliver or George Eliot in relation to their sexist societies, or when he failed to see that development itself, especially for girls, may be a controversial plot; the effect of doing so was nevertheless to man the barricades that were already under attack by feminist scholars.

To this mixed metaphorical account I would add a further observation about David Miles's "The Picaro's Journey to the Confessional: The Changing Image of the Hero in the German Bildungsroman," also published in 1974. As I have already noted, Miles argues that the *Bildungsroman* becomes progressively more introspective, reaching its logical culmination in Rainer Maria Rilke's *Die Aufzeichnungen des Malte Laurids Brigge* (1910), which takes the form of a confessional journal.[19] Even more than Buckley, Miles articulated a privatized notion of the *Bildungsroman*, to the point of suggesting that development takes place wholly in the twentieth-century hero's head. Construing the genre as a form of self-address, Miles forecloses on more dialogic narratives that might, for example, take the form of letters rather than journals. To consider, say, epistolary novels from *Evelina* to Alice Walker's *The Color Purple* might be to think of a young woman's formation as a process of exchange, an ongoing debate, a social relationship. The problem, therefore, goes beyond the fact that fictions of development such as *Evelina*, *To the Lighthouse*, and *The Color Purple* go unrecognized by the precepts of a Buckley or Miles. By neglecting these works one also neglects their invitation to reconceive identity in terms of interlocutory structures.

Unlike Sammons, I am not saying that the *Bildungsroman* is a "phantom" genre as opposed to "the actual German [or British] novel of the nineteenth century" (238). For while Sammons claims to see genres as "instrumental, not ontological" (230), he remains implicitly attached to the notion of an "actual," flesh and blood genre in some objective sense. If genres are simply pragmatic constructs then they are all phantoms, defined in the service of some explanation (and ideology) or another, and I would like to conclude this chapter and book by recurring to my own feminist phantom: the different way of reading for formation that I hope has haunted the preceding pages, that I have wanted, in relation to women writers, to conjure into being. I have been arguing that Maggie and *The Mill on the Floss* regard Tom's individualist *Bildungsroman* with some desire, but that its difficulty for Maggie estranges and ironizes it. This theme—Maggie's inability to enter the story of self-culture, her stubbornly relational mode—points further to the formal tendency of Eliot's novel, and of novels in general, to establish character interactively. The very structuring of the work as a series of colloquies, intimacies, disputes, suggests not a lone figure pushing past a painted backdrop, but a girl hedged in, defined at every point, by a specific cultural conversation. She is formed as a girl only in opposition to her brother's stubborn boyness (and vice versa), just as Bob's class identity emerges from the scuffle with his overpowering playmate, and Maggie's class and race from her condescending contact with the gypsies. Above and beyond its critique of the traditional *Bildungsroman*, *The Mill on the Floss* may, in its very dialogic form, offer to reformulate development as a matter of social context and conflict. [20]

Maggie's development, then, in the crucible of sibling conflict, consists of a series of transactions in the context of dominative male-female, among many other, social relations. But *The Mill on the Floss* is more than its struggles between brother and sister. It is also, like all the women's texts I have been discussing, a competition of narratives, referring less to the apprenticeship of a central figure than to a drama of dissonant ideas about just what formation is or should be. In rephrasing the genre, I have been recommending a shift away from character altogether—and especially from that Ur-character, Wilhelm Meister—and a turning of critical attention to those discourses of development at war in a given text. I have guessed that this approach might shed particular light on conduct materials and novels by women, whose representations of female formation are so typically beset by contradiction. I hope I have shown that when the ideology of *Bildung* is driven up against ideologies of femininity urging self-effacement one result may be precisely the splintering and counterpointing of narratives I have identified in Burney, Austen, and Brontë, and that appear with particular explicitness in *The Mill on the Floss*.

To recapitulate briefly, in relation to Eliot, these divergent narratives are succinctly invoked early in the novel in the episode of the dead rabbits. Maggie's neglect has killed Tom's pets, and now she nervously offers to pay for them. But Tom doesn't want *her* money, as he explains: "I always have half-sovereigns and sovereigns for my Christmas boxes, because I shall be a man, and you only have five-shilling pieces, because you're only a girl" (32). Here in a phrase—"I shall be a man"—is just that tale of individual agency and growth–associated–with–wealth played out, to its discredit, by Tom. And here in the figure of "only a girl" with little money and no future tense is the embittered, gothic story of repetition and diminution recognizable as Maggie's destiny. Revising an earlier precept, I am now proposing that the disjunction between these be thought of not as the space between genres but as the space within a genre for confusion, complaint, critique, and possibly compensation regarding issues of female development.

Eliot's controversial ending provides a final image of the relationship between Tom's conventional narrative of formation and Maggie's counternarrative. The moment when brother and sister are pulled beneath the waves in a dying embrace has been variously interpreted as androgynous reunion, incestuous orgasm, the climax of a long suicide or perhaps sororicide, and also as authorial revenge. Wishing neither to redeem Maggie's fate nor to discount Tom's, I suggest their simultaneous deaths mark a moment when their narratives collide for the last time, and now Tom's upward-bound *Bildungsroman* is fatally assimilated to Maggie's downward spiral. Little to celebrate except the negation of a story that, failing to work for Maggie, is finally discarded altogether. And yet—if self-centered *Bildung* is traumatically abandoned here, this conclusive grappling may nevertheless assert the inescapable relatedness of circumstances and subjectivities.

AFTERWORD

I began by asking, "Is there a female *Bildungsroman?*" Rather than simply answering this question in the negative, I have wished to consider the effects, the uses, the risks, of such a formulation. My concern has been that by placing "female" in complementary relation to "*Bildungsroman*" one risks closing down the critical distance between them, assimilating gender to genre and making it more difficult for the first to interrogate the second. I do not mean to underestimate the significance of those usually twentieth-century texts in which a girl is finally permitted to leave home, apprentice herself to the world, experiment with sex, and live to tell the tale. Yet this story of female equal access to *Bildung*, first scripted by the anomalous Moll Flanders and only much later revived by such heroines as Radclyffe Hall's Stephen Gordon and Erica Jong's Fanny Hackabout-Jones (see chapter 5, note 19), tends to take at face value the plot of toughing it out against a hostile society; the entry of women into the army of Romantic individualists cannot but strike us as a mixed blessing. On the other hand, those theories of female developmental fiction that recuperate a wholly different plot of spiritual growth and domestic relationships remain, in my view, too obligingly within the given contours of "women's culture," neglecting the troubling appeal and predominance of the *Bildungsroman* for female figures.

In contrast to these two ways of speaking about women and the novel of development, I have assembled narratives in which heroines are obstructed, humiliated, diverted from their early goals, and otherwise mocked by the project of *Bildung*. Occasionally a girl grows up in positive relation to other women and to her own author-ity. In all cases an exfoliation of narratives is typical, suggesting a veritable wilderness of confidences and anxieties about becoming female. I have wanted to tie these to the diversity of views on female development in the culture as a whole—views diversified in many cases by differences of gender and/or class position. In my reading, texts by and about women help us to a theory of the novel of development not as the story of a character, but as the story of a cultural moment, its uncertainties and desires concerning women and *Bildung*. My final chapter—whose title marks the way "critics" stand between Eliot's novel and a category such as the *Bildungsroman*—has proceeded to take its own chances at mediating between these two terms. If previous chapters questioned cultural axioms about female development and development generally (many of which persist to this day), chapter 5 has construed *The Mill on the Floss* as a more particular challenge to the *Bildungsroman* and some of its most influential theorists. This text, I have argued, regards self-interested *Bildung* as a tragic if not actually punishable project. It is decentered, as Tom Tulliver is decentered, by the novel's enactment of growing up as a persistent relatedness—rivalry, dependence, and embrace.

Where do we go from here? It would be possible, of course, to sketch the implications of my claims for later Victorian and early modern novels. Certainly the female and the *Bildungsroman* may be more happily conjoined in the twentieth century, as evidenced by the tendency of scholarship on female *Bildung* to focus on the modern period. But as I have said, I am less interested in renaturalizing the Germanic genre by finding recent female texts that fit the mold than in calling upon earlier works for the way they split it open. Moreover, this study does not, I have stressed, pretend to offer a revised genealogy of the form. What I would like to carry forward is not a tradition of texts but a set of exemplary readings that may prove useful to us in the present moment. It is a time, we know, of widespread backlash against feminism, of rapidly eroding reproductive rights and campaigns against feminist scholarship that threaten to recall the academic witch hunts of the 1950s. Sometime in the late 1980s, we entered an era gleefully dubbed "postfeminist" by the media, and even some of us raised on second-wave feminism have taken this diagnosis to heart, displacing women from the center of our concerns. Women's studies, once devoted to excavating forgotten female literature and history, has now given way to ostensibly less partisan work in "gender studies"—an area that not only includes excellent scholarship on male sexuality but also slips easily in the direction of Robert Bly's "men's movement" and other hardly less hysterical attempts to bring back unreconstructed masculinity.

Not surprising, then, that a casual glance at contemporary tales of female development is likely to make a feminist cringe. Conduct books in glossy paperback instruct women how to dress for success, to love but not too much, and to expect certain things when they're expecting. The sexual scripts of romance novels, movies, and television reproduce the old, dichotomized types: angelic, stay-at-home wife or horrendous fatal attraction. The working girl, too, is given by these texts a choice between two parts—winsome secretary or superbitch with power—and few women in the workplace are presumed entirely innocent. Even girls in their golden years are portrayed as blond and vacant or deep-voiced and smart, though at least these women stick together. Courtship narratives, cases of attempted love connection, routinely separate the good suitor from the bad in terms of chivalric capacity. And women who go on the road, by themselves or with another woman, suffer female difficulties in droves and usually end up dead.

I want to close by suggesting, however, that these conventional plots are no more monolithic or unresisted than the ones we encountered in earlier centuries. I would like this book to insist on the play of conflicting views in post- as well as premodern fictions of female development and help us to claim the most transgressive ones. I would like it to direct us particularly to women's texts, in search of today's unbecoming women—those who, by failing or defying the normative story, grow up in disconcerting ways. I would like it, finally, to answer those recent critics who term academic feminism a school of resentment. I say we represent a school of hope.

NOTES

1. Is There a Female *Bildungsroman?*

1. See Rick Altman's argument to this effect in his lucid "Introduction to the Theory of Genre Analysis" (6–7).

2. Among a great many others—Sandra Gilbert/Susan Gubar and Fredric Jameson, on the realist novel; Janice Radway and Tania Modleski on the Harlequin romance; Marianne Hirsch and Franco Moretti on the *Bildungsroman*; Michael Denning on the dime novel and spy story; Eve Sedgwick and Kate Ellis on the gothic novel.

3. For example, Jonathan Culler in "Towards a Theory of Non-Genre Literature." But see Ralph Cohen's reply that postmodern texts, however generically "blurred," never pass beyond genre altogether; even Derrida's attack on genre "falls within the genres of satire, parody and literary theory" (250).

4. Here I am building on the work begun by Abel, Hirsch, and Langland in their valuable anthology, *The Voyage In: Fictions of Female Development*, published in 1983. While my assumptions are less psychoanalytic (more socioeconomic) than theirs, and while I reinterpret their view of the genre as "the evolution of a coherent self" (13), my project is much indebted to their paradigm-smashing introduction and collection of essays.

5. G. B. Tennyson, for example, regards Dilthey as originary and translates the key passage (from his essay on Hölderlin) as follows: "[The *Bildungsroman*] examines a regular course of development in the life of the individual; each of its stages has its own value and each is at the same time the basis of a higher stage. The dissonances and conflicts of life appear as the necessary transit points of the individual on his way to maturity and

harmony" (136). François Jost mentions Morgenstern (first identified by Fritz Martini in 1961), and Randolph Shaffner points to Blanckenburg as well as Morgenstern, but both concur that the genre begins to be theorized in relation to Dilthey's later formulation (Jost, 101–102; Shaffner, 3). Martin Swales also opens his study of the German *Bildungsroman* with the passage from Dilthey just cited; by contrast, however, he credits nineteenth-century German novelists themselves with some theoretical awareness of the genre, putting particular emphasis on Morgenstern's coinage and on Blanckenburg's still earlier analysis of the *Bildungsroman* without naming it as such (12–14). My thanks to Rob Leventhal for clarifying Blanckenburg's role in this history.

6. I am indebted to Tennyson for the information concerning literary handbooks (135). Other discussions of the English *Bildungsroman* include those by Hans Wagner (1951), François Jost (1969), and Randolph Shaffner (1984). (The last two are comparative analyses.) Mikhail Bakhtin's influential work on the *Bildungsroman* focuses on Goethe but refers further to Fielding and Dickens as well as to French and Russian writers. Marianne Hirsch's 1979 essay on "The Novel of Formation as Genre" likewise contrasts German, English, and French manifestations of the genre, as does Franco Moretti's recent book-length study (1987). There have also been feminist revisions, with gender replacing nationality as controlling category, most of which have focused on twentieth-century texts: in addition to those essays collected in *The Voyage In* (1983), see Patricia Meyer Spacks's "The Adolescent as Heroine" (*The Female Imagination*, 1975); Annis Pratt and Barbara White's "The Novel of Development" (1981); Bonnie Hoover Braendlin's "Bildung in Ethnic Women Writers (1983); Joanne Frye's *Living Stories, Telling Lives* (1985); Esther Kleinbord Labovitz's *The Myth of the Heroine* (1987); and Rita Felski's "The Novel of Self-Discovery" (1989). For a comprehensive listing see Laura Sue Fuderer's *The Female Bildungsroman in English: An Annotated Bibliography of Criticism* (1990). See chapter 5 for more on Moretti and *The Voyage In*.

7. Howe's stated position is that, while the form did not originate with Goethe or even in Germany, "with Goethe this idea of *Bildung* took an especially comprehensive sweep" (24), and he is clearly her book's major point of reference and departure. Additional works mentioned by Howe and others as germinal to the tradition—though none so pervasively or exclusively as *Wilhelm Meister*—include Wolfram von Eschenbach's *Parzival* (1200), C. M. Wieland's *Agathon* (1766–67), Karl Philipp Moritz's *Anton Reiser* (1785–90), John Bunyan's *Pilgrim's Progress* (1678), Henry Fielding's *Tom Jones* (1749), and Rousseau's *Emile* (1762)—and these are only among the most frequently named.

Emile (though often regarded as an *Erziehungsroman*, or "novel of education" in the narrow sense) is defended by Jost as "le véritable précurseur français du *Bildungsroman*" (108), and its comparison of male and female educations makes it a telling intertext for the present study. As his title illustrates, Rousseau raises the issue of Sophie's education only to suppress it in favor of the eponymous hero's. Sophie's development is not even considered until the end of Rousseau's text when Emile is old enough to choose a mate, so that she appears, like Eve, solely in the capacity of companion to man. It was this, above all, that infuriated Mary Wollstonecraft: Rousseau's assertion (as cited in *A Vin-*

dication) that "the education of the women should be always relative to the men. To please, to be useful to us, to make us love and esteem them, to educate us when young, and take care of us when grown up, to advise, to console us, to render our lives easy and agreeable: these are the duties of women at all times, and what they should be taught in their infancy" (79). Thus *Emile* seems actually to make explicit the acute male-centeredness of a tradition that headlines Emile, Tom, and Wilhelm and habitually positions female development "relative" to theirs. As I elaborate later on in this chapter, my project could be described as an attempt to shift attention away from Emile—redirecting it not to Sophie but to the debates over female formation staged by women's texts. *A Vindication* is exemplary in this respect less for its interest in girls' education than for Wollstonecraft's heated *dialogue* with Rousseau. Many thanks to Paul Cantor for insisting on the relevance of *Emile*.

8. But see Georg Lukács, who would dispute its implicit conservatism. In *Goethe and His Age*, Lukács identifies *Wilhelm Meister*'s rejection of the bourgeois, appeal to the noble, and emphasis on developing the whole man as "a criticism of the capitalist division of labour" (52–53). Lukács recuperates Goethe's novel partly, I think, by conjoining the achievement of one man's "harmonious personality" to "harmonious co-operation between free men" (62); as in *The Theory of the Novel*, he reads *Wilhelm Meister* as a fantasy of communal rather than individual development (see chapter 5, note 6). He makes an analogous move in the 1947 "Preface" to *Goethe and his Age*, which debunks the myth of Goethe's irrationalism in order to salvage a humanist tradition for postwar Germany. Enlisting Goethe in his own rewriting of German national formation, Lukács once again assimilates *Wilhelm Meister*'s narrative of individual formation to a larger, collective one. Though I very much appreciate these hopeful views, my concern here is with the majority of uses to which the *Wilhelm Meister* story has been put, especially by critics of the English novel. Usually it has been culled for a depiction of personal development that, while said to be representative of an age, nevertheless stresses the unique and private individual.

9. I find Bakhtin provocative on this point. Defining the *Bildungsroman* as the novel of human emergence or becoming, he turns to Goethe for his superlative "visualizing of historical time" (26). In Goethe's eyes, says Bakhtin, even seemingly inanimate objects appear to be emerging, pulsating into the future, their position in space imbued with *time* (25–50). But what interests me here is that Bakhtin illustrates Goethe's innovative seeing-of-time-in-space with references primarily to his autobiographical *travel* writings. This makes me think that Goethe's sense of temporal dynamism arises in part from his own spatial dynamism: from his journeying to Italy where the past is so graphically strewn across space and, even more, from the suggestive momentum of travel itself. The temporalizing of space that Bahktin sees as characteristic of the *Bildungsroman* is, I would argue, inextricable in Goethe from its inverse, from the spatializing of time, the delightful laying out of moments along an itinerary of places—that is, from travel.

10. Mary Poovey, in her reading of *David Copperfield*, offers a compelling example of the way sequenced women map male development. In this case, David's passage to

manhood via Clara-Emily-Dora-Agnes involves the splitting off of Clara's sexual willfulness, lower-classness, and domestic incompetence, and the reembodiment of these by Emily and Dora, leaving behind the purified, middle-class domestic ideal that is finally represented by Agnes. As Poovey's discussion makes clear, Dickens's developing figure is typically the bourgeois male; what is more, the effect of Clara's multiple reincarnations is to situate the "good" woman firmly in the domestic sphere while punishing the woman with wandering desires (*Uneven Developments*, 89–125). This essay, although not about the *Bildungsroman* per se, also supports my previous remarks concerning this genre's role in producing the enterprising individual. Poovey implicates *David Copperfield*'s developmental fiction in "the textual construction of an individualist psychology," explaining that "this process was part of the legitimation and depoliticization of capitalist market and class relations" (89).

11. The introduction to *The Voyage In* makes similar points about the heroine's gendered relation to sexuality as well as to schooling and travel (7–8).

12. Marianne Hirsch takes the "Beautiful Soul" as a starting point for her 1983 reconception of the *Bildungsroman* along female lines. While acknowledging the failure of this story in worldly terms—it always, she explains, ends in death—Hirsch calls on such theorists as Nancy Chodorow in order to redeem its circular narrative of spiritual development and return to a kind of pre-oedipal symbiosis and fluidity. See chapter 5 for a closer look at Hirsch's strategy in relation to *The Mill on the Floss*.

13. Buckley, too, is more fully glossed in chapter 5.

14. David Miles contends that the texts and their heroes shift over time: from the relatively picaresque Wilhelm to Rainer Maria Rilke's more inward and confessional Malte, who also "merges with the figure of the artist" (989). Miles's emphasis on the latter supports my point that generic definitions have focused on the psychologized, often autobiographical character. I might note that Miles's reading of *Wilhelm Meister* downplays Wilhelm himself in favor of the more self-conscious narrator and, anticipating Hirsch, identifies not Wilhelm but the Beautiful Soul as Malte's precursor. Miles is discussed more fully in chapter 5.

15. I follow Poovey's *The Proper Lady and the Woman Writer*, which also links conduct books and novels as sites of ideological production about female "propriety," in stressing the unevenness of this production. Speaking of Mary Wollstonecraft, Mary Shelley, and Jane Austen, Poovey explains: "Implicitly, in both their works and their life choices, they also replicate the *tensions*, *paradoxes*, and *contradictions* that we see in the conduct material" (xiii; my emphasis). Three other studies come to mind in this regard, each of them placing early novels in relation to conduct literature and finding across genres a contradictory view of young women. *The Adolescent Idea* by Patricia Spacks attributes to eighteenth-century novelists and moralists alike a conflicted attitude toward youth and particularly adolescent girls, whom they perceive as "endangered but also as dangerous" (145). Ruth Yeazell's *Fictions of Modesty* describes the "modest woman" of novels and advice literature as a complex creature, modest by "instinct" yet needing to be schooled in modesty (5). Finally, Alison Sulloway's *Jane Austen and the Province of Womanhood* interprets this writer in the context of battles waged by

essays and conduct books as well as novels, disputing the boundaries of the feminine. Sulloway is one of the few critics who differentiates, as I will, between male and female conduct-book writers. But while Sulloway considers only what she calls "moderate feminist" or "radical feminist" writers (e.g., Mary Wollstonecraft, Clara Reeve, Elizabeth Hamilton), my own discussion includes such hardly feminist writers as Mrs. Chapone. By looking at some rather more obscure and inconclusive skirmishes over the province of womanhood, I suggest that conflicting ideologies about female formation play across the pages of even seemingly conservative women's texts.

16. Although the effect of Armstrong's argument is to treat class formation as the "real" story underlying what is merely a rhetoric or semiosis of gender, when she does consider the plight of middle-class women as *women*, she believes they are actually empowered by "domestication"—indeed, perniciously so (26). The problem as I see it is Armstrong's equation of the "feminine," its idealization as a category, with the women for whose lives this category had highly ambiguous implications. While I would stress the incoherence of the "feminine" in a way that allows it to be variously and sometimes subversively narrated, I do so within a feminist framework that assumes the *relative* disempowerment of women of all classes.

17. These two areas clearly correspond to the "erotic" and "ambitious" wishes that Nancy K. Miller (revising Freud) has identified as constitutive of women's fiction ("Emphasis"). I will be exploring not only the conflict between these two wishes and the plots they generate, but also the competing narratives operating within each term.

18. See Kristina Straub, whose fine work on Frances Burney first directed me to conduct materials for their critique of the romantic plot (9–11; 33–35; 63–65). While Straub and I both argue the "dividedness" of Burney's work in its representations of female formation, we differ somewhat on its relation to contemporaneous nonfiction for women. Whereas Straub seems to follow Pierre Macherey in privileging the literary work for its exposure of ideological contradictions (24–25), I see Burney's novels as largely continuous with courtesy texts, which are themselves divided in suggestive ways. Sulloway, too, mentions the antiromantic view of marriage circulated by women's conduct materials; she also addresses the wisdom of these texts on the issue of female friendship (69–77), an issue I explore shortly.

19. Austen's allusions to slavery serve a similar function: in *Emma*, Jane Fairfax describes those "places in town" where governesses inquire after work as "offices for the sale—not quite of human flesh—but of human intellect" (300), and in *Mansfield Park*, Sir Thomas Bertram's plantations in Antigua are a recurrent theme. As in Ellis, the comparison of governesses to slaves and the coincidence of slaveholder and English patriarch in Sir Bertram registers a subtle protest on behalf of white, middle-class English women. See Margaret Kirkham who expands upon this in her discussion of *Mansfield Park* (116–120). See also Karen Sanchez-Eppler for a more critical view of the similar intersection between feminist and abolitionist rhetoric in mid-nineteenth-century America. (For further discussion of slavery as a feminist metaphor, see chapter 4, note 8.)

Ellis's mariner image also has a literary correlate, in this case a later one: in chapter

81 of Eliot's *Middlemarch*, as Dorothea and Rosamond come together in an embrace that Gilbert and Gubar describe as the climax of the novel (518), we are told that "for a minute the two women clasped each other as if they had been in a shipwreck." This moment of female solidarity based on shared sorrow and eschewed rivalry is just what Ellis had in mind.

20. By way of contrast, neither the Reverend Fordyce (whose *Sermons to Young Women* went into fourteen editions in the years 1765–1814) nor Doctor Gregory (whose *A Father's Legacy* first appeared in 1774 and was reprinted constantly for the next fifty years, often in company with Chapone and occasionally with Pennington) have much to say about devoted affection between women. Fordyce calls for women to help protect each other from designing men (22), while Gregory says that compassion for other women, especially those ruined by men, is a quality men admire (27). There is no sense that women might choose each other in enduring friendship for reasons having little to do with male designs or approval, much less that an "electric chain of feeling" might unite them in more than an occasional way against male domination.

These two preeminent male courtesy writers do, on the other hand, help to articulate what I have called the antiromantic narrative of female development. Fordyce observes that unhappily married women are "commonly left to pine away in solitary misery. For them [as opposed to unhappy husbands] scarce any allowance is made; to them little or no pity is shown" (25). Gregory tells women, "Your whole life is often a life of suffering: you cannot plunge into business, or devote yourself to pleasure and excess, as men too often do when under the pressure of misfortunes; you must bear your sorrows in silence, unknown and unpitied" (17). Like Chapone, Gregory offers the consolation of religion, but in neither Gregory nor Fordyce do I find Chapone's heartaching lament for and implicit critique of the way girls' lives are apt to play out. Gregory, addressing his daughters, is worried about their marriages (he will increase their independence by leaving them money), but his concern for their happiness is everywhere compromised by his concern, as he puts it, to "render [them] most amiable and worthy of esteem in the eyes of my own sex" (15). So the male antiromance may be distinguished from the female mostly by tone: notwithstanding some guilt at double standards, male writers seem much less ambivalent about this story and are, indeed, apt to be invested in it. Not only do they express little sympathy for female misery, but their remarks about women's *unpitied* sorrow seem rather smug—sentimentalizing if not actually punitive. Sulloway comments similarly on the difference between male and female attitudes regarding spinsters: while both agree that spinsters suffer, male courtesy writers usually blame the women themselves, whereas female writers blame the circumstances that keep many women from marrying (23).

21. I use *homosocial* as a term that is broader than and inclusive of *homosexual*. As Sedgwick notes: "The adjective 'homosocial' as applied to women's bonds (by, for example, historian Carroll Smith-Rosenberg) . . . need not be pointedly dichotomized as against 'homosexual'; it can intelligibly denominate the entire continuum" (3). And if Sedgwick contends that today lesbianism may be seen as continuous with "the bond of

mother and daughter, for instance, the bond of sister and sister, women's friendship, 'networking,' and the active struggles of feminism" (2), Smith-Rosenberg has shown how much more coextensive female passion and friendship were in the nineteenth century.

22. In its introductory treatment of academic subjects and in its conversational form, Murry's guide clearly draws on another eighteenth-century genre: the educational dialogue. Her survey of the sciences seems, more specifically, to have anticipated what Ann Shteir describes as a boom in popular writing on science by and for women during the years 1790 to 1840. According to Shteir, these texts were usually dialogues set in the home, often involving "a powerful mother-figure (an actual mother, a governess, an aunt) who teaches children and exemplifies female knowledge and intellectual authority for adult readers" (312). Maria Jacson's *Botanical Dialogues: Between Hortensia and her Four Children* (1797), for example, resembles *Mentoria* in both its domestic setting and its maternal instructor. Shteir's discussion of this text points, moreover, to its occasional ambivalence about female intellectual development (314–15)—ambivalence that, as I elaborate later, was characteristic of women's conduct books and novels as well. Shteir herself notes that these three female-authored genres overlapped significantly (311), supporting my sense that (along with, say, Catherine Macaulay's 1790 polemic in favor of female education) "botanical dialogues" such as those by Maria Jacson joined conduct materials in providing women novelists of the late eighteenth and early nineteenth centuries with a usable set of narratives about the cultivation of girls' minds; of course, the relation among these materials is finally reciprocal. Thanks here to Michael Prince for suggesting I look at Shteir on botanical dialogues.

23. In a powerful reading of *Villette*, too often overshadowed by her more famous critique of Henry Miller and company, Millett says of the Bretton household: "Missy is the worshipful sister, Lucy the envious one. Together they represent the situation of the girl in the family. Bretton is both the spoiled son Graham, and the successful doctor John, and in both roles Lucy envies, loves and hates him" (140). And later: Lucy "envies every man his occupation, John his medicine, Paul his scholarship, just as she envied them their education" (144–45).

24. As the nineteenth century progressed, the figure of the doctor seems to have been invoked with increasing frequency in implicit relation to issues of professionalization. Given the parallel emergence in the early 1800s of doctors and writers as professionals—and the more complete consolidation of the status of doctors—it makes sense to me that Victorian writers, male as well as female, would articulate their own professional identities both through and against "the medical function." See, for example, Lawrence Rothfield's allusion to the professional congruence and competition between doctors and writers in *Madame Bovary*, there embedded in the oedipal drama between Flaubert and his surgeon-father (79). My own interest, of course, is in women's more specifically difficult relation to professional ambition, for while authorship in the mid-nineteenth century may have been "feminized" (imagined, like domestic labor, as unalienated and apart from the marketplace), it remained as much off-limits for actual

women as available to them (Poovey, *Uneven Developments*, 125). I am therefore very much taken by Naomi Schor's reading of *Madame Bovary*, in which she sees, underlying Emma's desire for a lover, the even more illicit desire "to be a famous novelist" (17).

2. Getting Waylaid in *Evelina*

1. In 1815, for example, J. W. Croker compared *The Wanderer* (1814) unfavorably to *Evelina*; the new book, he complained, had none of *Evelina*'s youthful innocence and charm. (Croker's review is cited by Claudia Johnson [xv].) Lillian and Edward Bloom have tried more recently to explain the "literary non-existence" of Burney's later works, which they attribute to a falling away from the consoling "fairy tale" mode of *Evelina* (1778) and *Cecilia* (1782).

2. Margaret Anne Doody, in her important 1988 biography of Burney, points out that her subject has been depreciated in part because she has been generically misconstrued. "Burney is further away from an imaginary realistic meridian than Jane Austen," Doody argues. Particularly in *The Wanderer*, Burney draws "upon the feminist and Gothic traditions" (3), and Doody goes on to suggest that the novels are further influenced by eighteenth-century stage farce (*Frances*, 49–51). I too will be arguing, though in somewhat different terms, that Burney makes better sense when one appreciates her apparent generic discontinuity. I also follow Doody in rejecting the diminutive first name "Fanny" and, revising a century-old tradition, restoring to Burney the full name that she herself used throughout the *Memoirs of Doctor Burney* (*Frances*, 6). Doody is among several recent critics whose feminist rereadings of *Evelina* and recuperations of Burney's later, disparaged novels and unpublished plays have radically transformed this writer. See especially Kristina Straub's *Divided Fictions: Fanny Burney and Feminine Strategy* (1987) and Julia Epstein's *The Iron Pen: Frances Burney and the Politics of Women's Writing* (1989).

3. James B. Vopat claims, for example, that "Evelina's marriage to Lord Orville . . . celebrates the fulfillment of her 'education'" (51). Lillian and Edward Bloom likewise argue that "Evelina moves . . . from trial to trial until she proves herself worthy of an eligible lord" (224). In a more theoretical formulation of Evelina's development, mapped in terms of pronominal reference, Catherine Parke also assumes that Evelina's education by Orville (taking her from a presocial "I" to a "third person" inserted into history and society) is unproblematically positive (166–69).

4. *Evelina* (1778) precedes *Wilhelm Meister* (1795) by seventeen years, and *Bildung* per se, as noted in chapter 1, would not emerge fully as a concept until the twentieth century. Nevertheless, *Wilhelm Meister* was clearly indicative as well as constitutive of a generally optimistic graphing of middle-class male development during the late eighteenth century. As Kristina Straub explains: "Middle-class young men [of Burney's era] are encouraged to look forward to their futures, to conceive of the shape of their lives on the model of progress" (4; see also 36–38). In keeping with Straub, I am arguing both that female development at this time was conceived along different, less triumphant lines and that the "male" model was, however, partially available to women, if only as the romantic myth of courtship as educational process. Where I differ from Straub is in

suggesting that conduct and other popular materials for women offered a complex range of female developmental narratives, not all of them simply dysphoric. (See chapter 1, note 18.)

5. Eve Sedgwick likewise describes as characteristically gothic the structure of "X within an X," one instance of which is "a prison from which there is escape into another prison" (*Coherence*, 34). My reference to the "gothic" shares with hers this emphasis on its *structures*, so that the paradigm of containment is more important than the symbolic resonance of any particular container—whether dungeon, monastery, or nobleman's carriage. Sedgwick further derives from the gothic a vividly *social* notion of identity: something not internal and inherent but inscribed (literally, in many gothic novels) onto a person's external surfaces (154–58). This tilts in a gothic direction my own view that women represent female formation as a manipulation of girls from the outside. The heroines I consider, rather than make their mark on the world, are more apt to be defaced by it. Finally, Sedgwick's discussion of repetition and doubling in the gothic is clearly relevant to the antiromantic narrative I trace out in *Evelina*.

Nina Auerbach has also explored the pattern of "double imprisonment." In Wollstonecraft's *The Wrongs of Woman: or, Maria* (1798), for example, the heroine is incarcerated by her husband in a madhouse; she flees, only to be trapped by another disastrous romance when her "rescuer" proves a villain. Auerbach sees this pattern persisting, as I do, in Jane Austen—"many of whose men can equally be perceived as redeemers/jailers, and whose gestures toward escape lead only to the ironic ubiquity of a double prison" ("Jane Austen," 18). Generally speaking, I share with Auerbach an interest in the darker, perverse side of realist fiction by nineteenth-century women, from the claustrophobia in Jane Austen to the gothic terror in George Eliot.

6. In her preface, Burney makes a point of distinguishing *Evelina*'s setting from those "fantastic regions of Romance, where Fiction is coloured by all the gay tints of luxurious Imagination, where Reason is an outcast, and where the sublimity of the *Marvellous* rejects all aid from sober Probability." Here I differ somewhat from Doody, who emphasizes Burney's distance from "realism," especially in the later novels. Except for *Jane Eyre* with its evident share of gothic claptrap, all of the novels I discuss eschew sensational settings and events while locating a gothic extremity of female distress in the ordinary everyday of women's lives. In doing so they may complicate not only what is meant by "novel of development," but also, implicitly, what is meant by "realism." Subsequent chapters will have more to say about the transaction between gothicism and realism.

7. For a suggestive reading of the opera in Burney as a fraught symbolic space—site of anxieties about the body, class status, and authorial voice—see Beth Kowaleski-Wallace's "A Night at the Opera," which juxtaposes *Evelina* with the *Early Diaries*.

8. Richardson's Pamela neatly inverts this paradox: if Evelina almost loses her status as virgin by being so obviously much one, Pamela protects that status by being, in terms of her sexual awareness, hardly one at all. The result is that, while Evelina's innocence is constantly threatened, Pamela's is constantly suspected. As Terry Eagleton explains in regard to Pamela, "The woman's very need to look sharp for sexual predators

entails an obsession with virginity at once necessary and compromising" (*Rape*, 33–34). Both Pamela and Evelina deconstruct their culture's fixation with female "innocence" by illustrating its impossibility. See also Ruth Yeazell on *Evelina*'s contradictory "fictions of modesty" (122–42).

9. *Evelina* is actually derived from an earlier manuscript entitled "Caroline Evelyn," so that the story of Evelina is generated by the mother story both inside and outside the novel. The burning of "Caroline Evelyn" in a fit of guilt and remorse (on Frances Burney's fifteenth birthday, June 13, 1767) is one of the more sensational moments in a career vexed by ambivalence toward female authorship. The reincarnation of this older, completed text as *Evelina*'s prehistory accounts for its unusual fullness. It has the effect, in keeping with my argument, of marking Evelina's entire life as *repetition*, her story but a doubling of her mother's. Thus the recurrence of constraint that organizes Evelina's single life also operates across women's lives, from one generation to the next.

10. Kowaleski-Wallace, for example, reads *Evelina* as an attempt to throw off the "phallic mother." She perceives both Madame Duval and the bluestocking, Mrs. Selwyn, as negative figures for whom the daughter has nothing but contempt ("*Evelina*"). And Margaret Doody, though she regards Mrs. Selwyn in a positive light, associates Madame Duval with a maternal legacy of helplessness: "The discovery of the mother, of the inevitable female descent and fate, is very bad news. . . . Surrounded by mothers (Madame Duval and the encircling Mrs. Mirvan), Evelina undergoes her most truly terrible experience" (*Frances*, 51). But as I will explain, I think mothers in *Evelina* (and especially Madame Duval) represent, at least potentially, emancipation as well as repetition.

11. If this is the original wrong the narrative strives (and, I believe, fails) to repair, then its underlying agenda may be not the misleading and redundant search for the father but the search (more integrally tied to female identity) for the mother. Perhaps Evelina does not advance in part because she misconstrues her quest. Mary Poovey is one of the few critics who shares my sense of *Evelina*'s desire for mother-daughter solidarity; indeed, while I see this desire as barely expressed and never satisfied, Poovey argues that Evelina is in fact the efficient agent of her mother's revenge ("Fathers," 46–47). Chapter 4 will elaborate on this narrative of the female homosocial—beginning with the voicing of female identity in relation to the mother—in its consideration of *Jane Eyre*.

12. In *A Vindication of the Rights of Woman*, Wollstonecraft demands: "If then women are not a swarm of ephemeron triflers, why should they be kept in ignorance under the specious name of innocence?" (19)

13. See Irene Fizer on the implicit threat of incest posed to Evelina by Sir John Belmont, the "lawless" paternal libertine. Although Fizer acknowledges the creepy, erotic undertones of Villars's possessiveness, she argues that the aging clergyman is actually "emasculated" and "poses no sexual threat" (100–3). I am insisting, by contrast, on the continuity among the many paternal figures in *Evelina*, all of whom may be seen to menace the heroine's apprenticeship in one way or another.

14. Speaking of names, it is worth noting that "Evelina," followed by an erased

patronym, is a transposition of the maternal *nom de famille* (Caroline "Evelyn") into a *nom de fille*. (See Doody on the anagrammatic implications of "Evelina," including "Eve" and "Elle" [*Frances*, 40–41].) This reminds me of the writer who, born Gabrielle Sidonie Colette and having accumulated the names of more than one husband, finally returns simply to "Colette," appropriating the patronym as a single, sufficient female name. In Evelina's case, however, this development is reversed: beginning with a single, free-floating female name, "Evelina" gradually acquires a ball and chain of patronyms.

15. Thus Burney participates in what Eagleton describes as a general critique of aristocratic culture by the eighteenth-century middle class: "pitting the values of thrift, peace and chastity against a violent and profligate nobility" (*Rape*, 6). In Burney's hands, as in Richardson's, the eighteenth-century novel helped to formulate this critique.

16. Straub agrees that the race sequence "underscores the powerlessness of women and the insensitivity of Burney's culture to female pain by giving both a rough, physical presence in the novel" (44). Straub sees Orville, however, as less culpable than enigmatically removed: his withdrawal "leaves a gap, an empty moral space that may be the possibility of sympathy with Evelina's feelings—or merely silent dissociation from her" (51).

17. In this Lovel foreshadows the protagonist of Burney's unpublished comedy, *The Woman Hater* (1799), another satirized misogynist whose attitude stems from his rejection by a woman. This play, a rewriting of *The Witlings* (1779), makes clear what *The Witlings* left uncertain: that the object of Burney's satire was less the bluestockings than the men who hate them. *The Witlings* was also unpublished; both manuscripts are in the New York Public Library's Berg Collection.

18. Judith Lowder Newton discusses at length the connection between men's money and their power over women in *Evelina*. She contends, however, that Burney admits this connection only in regard to the trading classes (30–33)—for example, Branghton Junior's attempt to control Evelina by spending money on her: "If I pay, I think I've a right to have it my own way" (172). Newton feels that Burney preserves a "courtly fiction" about the operation of money among the gentry, and her overriding conclusion is that Orville's "consistent courtliness . . . tends to justify ruling-class male control" (44). I am arguing, on the other hand, that Burney's novel both represents *and* interrogates courtly fictions; the consistency of Orville's courtliness, as I have shown, is open to debate.

19. Marivaux wrote a preface to the original *Evelina*, and a comparison between *Evelina* and *La Vie de Marianne* (1731) is suggestive. Both feature heroines who arrive in the city unknown and unprotected, their "innate virtue" bespeaking what turns out to be their noble rank. Both are aggressed by the men who offer to protect them. But while Orville's inconsistency is only hinted at, Marianne's lover Valville actually betrays her, and while Evelina accumulates fathers but never a mother, Marianne finds, instead of a man, a loyal maternal figure. As Nancy K. Miller sums up the outcome of *La Vie de Marianne*: "Supported by a mother, whose sole function is to approve of her,

without a constraining father or husband, possessed of an independent income, Marianne has the power to operate alone" (*Heroine*, 35). Marivaux seems actually to play out what in Burney remains at the level of intimation. Supporting the hypothesis that male writers more easily imagine empowered female characters than do women writers themselves, Marivaux's novel ends, Miller explains, unfinished and open to possibility, a "point of departure" (35). I will be suggesting that Burney's conclusion, by contrast, is marked by a sense of depressing finality.

20. Doody agrees with me that "a woman has to leave the paternal protection, the tender burial of a Berry (or Bury) Hill. Without stepping out into life and the world there is no identity" (*Frances*, 65). But while I have been describing a narrative of continual reburial—and after all, the book's last sentence asserts: "The chaise now waits which is to conduct me to dear Berry Hill" (388)—Doody sees *Evelina*, nevertheless, as a successful stepping out (45–46; 64–65). Notwithstanding her insistence on Evelina's achieved maturity, Doody does quote Lord Merton—"I don't know what the devil a woman lives for after thirty"—and notes that "this is an extremely ironic remark within a *Bildungsroman*, for it indicates that the *Bildung* is completely unnecessary" (55). My study could be seen in one sense as a compendium of this and other such ironic remarks about the *Bildungsroman* on the part of women writers, culminating with Eliot's sustained critique of the genre associated with *Wilhelm Meister*.

21. Thanks are due to Susan Winnett, who made this point in a conversation we had early on in this project.

22. "A child to appear against the father!" (116) Villars exclaims in response to the prospect of a suit against Sir John. Taking the nobleman's side against the women he has wronged, here Villars is once again identified with the immoral father. I am arguing, of course, that *Evelina* puts Villars as well as Belmont on trial for paternal crimes, offering its heroine's double-voiced letters as testimony for both sides, at once defending and accusing the male guardian.

3. The Humiliation of Elizabeth Bennet

1. Claudia Johnson derives the picture of Austen as a political innocent from R. W. Chapman, who credited the writer with little self-consciousness about either her work or world; Johnson names Lord David Cecil and even Marilyn Butler as other critics who essentially read off a conservative politics from Austen's class position, assuming her passivity in relation to dominant cultural views. As Johnson notes, and as I elaborate shortly, "subversive" critic John Halperin likewise casually deduces Austen's irony from her sorry status as an unmarried woman, as if Austen were unable to achieve and inhabit this status against the grain of received beliefs (xvi–xix). See Johnson, too, for her argument that the family was invoked not only allegorically, but as a matter of concern in its own right during the debates about patriarchal authority that followed the French Revolution (1–11); it is perhaps the similar centrality of "family issues" in political debates today that makes us turn so naturally to Austen in seeking our own relation to these issues. In addition to Johnson's invaluable *Jane Austen: Women, Politics, and the Novel* (1988), other recent feminist volumes on Austen include Margaret Kirkham's *Jane Aus-*

ten, *Feminism, and Fiction* (1983), Janet Todd's collection, *Jane Austen: New Perspectives* (1983), Mary Poovey's *The Proper Lady and the Woman Writer: Ideology and Style in the Works of Mary Wollstonecraft, Mary Shelley, and Jane Austen* (1985), Mary Evans's *Jane Austen and the State* (1987), and Alison Sulloway's *Jane Austen and the Province of Womanhood* (1989).

2. It could be said in Halperin's defense that he cites only book-length monographs on Austen and that the feminist analyses I mention are essays or chapters in books that treat Austen under some broader rubric—in the context, for example, of a female literary tradition. Yet the preference for monographs is itself ideologically (and methodologically) suspect, of a piece with Halperin's reluctance to situate Austen's satirical views within a larger, oppositional discourse, thereby reducing them to a merely private bitterness.

3. The exception is Nina Auerbach who—at least in her 1978 *Communities of Women*—does, I agree with Brown, disparage *Pride and Prejudice* for its allegedly negative view of the mother and of female community. Yet Brown seems most upset by Auerbach's "lack of taste" in daring "to compare a novel by Jane Austen to one that puts anyone over the age of fourteen asleep": Louisa May Alcott's *Little Women*. This is an aesthetic point that, Brown eventually admits, relies upon questionable assumptions about intrinsic literary value ("Feminist," 304–5). More important, Brown neglects to mention that elsewhere and at great length Auerbach admires Austen for her "revolutionary" spirit; as early as 1972, she linked *Persuasion* to the redemptive mood of *The Tempest*, to the "passion and vision" of Shelley and Keats, and to the radical feminism of Wollstonecraft's *Vindication* ("O Brave New World: Evolution and Revolution in *Persuasion*"). Auerbach's feminist argument for Austen's "Romantic" preoccupation with confinement and escape is further elaborated in the 1981 essay, "Jane Austen and Romantic Imprisonment."

4. See Patricia Meyer Spacks's enlivening essay on female boredom in *Emma* and *Madame Bovary*. Spacks notes how potentially dangerous (and implicitly feminist) such boredom, as a spur to alleviating action, may be: "Emma [Woodhouse] seems sufficiently active, and sufficiently threatened, to do dreadful things" ("Women," 201). But whereas I see marriage as subtly discredited by being invoked as an antidote to boredom, Spacks emphasizes the extent to which Austen endorses marriage for its ability to keep Emma within bounds.

5. Sandra Gilbert and Susan Gubar point to Lloyd W. Brown's *Bits of Ivory: Narrative Techniques in Jane Austen's Fiction* for "the most sustained discussion of Austen's ironic undercutting of her own endings" (667). Karen Newman also sees the happy ending in Austen as parodic. Despite its comic effect, Newman argues there remain "unresolved contradictions between romantic and materialist notions of marriage" (695). My own reading accords a good deal with Newman's, though I am less confident than she that Austen's heroines manage nevertheless to "live powerfully within the limits imposed by ideology" (705). D. A. Miller, too, has made an attractive case for the irresolution of Austen's endings, which he derives from a conflict between Austen's "ideological" desire for closure and a built-in formal or "constructional" resistance to it, arising from

the very nature of narrative (54). As should be clear by now, I would describe this instead as a conflict between two ideological impulses, corresponding to two versions of how a girl's life unfolds.

6. I am indebted to Beth Kowaleski-Wallace's "Milton's Daughters: The Education of Eighteenth-Century Women Writers" for its illuminating discussion of the Lockean father's ambiguous relation to the literary daughter, and also for the reference to Fliegelman.

7. The relevant essays are "The Dissolution of the Oedipus Complex" (1924), "Some Psychical Consequences of the Anatomical Distinction between the Sexes" (1925), "Female Sexuality" (1931), and "Femininity" (1932). Nancy Chodorow offers a helpful recapitulation of Freud on fathers and daughters (94, 114–116); see also Sarah Kofman for a further glossing of the Oedipus and masculinity complexes (199–206).

8. In a letter to a favorite niece, Austen more explicitly and bitterly represents marriage as a loss for women, ushering in a period of inactivity: "Oh, what a loss it will be when you are married. You are too agreable in your single state, too agreable as a Neice [sic]. I shall hate you when your delicious play of Mind is settled down into conjugal and maternal affections" (*Letters*, 478–79).

9. According to Lynda E. Boose in "The Father and the Bride in Shakespeare," Lear's faux pas is his unwillingness to release Cordelia—he "casts her away not to let her go but to prevent her from going" (333)—thereby obstructing the ritual process of her marriage to France. The reference to Bataille is thanks to Boose.

10. In these terms, *Emma*'s matrilocal solution may have certain advantages for its heroine. It is true that Emma defers to Knightley's worldview much as Elizabeth does to Darcy's, but bringing Knightley home to live under Mr. Woodhouse's roof preserves some of the authority Emma has enjoyed both in the household and in the community at large by being her father's daughter.

11. Many thanks to Patsy Yaeger for pointing out the way my reading of Elizabeth comments on Sedgwick's paradigm.

12. Thus Austen's famous defense in *Northanger Abbey* of the novel as a "work in which the greatest powers of the mind are displayed . . . the most thorough knowledge of human nature . . . [as well as] the liveliest effusions of wit and humour" (38).

13. John Halperin is particularly complacent before this formulation: "It is unnecessary to rehearse again the process by which Darcy's pride is humbled and Elizabeth's prejudices exposed—'*your* defect is a propensity to hate every body,' she tells him early in the novel; 'And yours . . . is wilfully to misunderstand them,' he replies" (70). Alison Sulloway, by contrast, revises the cliché by historicizing the terms *pride* and *prejudice*, demonstrating their embeddedness in eighteenth-century feminist texts (66–69); in the polemical writings of Mary Astell, Catherine Macaulay, Mary Wollstonecraft, and Mary Hays, as in novels by Burney, Edgeworth, and Austen, these frequently used terms come to operate as "code words to describe men's pride in their dominion and their prejudice against the sex they dominated" (66).

14. My remarks throughout this section are indebted to the body of work on looking and power developed in the past fifteen years primarily by feminist film theorists.

Much of this work, following the lead of Laura Mulvey's "Visual Pleasure and Narrative Cinema" (1975), has emphasized the aggressive "maleness" of the gaze intrinsic to classical cinema's way of seeing. More recently, however, critics like Judith Mayne, Mary Ann Doane, Linda Williams, and Mulvey herself have raised questions about women as spectators—for example, as the audience addressed by the "woman's film" of the 1940s (Doane); as classical and avant-garde filmmakers (Mayne); and as female characters whose active looking and desiring is often violently punished (Williams). These last may have something in common with the investigative Elizabeth Bennet, well aware of her crime against propriety in gazing on Pemberley and an image of its master, without herself being seen. In the terms suggested by Williams's "When the Woman Looks," Elizabeth's humiliation may be the punitive fate of a woman who dares to look aggressively; I have been arguing, however, that Austen leads her readers to question the naturalness and rightness of this fate. The essays by Mayne, Doane, and Williams can be found in *Re-vision: Essays in Feminist Film Criticism* (1984); see also *Feminism and Film Theory* (1988), edited by Constance Penley.

15. I have in mind D. W. Harding and Marvin Mudrick, old guard of the subversive school. While I am indebted to this tradition, I disagree with Harding's and Mudrick's view that Austen challenges her society by having Elizabeth transcend it. Mudrick contends, for instance, that "the central fact for Elizabeth remains the power of choice" (124); to his liberal imagination, Elizabeth represents the "free individual" (126). In my opinion, *Pride and Prejudice* is about the heroine's inextricability from the social context, not her independence of it.

16. It is interesting that Hollywood—of venal habits and puritanical tastes— should recognize and be uneasy with the suspiciousness of Elizabeth's position as Austen wrote it. In the 1940 film version of *Pride and Prejudice* (directed by Robert Z. Leonard, with a screenplay by Aldous Huxley and Jane Murfin), Lady Catherine De Bourgh threatens to cut Darcy out of her will if he goes ahead and marries a Bennet. Elizabeth proves her romantic integrity by vowing to marry him anyway. Needless to say, Austen conspicuously chose *not* to test Elizabeth in such a manner. Agreeing that "Austen is at pains from early in the novel to show us Elizabeth's response to Darcy's wealth," Karen Newman adds that critics as early as Sir Walter Scott remarked on the heroine's fascination with Pemberley (698).

4. Jane Eyre's Fall from Grace

1. See also the alarmist review of April 1848 in the *Christian Remembrancer*, and the attack by Edwin Percy Whipple on the books of all three Brontës, which appeared in October 1848.

2. Discussions of Charlotte Brontë and her work in psychosexual terms range from Lucile Dooley's "Psychoanalysis of Charlotte Brontë, As a Type of the Woman of Genius" (1920) to Charles Burkhart's *Charlotte Brontë: A Psychosexual Study of Her Novels* (1973) to Linda Kauffman's "*Jane Eyre*: The Ties That Blind" (1986). In a related critical mode, there has also been much said about Brontë's use of archetypal materials, reworking of fairy tales, allusions to *King Lear* and *Paradise Lost*, etc. See, for example, the

section on *Jane Eyre* of Robert Bernard Martin's *The Accents of Persuasion: Charlotte Brontë's Novels* (1966); Paula Sullivan's "Fairy Tale Elements in *Jane Eyre*" (1978); and Karen E. Rowe's "'Fairy-born and human-bred': Jane Eyre's Education in Romance" (1983). What most of these share is an emphasis on internal, mythic rather than historical landscapes. Other critics resent what they see as Brontë's retreat into myth and consequent mystification of history. Jina Politi (1982) blames *Jane Eyre* for shifting from a realist mode, capable of social critique, into an evasive, "a-temporal fantasy mode" (64). Nancy Armstrong (1987) also accuses *Jane Eyre* (and domestic fiction in general) of turning "political information" into "psychological information" (204), reducing historical social relations to psychosexual fantasies. As I go on to elaborate, I disagree that Brontë's representation of female subjectivity precludes a political referent.

3. Alan Shelston, in his notes to Elizabeth Gaskell's *The Life of Charlotte Brontë*, explains her feelings thus: as a Tory, Brontë "would naturally tend to sympathize with the established order, particularly where the Irish were concerned." But Brontë supports the Italian and German rebellions because "these were predominantly nationalistic enterprises" involving "the removal of the Catholic hegemony of the Austrian Empire" (597). I want to argue that Brontë's "natural sympathies" were more complex than this—to identify, not only in her letters but also in *Jane Eyre*, a deeper ambivalence toward the "established order" than Shelston allows.

4. Thompson offers a historical account of the attack on Cartwright's mill and goes on to discuss *Shirley*'s relation to it. Praising Brontë's faithful characterization of the mill owner and conservative parson, Thompson identifies the novel as "a true expression of the middle-class myth" (561), limited by its unsympathetic view of the Luddites and their supporters. My own view of *Shirley*—as somewhat more conflicted in its class attitudes and feelings about revolution—is consistent with Raymond Williams's characterization of other industrial novels. In *Hard Times* and *Felix Holt*, for example, Williams finds at once a genuine sympathy with the plight of workers and a middle-class retreat from the specter of violent protest (87–109).

5. See Woolf, *A Room of One's Own* (1929); Linton Andrews, "Charlotte Brontë: The Woman and the Feminist" (1955); P. P. Sharma, "Charlotte Brontë: Champion of Woman's Economic Independence" (1965); Carol Ohmann, *Charlotte Brontë: The Limits of Her Feminism* (1972); Margaret Blom, "Charlotte Brontë, Feminist *Manquée*" (1973). Also notable are Adrienne Rich's fine piece of early feminist criticism, "Jane Eyre: The Temptations of a Motherless Woman" (1973) and Elaine Showalter's chapter in *A Literature of Their Own* (1977). Since Gilbert and Gubar there have been many other significant feminist readings of Charlotte Brontë; later footnotes indicate those with whom this chapter is particularly in dialogue.

6. See especially Jina Politi's "*Jane Eyre* Class-ified" (1982), Gayatri Spivak's "Three Women's Texts and a Critique of Imperialism" (1985), and Penny Boumelha's "'And What Do the Women Do?': Jane Eyre, Jamaica, and the Gentleman's House" (1988). Boumelha's excellent essay does close by stressing—in spite of what she sees as a highly conservative ending—the "range of narrative possibilities intimated in the course of

the text" (119). But Boumelha describes these as "explorations . . . of the kinds and limits of power available to a middle-class white woman" (119), demonstrating Jane's ability to choose among several possible options, almost as if she were the male hero of a *Bildungsroman* (119). My own reading, by contrast, will emphasize a narrative possibility whose defiance of gender norms is coextensive with its defiance of class norms and, for that matter, the generic norms of the *Bildungsroman*. Susan Meyer's "Colonialism and the Figurative Strategy of *Jane Eyre*" (1990) and Cora Kaplan's forthcoming article on *Jane Eyre* and British nationalism also address the conservative class and racial implications of Brontë's novel.

7. I want both to invoke and, in some sense, to distance myself from Peter Brooks's narratological notion of the "primal scene." His appropriation of this term to characterize narrative material whose semantic urgency is tied to its temporal priority, and whose repression proceeds from its illicitness, helps me to suggest the weight I would give to *Jane Eyre*'s first chapters. In fact, my reading of Brontë's novel is in many ways congruent with Brooks's of *Great Expectations* (113–42). Like Brooks, I privilege a child's early communion with a marginal figure (the convict/the servant); trace the binding of this "criminal" plot by a more decorous "official" one (apprenticeship/courtship); and point to the uncanny return of the prohibited material. I differ from Brooks, however, in my attention to female instead of male development, female rather than male "deviance." (See chapter 5, note 11 for more on the gender specificity of *Great Expectations*, in contrast to *The Mill on the Floss*.) In addition, if Brooks's "masterplot" is psychoanalytic, mine is essentially political and Marxist-feminist; if his repressive force is ultimately the local, internalized superego, mine is the material coercion of ideology as well as juridical, social, and economic relations.

8. Boumelha makes a strong case for Jamaican slavery as *Jane Eyre*'s repressed—the shameful, unspoken source of Uncle Eyre's and Rochester's wealth. The frequent references to slavery in relation to Jane's own position are, in this view, but displaced allusions to and evasions of this fact. Susan Meyer and Cora Kaplan see the racial discourse in *Jane Eyre* as somewhat more conflicted. Meyer argues that "what begins . . . as an implicit critique of British domination and an identification with the oppressed collapses into merely an appropriation of the metaphor of 'slavery'" (250). Kaplan, too, sees Brontë's references to slavery as sites of contradiction. Juxtaposing *Jane Eyre* with the racial theories of its time, she suggests that Jane's association with the "savage" both crosses and reasserts racial boundaries ("'White Skin'"). In my view this degree of complicity with imperialist attitudes needs to be seen alongside the slavery metaphor's empowering and explanatory value for nineteenth-century feminists. (See chapter 1, note 19.)

9. For more on Jane Eyre and mothers see Rich's essay on "the temptations of a motherless woman," in which Jane is enabled to resist conventional femininity by a series of powerful maternal figures, from Bessie to Diana and Mary Rivers. See also Marianne Hirsch (*Mother/Daughter*, 43–50), who cites Rich to the effect that the absence of her real mother is freeing for Jane (44). While this seems right to me, I would qualify Hirsch's further claim that mothers are altogether "silenced, denigrated, sim-

ply eliminated, or written out" of *Jane Eyre* and other Victorian novels by women (47). As Rich implies, the result of Jane's initial motherlessness may be less an elimination than proliferation of mothers; what interests me is the competing class interests and developmental schemes they represent.

10. Bruce Robbins, in his valuable book on "the servant's hand" in nineteenth-century novels, notes that eavesdropping or "indiscreet listening" is a common trope in representations of servants (66). This trope involves not only, as Bakhtin suggested, the usefulness of a servant's keyhole perspective to a literature of the private life, but also what Robbins describes as a middle-class anxiety about being overheard and spied upon by servants (108). Thus Jane's role as eavesdropper (and she does pry open family secrets at Thornfield even as she exposes moral failings at Gateshead) marks her, in one sense, as a member of the servant class. On the other hand, I am proposing that her eavesdropping *on servants* in the passages I have cited reverses the usual master-servant economy. Though servants may be spied on and listened to for purposes of surveillance and titillation, here the reversal has, I think, the more radical implication that what servants, and not masters, say may be a source of knowledge, community, and power. Robbins also helps to tie Jane's "fit" in the red-room with conventional depictions of impertinence on the part of servants. He lists "epileptic fits" and "terror" along with drunkenness and other altered states that allow servants to speak freely, "to comment against the grain instead of responding submissively" (65). While Jane's insubordination seems to cause her fit, rather than the other way around, the juxtaposition of these still, to my mind, points to Robbins's tradition of servant back talk.

11. In his extraordinary work on Victorian pornographic discourse, Marcus—citing a chilling description of a field hand who is raped by her employer's nephew—goes on to remark: "*This* is the kind of thing, one wants to say, that it was all about; *this* is the kind of thing that the Victorian novelists could not but be aware of—even though their explicit dealings with it were very circumspect—that their work as a whole was directed against" (138). I would add only that, if this is indeed what realist fiction is all about—and the notion is compelling—its view of class and gender is rarely, in my view, so oppositional as Marcus assumes; even George Eliot in *Adam Bede* has trouble recuperating the seduced dairy maid, Hetty Sorrel. But the final assertion has, perhaps, more validity if we specify *female* novelists, who as a group were generally (if sometimes tentatively) impatient with double sexual standards: one for men, another for women; one for proper ladies, another for working women.

12. See also in *Shirley*, in spite of its ambivalence toward the "operative class," Brontë's portrayal of the Farrens. Though poor, their decency is evinced not least by the fastidiousness of Mrs. Farren: "a raight cant body, and as clean—! ye might eat your porridge off th' house floor" (162). At the same time, the death of Jane's parents from typhus caught while visiting the urban poor, and also the decimation of Lowood's charity-student population by the same disease, seem to call upon the period's association of dirt and disease with massings of poor people, who are always potentially a "mob." See Cora Kaplan's "'Like a Housemaid's Fancies': The Representation of Working-Class Women in Nineteenth-Century Writing" for more on the nexus of gen-

der, class, sex, dirt, and danger in Brontë's time (65–75); here, as in "Pandora's Box," Kaplan explores the ambivalent attitudes of middle-class female writers toward working women.

13. As Shirley Keeldar might explain—flatly refusing her sixth proposal—"almost" in matters of matrimony is not good enough. Brontë herself died less than a year after marrying an almost worthy man.

14. The term *high feminist criticism* is Gayatri Spivak's, reproving the tendency to celebrate white female subjectivity at the expense of Third World subjects: "A basically isolationist admiration for the literature of the female subject in Europe and Anglo-America establishes the high feminist norm" (262). In her influential critique of *Jane Eyre*, Spivak sees Bertha as the "native female," whose death is the price of Jane's constitution as a female "individualist" in an age of imperialism (262–263). I am suggesting, however, that Jane's formation as individualist is interrogated by another suppressed but nonetheless dissenting developmental story; the text itself may share some of Spivak's qualms. Further, without disputing Spivak's characterization of Bertha as "native," I have chosen to focus on Grace Poole, the madwoman as working-class. As I will argue, Grace is both continuous with Bertha and, insofar as the Creole is aristocratic, opposed to her. Hardly a self-consistent signifier, the madwoman can, I think, sustain the weight of these plural meanings.

15. Here I would note that arson, as Robbins credits E. P. Thompson with remarking, was a crime typically associated with servants (191).

16. See Catherine Gallagher's incisive analysis of Mayhew's *London Labour and the London Poor* (1861), in which Mayhew develops the distinction between feeble-bodied, fixed industrial workers, on the one hand, and threateningly robust, itinerant workers, on the other. This seems as good a place as any to observe a related distinction between domestic servants—objects of increasingly nervous scrutiny as the nineteenth-century progressed—and the urban proletariat (Robbins 109–12). Both polarities attempt to preserve a category of the *controllable worker* (proletarian or servant) in opposition to a category evoking middle-class fears about striking, out-of-control workers (itinerant worker or proletarian), and together they illustrate in what contradictory ways the proletariat was represented. For my purposes, of course, the most salient subcategory of worker is the servant. While her presence in Victorian fiction may have involved, as Robbins suggests, displaced anxieties about those industrial workers outside the purview of the patriarchal family (and, usually, the novel) it also, I would add, involved particular anxieties about working *women*, the vast majority of whom were domestic workers; clearly the distinction between servant and proletarian is also a gendered one.

17. Brontë first represents the eroticized student-teacher relationship in her tormented letters to Monsieur Heger, the married professor she fell in love with while studying in Belgium (1842–43). (See Linda Kauffman on this epistolary discourse of desire later transposed, she suggests, into *Jane Eyre*.) The dyad reappears in *The Professor* (written in 1846, published in 1857), a kind of pre-text for *Villette* (1853) told, however, from the professor's masculine perspective. The relationship takes what is probably its mildest form in *Jane Eyre* and its fiercest in *Shirley*. There the classroom becomes

a charged erotic space in which class differences between a poor tutor and his aristocratic pupil are finally suspended as gender differences take over.

18. See Linda Kauffman for a longer and uniquely damning view of Rochester: "Like Lovelace," she argues, "he will employ every trick, every disguise, every artifice to win the game" (192). Denying Jane's judgment and dismissing her fears, "he prefers to make Jane doubt her own sanity, rather than reveal his duplicity" (191), Kauffman observes. She, too, likens Rochester to Rivers: "Their similarities, though less obvious than their differences, are no less important. Both exercise the same male prerogatives where speech and silence, reason and madness are concerned" (198).

19. It is disturbing, too, to be told that Jane has no time for anyone but Rochester, not even for Adèle—not even, by implication, for herself. As Karen Chase pointedly remarks, "When [Jane] tells us in these last pages that 'I know no weariness of my Edward's society,' that, 'We talk, I believe, all day long' (ch. 38), then we must wonder when she has time to write" (75).

20. See Robbins on "the servant in the ending" of both *Jane Eyre* and *Shirley*, a trope he associates with a vague utopianism, irresolute longings in the direction of a broader community (190–91; 128–29).

5. *The Mill on the Floss*, the Critics, and the *Bildungsroman*

1. Haight concludes that Eliot, while accepting Darwin's theory, refused to celebrate a process of selection based on biological criteria alone, to the exclusion of moral factors—thus Maggie's ultimate rejection of Stephen (xix). Yet Haight's interpretive schema remains an evolutionary one, invested in the procreative couple.

It is tempting, I might add, to see the accumulation of critical language around Stephen, the repeated assigning and analyzing of desire including Eliot's own, as an attempt to gain control over the specter of female sexuality raised by Maggie's elopement.

2. Hagan sums up Maggie's quandary as an impossible choice among men: "Had she gone on to love and marry Philip against her father's and Tom's wishes" or "had she run away and married Stephen" she would, in either case, have betrayed someone's trust (54). Hagan argues, I should note, that readers are meant to value Maggie's loyalty to her earliest ties and duties, not to Tom per se—in fact Hagan blames Tom for making family loyalty and erotic love mutually exclusive for Maggie. Underlining the concept of "division" between "the large-souled woman . . . and the narrow-souled father and brother" (62), he could be said to anticipate feminist discussions of "difference" in George Eliot.

3. The problem of Maggie's destiny might have been solved, Knoepflmacher points out, had she been either a man or, like her mother, a less gifted woman. But he undercuts the feminist implications of this perception by agreeing with Mr. Tulliver that Maggie's female intelligence was a genetic fluke; her frustration and eventual sacrifice are therefore the result less of character or social conditions than of "hereditary caprice" (213). For Knoepflmacher, this makes her story unsuccessful as "tragedy."

4. Spacks's appropriation of conventionally feminine values for feminist purposes is a strategy descended from Eliot's time to our own. It is especially characteristic of "cultural feminism," emergent in the 1970s and exemplified by such diverse figures as Adrienne Rich, Carol Gilligan, and Hélène Cixous.

5. In *Woman and the Demon* (1982), by contrast, Auerbach goes on to read through the Victorian myth of the feminized demon to a fantasy of empowered womanhood. But the 1975 essay lacks the historical analysis that distinguishes her later book, and in this it resembles still another strain of seventies work—so-called images of women criticism—of which Kate Millett's *Sexual Politics* (1970) is the most notable example. Calling attention in important ways to misogynist characterizations of women, particularly in writing by men, this approach tended initially to produce lists of "virgins" and "bitches" without considering how such categories function in a specific context.

6. This observation by Steinecke (*Romantheorie und Romankritik in Deutschland*, I, 27) is cited by Jeffrey L. Sammons in "The Mystery of the Missing *Bildungsroman*" (232–33). As I discuss later, Sammons offers a very suggestive metacommentary on the popularization of the *Bildungsroman* as a critical category in the early twentieth century. I take my lead from Sammons as well as Jameson in speculating about more recent uses of the term and their implied political agendas. Here I want also to note Georg Lukács's dissenting view, at least about *Wilhelm Meister* itself. In *The Theory of the Novel*, Lukács stresses that Wilhelm is representative not unique, that Goethe's novel is not about individual development so much as "common destinies and life-formations" (135). It is the "modern" novel of education that has, to his regret, become a merely "private memoir of how a certain person succeeded in coming to terms with his world" (137). Lukács expresses similar views in *Goethe and His Age*; see chapter 1, note 8.

7. Franco Moretti phrases this as a tension between "dynamism and limits, restlessness and the 'sense of an ending'" (6). Though weakened by a disregard for gender differences, Moretti's recent book on the *Bildungsroman* makes an important case for the genre's "*intrinsically contradictory*" nature (6). While for me this makes it the locus of struggle and dissent, Moretti sees it as implicitly conservative, an attempt to gain consent to the contradictions of modern bourgeois culture. We differ on Eliot as well, for Moretti does not consider *The Mill on the Floss*, and his discussions of *Middlemarch*, *Felix Holt*, and *Daniel Deronda* all privilege the stories of male destiny. What we share, however, is an interest in the *Bildungsroman* as the "symbolic form" of a particular time and place (5), thus an attention to its ideological components.

8. See Hegel's *Vorlesungen über die Aesthetik, II* in *Werke in zwanzig Bänden*, XIV (Frankfurt: Suhrkamp, 1970), 220, a reference called to my attention by David Miles (981).

9. Eliot wrote about *Wilhelm Meister* for the *Leader* ("The Morality of *Wilhelm Meister*," July 21, 1855), and George Lewes was no less than Goethe's biographer.

10. In her work on gender and genre, Celeste Schenck has suggested that female interventions into masculinized genres involve both deconstruction and reconstruction. In these terms, I associate all of my four female novelists, and especially Eliot,

primarily with the first project—in Schenck's words (speaking here of the elegy), "the deliberate undoing of generic conventions . . . the despoiling of generic purity by recourse to attenuated, incomplete, even parodic renderings" (23).

11. Since I am making feminist criticism's usual assumption about the gender specificity of George Eliot's text, let me briefly extend this comparison of *The Mill on the Floss* to *Great Expectations*. Dickens's novel, one might easily observe, similarly invokes a conventional version of *Bildung* only to debunk it. Nevertheless, Pip's story of ties broken and money made, although criticized, is still taken more seriously and made more central than Tom's; however wrong-headed, it always dominates the text and finally proves redeemable, even therapeutic, in a way Tom's never is. It is also worth noting that Estella, quite like Maggie, is a girl whose story of expectations is appropriated by a boy—Magwitch is, after all, *her* father. Yet Estella's inability to have a *Bildung* of her own is not an issue for *Great Expectations*. I will be arguing that Maggie's comparable exclusion from the male *Bildungsroman* (denying her Pip's chance to live out, if only to reject, this plot) is by contrast a major issue for *The Mill on the Floss*. In short, Eliot's distance from the normative genre seems to me more dramatic than Dickens's, her stake in critique more profound.

12. As I have mentioned, Auerbach is also intrigued by the gothic elements of Eliot's novel, which she agrees are embodied by Maggie. She makes the helpful biographical observation that "just before beginning *The Mill on the Floss*, [George Eliot] turned from the rather overinsistent naturalism of *Scenes of Clerical Life* and *Adam Bede* to write 'The Lifted Veil,' a short story in which Gothic fantasies run wild" ("Power," 235). But whereas Auerbach discusses Maggie as a type of the gothic uncanny (witch, vampire, lamia), I am interested in the unluckily gothic orbit of Maggie's narrative, its downward, drowning spiral. (For more on the gothic pattern of repeated imprisonment, see chapter 2, note 5.) Judith Wilt is another critic in pursuit of "ghosts of the gothic" in Eliot. Wilt identifies Maggie's fatal relation to Tom, their inevitable double death, as evidence of a distinctly gothic "machine" (whose operation she explores in "The Lifted Veil," *Romola*, *Middlemarch*, and *Daniel Deronda*): the murderous marriage (187, 195). I disagree somewhat in arguing that Maggie's plot *as opposed to* Tom's is controlled by a gothic logic of repeated imprisonment, though in the very last pages this logic subsumes Tom as well.

13. It is true that Goodman sets out to redefine the genre in relation to the male-female pair in novels by women—Emily Brontë, George Eliot, Willa Cather, Jean Stafford, and Joyce Carol Oates. But her mapping posits an initial "prelapsarian" unity, followed by separation and ending with a return to "androgynous wholeness" (30–31). Her mythification of *The Mill on the Floss* still pulls toward the formation of a single, "whole" individual, thereby neutralizing what I see as the critical struggle between Maggie's narrative and Tom's.

14. Virtually all of George Eliot's novels, in spite of their titles, are similarly decentered. *Adam Bede* is parceled out among Adam, Hetty, and Dinah; Book 1 of *Romola* focuses on Tito; *Felix Holt* is divided between Felix and Mrs. Transome, as *Middlemarch*

is between Dorothea and Lydgate; and the right to the title of *Daniel Deronda* is notoriously contested by Gwendolen Harleth. Austen's *Sense and Sensibility*, *Mansfield Park*, and Charlotte Brontë's *Shirley* happen also to feature dueling protagonists. Sandra A. Zagarell explores a related diffuseness in what she calls "narratives of community." This genre is dominated by women writers and includes nineteenth-century novels by Elizabeth Gaskell, George Eliot, Harriet Beecher Stowe, and Sarah Orne Jewett.

Jonathan Arac has also commented on the decenteredness of *The Mill on the Floss*. His sense of two patterns at work in Eliot's novel—one suggesting harmony, unity, stability, while the other (associated with the figure of "hyperbole") suggests excess, incoherence, and instability—is similar to my sense of the book's generic dialectic. Though Arac does not see these patterns as gendered, he does at one point tie hyperbolic speech to Maggie, insofar as her language and desires exceed masculine norms (680).

15. Newton makes the similar point that "Maggie's notion of life among the gypsies is essentially a fantasy of power and significance—and a rather 'masculine' fantasy at that" (144). I want to elaborate on this and also on her remark that Maggie's "sojourn among the gypsies ends, predictably enough, in confirmation not of her power but of her powerlessness" (144–45).

16. It was a student of mine, Carolyn Price, who first called my attention to the importance of this scene as a rite of female initiation. In a highly provocative reading, Price stressed the sexual subtext of the manifold cloaking and mystification of the obviously symbolic bonnet. The incident, she argued, introduces the two girls both to the shrouding of female sexuality and, in aunt Pullet's flirtatious modeling of her hat, to the forms of sexual displacement.

17. Notable early essays on the English genre are those by G. B. Tennyson (1968) and François Jost (1969); see chapter 1 and particularly note 6 for more on these and other treatments of the English *Bildungsroman*.

18. Lily's relatively advanced age might seem to disqualify her altogether from a genre conventionally associated with youth. But as the editors of *The Voyage In* have argued, attention to female protagonists suggests a different pattern. Observing that often "fiction shows women developing later in life" (7), they include in their collection essays on such late bloomers as Emma Bovary, Edna Pontellier, and Mrs. Dalloway.

19. Abel et al. observe in reference to Miles that fictions of female development seem to move in the opposite direction, "from introspection to activity" (13), culminating today in worldly texts such as Erica Jong's *The Adventures of Fanny Hackabout-Jones* (13). Clearly Miles's schema both assumes and assures the exclusion of works such as Jong's.

20. Like the editors of *The Voyage In*, I would draw on feminist object-relations theorists such as Nancy Chodorow to question the possibility and desirability of "autonomy" as a developmental goal. I want to stress, however, that formation is relational in a socioeconomic as well as psychological sense, to a degree that may ultimately be more Marxist than psychoanalytic. My view of the novel as dialogic is obviously in-

debted to Bakhtin and implies not simply conversation but a roar of antagonistic social voices: male and female, dominant and laboring classes, white and "gypsy." Like Bakhtin, I want to build on the Marxist perception that, as Jameson puts it, "classes must always be apprehended relationally" (83)—and I would add that the same goes for genders.

WORKS CITED

Abel, Elizabeth, Marianne Hirsch, and Elizabeth Langland, eds. *The Voyage In: Fictions of Female Development*. Hanover, N.H.: University Press of New England, 1983.

Adelstein, Michael. *Fanny Burney*. New York: Twayne, 1968.

Altman, Rick. "An Introduction to the Theory of Genre Analysis." *The American Film Musical*. Bloomington: Indiana University Press, 1987, pp. 1–15.

Andrews, Linton. "Charlotte Brontë: The Woman and the Feminist." *Brontë Society Transactions* 12, no. 5 (1955): 351–60.

Arac, Jonathan. "Rhetoric and Realism in Nineteenth-Century Fiction: Hyperbole in *The Mill on the Floss*." *Journal of English Literary History* [hereafter *ELH*] 46, no. 4 (1979): 673–92.

Armstrong, Nancy. *Desire and Domestic Fiction: A Political History of the Novel*. New York: Oxford University Press, 1987.

Auerbach, Nina. *Communities of Women: An Idea in Fiction*. Cambridge: Harvard University Press, 1978.

———"Jane Austen and Romantic Imprisonment." *Jane Austen in a Social Context*. Ed. David Monaghan. London: Macmillan, 1981, pp. 9–27. Reprinted in *Romantic Imprisonment: Women and Other Glorified Outcasts*. New York: Columbia University Press, 1985, pp. 3–21.

———"O Brave New World: Evolution and Revolution in *Persuasion*." *ELH* 39, no. 1 (1972): 112–28.

———"The Power of Hunger: Demonism and Maggie Tulliver." *Nineteenth-Century*

Fiction 30, no. 2 (1975): 150–71. Reprinted in *Romantic Imprisonment: Women and Other Glorified Outcasts*. New York: Columbia University Press, 1985, pp. 230–39.

———*Woman and the Demon: The Life of a Victorian Myth*. Cambridge: Harvard University Press, 1982.

Austen, Jane. *Jane Austen's Letters to Her Sister Cassandra and Others*. Ed. R. W. Chapman. 2d ed. London: Oxford University Press, 1932.

———*Minor Works*. Ed. R. W. Chapman. London: Oxford University Press, 1954.

———*Northanger Abbey*. 1818. Ed. R. W. Chapman. 3d ed. London: Oxford University Press, 1933.

———*Pride and Prejudice*. 1813. Ed. R. W. Chapman. 3d ed. London: Oxford University Press, 1932.

Bakhtin, M. M. "The *Bildungsroman* and Its Significance in the History of Realism (Toward a Historical Typology of the Novel)." *Speech Genres and Other Late Essays*. Ed. Caryl Emerson and Michael Holquist, Vern W. McGee, trans. Austin: University of Texas Press, 1986, pp. 10–59.

———*The Dialogic Imagination*. Trans. Caryl Emerson and Michael Holquist. Ed. Michael Holquist. Austin: University of Texas Press, 1981.

Barthes, Roland. *The Pleasure of the Text*. Trans. Richard Miller. New York: Hill, 1975.

Bataille, Georges. *Death and Sensuality: A Study of Eroticism and the Taboo*. New York: Arno, 1977.

Berger, John. *Ways of Seeing*. London: British Broadcasting and Penguin, 1972.

Blom, Margaret. "Charlotte Brontë, Feminist Manquée." *Bucknell Review* 21, no. 1 (1973): 87–102.

Bloom, Edward A., and Lillian D. Bloom. "Fanny Burney's Novels: The Retreat from Wonder." *Novel* 12, no. 3 (1979): 215–35.

Boose, Lynda E. "The Father and the Bride in Shakespeare." *PMLA* 97, no. 3 (1982): 325–47.

Borcherdt, Hans Heinrich. "Bildungsroman." *Reallexikon der deutschen Literaturgeschichte*. Ed. Werner Kohlschmidt and Wolfgang Mohr. Berlin: De Gruyter, 1955. I, 174–78.

Boumelha, Penny. "'And What Do the Women Do?': Jane Eyre, Jamaica and the Gentleman's House." *Southern Review* 21, no. 2 (1988): 111–22.

Braendlin, Bonnie Hoover. "Bildung in Ethnic Women Writers." *Denver Quarterly* 17, no. 4 (1983): 75–87.

Brontë, Charlotte. *Jane Eyre*. 1847. Ed. Richard J. Dunn. New York: Norton, 1971.

———*Shirley*. 1849. Ed. Andrew Hook and Judith Hook. New York: Penguin, 1974.

Brooks, Peter. "Repetition, Repression, and Return: The Plotting of *Great Expectations*." *Reading for the Plot: Design and Intention in Narrative*. New York: Knopf, 1984, pp. 113–42.

Brown, Julia Prewitt. "The Feminist Depreciation of Austen: A Polemical Reading." *Novel* 23, no. 3 (1990): 303–13.

Works Cited

————*Jane Austen's Novels: Social Change and Literary Form*. Cambridge: Harvard University Press, 1979.

Brown, Lloyd W. *Bits of Ivory: Narrative Techniques in Jane Austen's Fiction*. Baton Rouge: Louisiana State Press, 1973.

Brownstein, Rachel M. *Becoming a Heroine: Reading About Women in Novels*. New York: Viking, 1982.

Buckley, Jerome Hamilton. *Season of Youth: The Bildungsroman from Dickens to Golding*. Cambridge: Harvard University Press, 1974.

Burkhart, Charles. *Charlotte Brontë: A Psychosexual Study of Her Novels*. London: Gollancz, 1973.

Burney, Frances. *Evelina; or, The History of a Young Lady's Entrance into the World*. 1778. New York: Norton, 1965.

Butler, Judith. "Variations on Sex and Gender: Beauvoir, Wittig, and Foucault." *Feminism as Critique: On the Politics of Gender*. Ed. Seyla Benhabib and Drucilla Cornell. Minneapolis: University of Minnesota Press, 1987, pp. 128–42.

Chapone, Hester. "Letter to a New-Married Lady." Reprinted with *A Father's Legacy to His Daughters*. Dr. John Gregory. London: John Sharpe, 1828, pp. 99–122.

————*Letters on the Improvement of the Mind*. 1772. London: J. Walter, J. Scatcherd, T. N. Longman, and O. Rees, 1801.

Chase, Karen. *Eros and Psyche: The Representation of Personality in Charlotte Brontë, Charles Dickens, George Eliot*. New York: Methuen, 1984.

Chodorow, Nancy. *The Reproduction of Mothering: Psychoanalysis and the Sociology of Gender*. Berkeley: University of California Press, 1978.

Cohen, Ralph. "Do Postmodern Genres Exist?" *Genre* 20, nos. 3–4 (1987): 241–57.

Culler, Jonathan. "Towards a Theory of Non-Genre Literature." *Surfiction*. Ed. Raymond Federman. 1975. 2d ed. Chicago: Swallow Press, 1981, pp. 255–62.

Cutting, Rose Marie. "Defiant Women: The Growth of Feminism in Fanny Burney's Novels." *Studies in English Literature* [Texas] 17, no. 3 (1977): 519–30.

De Lauretis, Teresa. "Upping the Anti (sic) in Feminist Theory." *Conflicts in Feminism*. Ed. Marianne Hirsch and Evelyn Fox Keller. New York: Routledge, 1990, pp. 255–70.

Denning, Michael. *Cover Stories: Narrative and Ideology in the British Spy Thriller*. London: Routledge, 1987.

————*Mechanic Accents: Dime Novels and Working-Class Culture in America*. London: Verso, 1987.

Dilthey, Wilhelm. *Das Erlebnis und die Dichtung: Lessing, Goethe, Novalis, Hölderlin*. 1906. 14th ed. Göttingen: Vandenhoeck und Ruprecht, 1965.

————*Das Leben Schleiermachers*. 1870. 2d ed. Berlin: De Gruyter, 1922.

Doane, Mary Ann. "The 'Woman's Film': Possession and Address." *Re-vision: Essays in Feminist Film Criticism*. Ed. Mary Ann Doane, Patricia Mellencamp, and Linda Williams. Frederick, Md.: University Publications of America, 1984, pp. 67–82.

Doody, Margaret Anne. "Deserts, Ruins and Troubled Waters: Female Dreams in Fiction and the Development of the Gothic Novel." *Genre* 10, no. 4 (1977): 529–72.

————*Frances Burney: The Life in the Works*. New Brunswick: Rutgers University Press, 1988.

Dooley, Lucile. "Psychoanalysis of Charlotte Brontë, As a Type of the Woman of Genius." *American Journal of Psychology* 31, no. 3 (1920): 221–72.

Eagleton, Terry. *Myths of Power: A Marxist Study of the Brontës*. New York: Knopf, 1975.

————*The Rape of Clarissa: Writing, Sexuality, and Class Struggle in Samuel Richardson*. Minneapolis: University of Minnesota Press, 1982.

Edgeworth, Maria. *Belinda*. 1801. London: Pandora, 1986.

Eliot, George. *The Mill on the Floss*. 1860. Ed. Gordon S. Haight. Boston: Houghton, 1961.

Ellis, Kate Ferguson. *The Contested Castle: Gothic Novels and the Subversion of Domestic Ideology*. Urbana: University of Illinois Press, 1989.

Ellis, Sarah Stickney. *The Daughters of England: Their Position in Society, Character and Responsibilities*. New York: D. Appleton, 1842.

Ellmann, Mary. *Thinking About Women*. New York: Harcourt, 1968.

Epstein, Julia. *The Iron Pen: Frances Burney and the Politics of Women's Writing*. Madison: University of Wisconsin Press, 1989.

Ermarth, Elizabeth. "Maggie Tulliver's Long Suicide." *Studies in English Literature* 14, no. 4 (1974): 587–601.

Evans, Mary. *Jane Austen and the State*. London: Tavistock, 1987.

Felski, Rita. "The Novel of Self-Discovery: Integration and Quest." *Beyond Feminist Aesthetics: Feminist Literature and Social Change*. Cambridge: Harvard University Press, 1989, pp. 122–53.

Fizer, Irene. "The Name of the Daughter: Identity and Incest in *Evelina*." *Refiguring the Father: New Feminist Readings of Patriarchy*. Ed. Patricia Yaeger and Beth Kowaleski-Wallace. Carbondale: S. Illinois University Press, 1989, pp. 78–107.

Fliegelman, Jay. *Prodigals and Pilgrims: The American Revolution Against Patriarchal Authority*. Cambridge: Cambridge University Press, 1982.

Fordyce, James. *Sermons to Young Women*. 1765. 5th ed. London: D. Payne, 1770.

Freud, Sigmund. *The Standard Edition of the Complete Psychological Works of Sigmund Freud*. Ed. James Strachey. 24 vols. London, 1953–74.

Frye, Joanne S. *Living Stories, Telling Lives: Women and the Novel in Contemporary Experience*. Ann Arbor: University of Michigan Press, 1986.

Frye, Northrop. *Anatomy of Criticism: Four Essays*. Princeton: Princeton University Press, 1957.

Fuderer, Laura Sue. *The Female Bildungsroman in English: An Annotated Bibliography of Criticism*. New York: MLA, 1990.

Gallagher, Catherine. "The Body Versus the Social Body in the Works of Thomas Malthus and Henry Mayhew." *Representations* 14 (1986): 83–106.

Gaskell, Elizabeth. *The Life of Charlotte Brontë*. 1857. Ed. Alan Shelston. New York: Penguin, 1975.

Gilbert, Sandra M., and Susan Gubar. *The Madwoman in the Attic: The Woman Writer and the Nineteenth-Century Literary Imagination*. New Haven: Yale University Press, 1979.

Works Cited

Glock, Waldo S. "Appearance and Reality: The Education of Evelina." *Essays in Litera-ture* 2, no. 1 (1975): 32–41.

Goodman, Charlotte. "The Lost Brother, the Twin: Women Novelists and the Male Female Double *Bildungsroman.*" *Novel* 17, no. 1 (1983): 28–43.

Gregory, John. *A Father's Legacy to His Daughters.* 1774. Ed. Gina Luria. New York: Garland, 1974.

Gubar, Susan. "Sane Jane and the Critics: 'Professions and Falsehoods.'" *Novel* 8, no. 3 (1975): 246–59.

Hagan, John. "A Reinterpretation of *The Mill on the Floss.*" *PMLA* 87, no. 1 (1972): 53–63.

Haight, Gordon S. Introduction. *The Mill on the Floss.* By George Eliot. Boston: Houghton, 1961. v–xxi.

Halperin, John. *The Life of Jane Austen.* Baltimore: Johns Hopkins University Press, 1984.

Harding, D. W. "Regulated Hatred: An Aspect of the Work of Jane Austen." *Scrutiny* 8, no. 4 (1940). Reprinted in *Jane Austen: A Collection of Critical Essays.* Ed. Ian Watt. Englewood Cliffs: Prentice, 1963, pp. 166–79.

Hardy, Barbara. *The Novels of George Eliot: A Study in Form.* New York: Oxford University Press, 1959.

Heilbrun, Carolyn G. *Toward a Recognition of Androgyny.* New York: Knopf, 1973.

Heilman, Robert B. "Charlotte Brontë's 'New' Gothic." *From Jane Austen to Joseph Conrad.* Ed. Robert Rathburn and Martin Steinmann, Jr. Minneapolis: University of Minnesota Press, 1958, pp. 118–32. Reprinted in *Jane Eyre.* Ed. Richard J. Dunn. New York: Norton, 1971, pp. 457–62.

Hemlow, Joyce. "Fanny Burney and the Courtesy Books." *PMLA* 65, no. 5 (1950): 732–61.

Hirsch, Marianne. *The Mother/Daughter Plot: Narrative, Psychoanalysis, Feminism.* Bloomington: Indiana University Press, 1989.

———. "The Novel of Formation as Genre: Between Great Expectations and Lost Illusions." *Genre* 12, no. 3 (1979): 293–311.

———. "Spiritual *Bildung*: The Beautiful Soul as Paradigm." *The Voyage In: Fictions of Female Development.* Ed. Elizabeth Abel, Marianne Hirsch, and Elizabeth Langland. Hanover, N.H.: University Press of New England, 1983, pp. 23–48.

Howe, Susanne. *Wilhelm Meister and His English Kinsmen: Apprentices to Life.* New York: Columbia University Press, 1930.

Jacobus, Mary. "The Question of Language: Men of Maxims and *The Mill on the Floss.*" *Critical Inquiry* 8, no. 2 (1981): 207–22. Reprinted in *Reading Woman: Essays in Feminist Criticism.* New York: Columbia University Press, 1986, pp. 62–79.

Jacson, Maria. *Botanical Dialogues: Between Hortensia and Her Four Children.* London: Joseph Johnson, 1797.

Jameson, Fredric. *The Political Unconscious: Narrative as a Socially Symbolic Act.* Ithaca: Cornell University Press, 1981.

Johnson, Claudia L. *Jane Austen: Women, Politics, and the Novel.* Chicago: University of Chicago Press, 1988.

Works Cited

Jost, François. "La Tradition du *Bildungsroman*." *Comparative Literature* 21, no. 2 (1969): 97–115.

Kaplan, Cora. "'Like a Housemaid's Fancies': The Representation of Working-Class Women in Nineteenth-Century Writing." *Grafts: Feminist Cultural Criticism*. Ed. Susan Sheridan. London: Verso, 1988, pp. 55–75.

———"Pandora's Box: Subjectivity, Class and Sexuality in Socialist Feminist Criticism." *Sea Changes: Culture and Feminism*. London: Verso, 1986, pp. 147–76.

——— "'White Skin': *Jane Eyre* and the Making of British Nationality, 1840–1850." *New Literary History* (forthcoming).

Kauffman, Linda S. "*Jane Eyre*: The Ties That Blind." *Discourses of Desire: Gender, Genre, and Epistolary Fiction*. Ithaca: Cornell University Press, 1986, pp. 159–201.

Kirkham, Margaret. *Jane Austen, Feminism and Fiction*. Brighton: Harvester; Totowa: Barnes, 1983.

Knoepflmacher, U. C. *George Eliot's Early Novels: The Limits of Realism*. Berkeley: University of California Press, 1968.

Kofman, Sarah. *The Enigma of Woman: Woman in Freud's Writings*. Trans. Catherine Porter. Ithaca: Cornell University Press, 1985.

Kowaleski-Wallace, Beth. "*Evelina*: Mother's Text, Daughter's Image." Unpublished essay, 1984.

———"Milton's Daughters: The Education of Eighteenth-Century Women Writers." *Feminist Studies* 12, no. 2 (1986): 275–93.

———"A Night at the Opera: The Body, Class, and Art in *Evelina* and Frances Burney's *Early Diaries*." *Historicizing Gender: Feminist Historical Criticism of British Literature, 1690–1820*. Ed. Beth Fowkes Tobin. Forthcoming.

Labovitz, Esther Kleinbord. *The Myth of the Heroine: The Female Bildungsroman in the Twentieth Century: Dorothy Richardson, Simone de Beauvoir, Doris Lessing, Christa Wolf*. New York: Lang, 1987.

Leavis, F. R. *The Great Tradition*. 1948. New York: New York University Press, 1960.

Leavis, Q. D. "A Critical Theory of Jane Austen's Writings." *Scrutiny* 10, no. 1 (1942): 61–87. Reprinted as "*Pride and Prejudice* and Jane Austen's Early Reading and Writing." *Pride and Prejudice*. Ed. Donald J. Gray. New York: Norton, 1966, pp. 293–305.

Lévi-Strauss, Claude. *The Elementary Structures of Kinship*. 1949. Boston: Beacon, 1969.

Lewis, C. S. "A Note on Jane Austen." *Essays in Criticism* 4, no. 4 (1954): 359–71. Reprinted in *Jane Austen: A Collection of Critical Essays*. Ed. Ian Watt. Englewood Cliffs: Prentice, 1963, pp. 25–34.

Locke, John. *Some Thoughts Concerning Education*. 1693. New York: Oxford University Press, 1989.

Lukács, Georg. *Goethe and His Age*. 1947. Trans. Robert Anchor. New York: Grosset, 1969.

———*The Theory of the Novel*. 1920. Trans. Anna Bostock. Cambridge: Massachusetts Institute of Technology Press, 1971.

Works Cited

Macaulay, Catherine. *Letters on Education: With Observations on Religious and Metaphysical Subjects*. 1790. Ed. Gina Luria. New York: Garland, 1974.

Marcus, Steven. *The Other Victorians: A Study of Sexuality and Pornography in Mid-Nineteenth-Century England*. 1964. New York: Norton, 1985.

Marivaux, Pierre Carlet. *La Vie de Marianne*. 1731. Paris: Garnier, 1971.

Martin, Robert Bernard. *The Accents of Persuasion: Charlotte Brontë's Novels*. New York: Norton, 1966.

Martini, Fritz. "Der Bildungsroman: Zur Geschichte des Wortes und der Theorie." *Deutsche Vierteljahrsschrift für Literaturwissenschaft und Geistesgeschicte* 35 (1961): 44–63.

Maynard, John. *Charlotte Brontë and Sexuality*. New York: Cambridge University Press, 1984.

Mayne, Judith. "The Woman at the Keyhole: Women's Cinema and Feminist Criticism." *Re-vision: Essays in Feminist Film Criticism*. Ed. Mary Ann Doane, Patricia Mellencamp, and Linda Williams. Frederick, Md.: University Publications of America, 1984, pp. 49–66.

Meyer, Susan L. "Colonialism and the Figurative Strategy of *Jane Eyre*." *Victorian Studies* 33, no. 2 (1990): 247–68.

Michie, Helena. *The Flesh Made Word: Female Figures and Women's Bodies*. New York: Oxford University Press, 1987.

Miles, David H. "The Picaro's Journey to the Confessional: The Changing Image of the Hero in the German Bildungsroman." *PMLA* 89, no. 5 (1974): 980–92.

Miller, D. A. *Narrative and Its Discontents: Problems of Closure in the Traditional Novel*. Princeton: Princeton University Press, 1981.

Miller, Nancy K. "Emphasis Added: Plots and Plausibilities in Women's Fiction." *PMLA* 96, no. 1 (1981): 36–48. Reprinted in *Subject to Change: Reading Feminist Writing*. New York: Columbia University Press, 1988, pp. 25–46.

——*The Heroine's Text: Readings in the French and English Novel, 1722–1782*. New York: Columbia University Press, 1980.

——"*Justine*, Or The Vicious Circle." *Studies in Eighteenth-Century Culture* 5 (1976): 215–28.

Millett, Kate. *Sexual Politics*. New York: Doubleday, 1970.

Modleski, Tania. *Loving with a Vengeance: Mass-Produced Fantasies for Women*. 1982. New York: Methuen, 1984.

Moers, Ellen. *Literary Women*. New York: Doubleday, 1976.

Moglen, Helene. *Charlotte Brontë: The Self Conceived*. Madison: University of Wisconsin Press, 1984.

Moretti, Franco. *The Way of the World: The Bildungsroman in European Culture*. London: Verso, 1987.

Mudrick, Marvin. *Jane Austen: Irony as Defense and Discovery*. Berkeley: University of California Press, 1974.

Mulvey, Laura. "Afterthoughts on 'Visual Pleasure and Narrative Cinema' inspired by King Vidor's *Duel in the Sun* (1946)." *Visual and Other Pleasures*. Bloomington: Indiana University Press, 1989, pp. 29–38.

————"Visual Pleasure and Narrative Cinema." *Screen* 16, no. 3 (1975): 6–18. Reprinted in *Visual and Other Pleasures*. Bloomington: Indiana University Press, 1989, pp. 14–26.

Murry, Ann. *Mentoria; or, The Young Ladies Instructor: in Familiar Conversations, on Moral and Entertaining Subjects. Calculated to Improve Young Minds in the Essential as well as Ornamental Parts of Female Education*. 1778. 7th ed. London: C. Dilly, 1794.

Newman, Karen. "Can This Marriage Be Saved: Jane Austen Makes Sense of an Ending." *ELH* 50, no. 4 (1983): 693–710.

Newton, Judith Lowder. *Women, Power, and Subversion: Social Strategies in British Fiction, 1778–1860*. 1981. New York: Methuen, 1985.

Ohmann, Carol. *Charlotte Brontë: The Limits of Her Feminism*. Old Westbury, N.Y.: The Feminist Press, 1972.

Olshin, Toby A. "'To Whom I Must Belong': The Role of the Family in *Evelina*." *Eighteenth-Century Life* 6, no. 1 (1980): 29–42.

O'Neill, Judith. Introduction. *Critics on Jane Austen: Readings in Literary Criticism*. Ed. Judith O'Neill. London: George Allen, 1970.

Parke, Catherine. "Vision and Revision: A Model for Reading the Eighteenth-Century Novel of Education." *Eighteenth-Century Studies* 16, no. 2 (1982–83): 162–74.

Penley, Constance, ed. *Feminism and Film Theory*. New York: Methuen, 1988.

Pennington, Lady Sarah. *An Unfortunate Mother's Advice to Her Absent Daughters*. 1761. Reprinted as *A Mother's Advice to Her Absent Daughters: With an Additional Letter on the Management and Education of Infant Children*. 1817. Ed. Gina Luria. New York: Garland, 1986.

Politi, Jina. "*Jane Eyre* Class-ified." *Literature and History* 8, no. 1 (1982): 56–66.

Poovey, Mary. "Fathers and Daughters: The Trauma of Growing Up Female." *Men By Women: Women and Literature, Volume Two*. Ed. Janet Todd. New York: Holmes, 1981, pp. 39–58.

————*The Proper Lady and the Woman Writer: Ideology as Style in the Works of Mary Wollstonecraft, Mary Shelley, and Jane Austen*. Chicago: University of Chicago Press, 1984.

————*Uneven Developments: The Ideological Work of Gender in Mid-Victorian England*. Chicago: University of Chicago Press, 1988.

Pratt, Annis and Barbara White. "The Novel of Development." *Archetypal Patterns in Women's Fiction*. Bloomington: Indiana University Press, 1981, pp. 13–37.

Radway, Janice A. *Reading the Romance: Women, Patriarchy, and Popular Literature*. Chapel Hill: University of North Carolina Press, 1984.

Review of *Jane Eyre*. *Christian Remembrancer* 15 (April 1848): 396–409.

Rich, Adrienne. "Compulsory Heterosexuality and Lesbian Existence." *Signs* 5, no. 4 (1980). Reprinted in *Blood, Bread, and Poetry: Selected Prose 1979–1985*. New York: Norton, 1986, pp. 23–75.

————"Jane Eyre: The Temptations of a Motherless Woman." *Ms.* 2, no. 4 (Oct. 1973). Reprinted in *On Lies, Secrets, and Silence: Selected Prose 1966–1978*. New York: Norton, 1979, pp. 89–106.

Works Cited

Rigby, Elizabeth. Review of *Jane Eyre*. *Quarterly Review* 15 (April 1848): 396–409. Reprinted in *Jane Eyre*. Ed. Richard J. Dunn. New York: Norton, 1971, pp. 449–53.

Robbins, Bruce. *The Servant's Hand: English Fiction From Below*. New York: Columbia University Press, 1986.

Robinson, Lillian. "Why Marry Mr. Collins?" *Sex, Class, and Culture*. Bloomington: Indiana University Press, 1978, pp. 178–99.

Ross, Marlon B. "Romantic Quest and Conquest: Troping Masculine Power in the Crisis of Poetic Identity." *Romanticism and Feminism*. Ed. Anne K. Mellor. Bloomington: Indiana University Press, 1988, pp. 26–51.

Rothfield, Lawrence. "From Semiotic to Discursive Intertextuality: The Case of *Madame Bovary*." *Novel* 19, no. 1 (1985): 57–81.

Rowe, Karen E. "'Fairy-born and human-bred': Jane Eyre's Education in Romance." *The Voyage In: Fictions of Female Development*. Ed. Elizabeth Abel, Marianne Hirsch, and Elizabeth Langland. Hanover, N.H.: University Press of New England, 1983, pp. 69–89.

Rubin, Gayle. "The Traffic in Women: Notes on the 'Political Economy' of Sex." *Toward an Anthropology of Women*. Ed. Rayna R. Reiter. New York: Monthly Review, 1975, pp. 157–210.

Sammons, Jeffrey L. "The Mystery of the Missing *Bildungsroman*, or: What Happened to Wilhelm Meister's Legacy?" *Genre* 14, no. 2 (1981): 229–46.

Sanchez-Eppler, Karen. "Bodily Bonds: The Intersecting Rhetorics of Feminism and Abolition." *Representations* 24 (1988): 28–59.

Schenck, Celeste M. "Feminism and Deconstruction: Re-Constructing the Elegy." *Tulsa Studies in Women's Literature* 5, no. 1 (1986): 13–27.

Schor, Naomi. *Breaking the Chain: Women, Theory, and French Realist Fiction*. New York: Columbia University Press, 1985.

Schorer, Mark. "The Humiliation of Emma Woodhouse." *The Literary Review* 2, no. 4 (1959): 547–63. *Jane Austen: A Collection of Critical Essays*. Ed. Ian Watt. Englewood Cliffs: Prentice, 1963, pp. 98–111.

Sedgwick, Eve Kosofsky. *Between Men: English Literature and Male Homosocial Desire*. New York: Columbia University Press, 1985.

———*The Coherence of Gothic Conventions*. 1980. New York: Methuen, 1986.

Shaffner, Randolph P. *The Apprenticeship Novel: A Study of the "Bildungsroman" as a Regulative Type in Western Literature with a Focus on Three Classic Representatives by Goethe, Maugham, and Mann*. New York: Peter Lang, 1984.

Sharma, P. P. "Charlotte Brontë: Champion of Women's Economic Independence." *Brontë Society Transactions* 14 (1965): 38–40.

Showalter, Elaine. *A Literature of Their Own: British Women Novelists from Brontë to Lessing*. Princeton: Princeton University Press, 1977.

Shteir, Ann B. "Botanical Dialogues: Maria Jacson and Women's Popular Science Writing in England." *Eighteenth-Century Studies* 23, no. 3 (1990): 301–17.

Smith, Barbara. "Toward a Black Feminist Criticism." *Conditions: Two* 1, no. 2 (1977).

Reprinted in *The New Feminist Criticism: Essays on Women, Literature and Theory*. Ed. Elaine Showalter. New York: Pantheon, 1985, pp. 168–85.

Smith-Rosenberg, Carroll. "The Female World of Love and Ritual: Relations Between Women in Nineteenth-Century America." *Signs* 1, no. 1 (1975): 1–29. Reprinted in *Disorderly Conduct: Visions of Gender in Victorian America*. New York: Oxford, 1985, pp. 53–76.

Spacks, Patricia Meyer. *The Adolescent Idea: Myths of Youth and the Adult Imagination*. New York: Basic Books, 1981.

———— "Ev'ry Woman is at Heart a Rake." *Eighteenth-Century Studies* 8, no. 1 (1974): 27–46.

————*The Female Imagination*. New York: Knopf, 1975.

————"Female Resources: Epistles, Plot, and Power." *Persuasions* 9 (1987): 88–98.

————*Imagining A Self*. Cambridge: Harvard University Press, 1976.

————"Women and Boredom: The Two Emmas." *Yale Journal of Criticism* 2, no. 2 (1989): 191–205.

Spivak, Gayatri Chakravorty. "Three Women's Texts and a Critique of Imperialism." *Critical Inquiry* 12, no. 1 (1985). Reprinted in *"Race," Writing, and Difference*. Ed. Henry Louis Gates, Jr. Chicago: University of Chicago Press, 1986, pp. 262–80.

Starr, G. A. "'Only a Boy': Notes on Sentimental Novels." *Genre* 10, no. 4 (1977): 501–27.

Staves, Susan. "*Evelina* or Female Difficulties." *Modern Philology* 73, no. 4 (1976): 368–81.

Steinecke, Hartmut. *Romantheorie und Romankritik in Deutschland*. Stuttgart: Metzler, 1975.

Straub, Kristina. *Divided Fictions: Fanny Burney and Feminine Strategy*. Lexington: University Press of Kentucky, 1987.

Sullivan, Paula. "Fairy Tale Elements in *Jane Eyre*." *Journal of Popular Culture* 12, no. 1 (1978): 61–74.

Sulloway, Alison G. *Jane Austen and the Province of Womanhood*. Philadelphia: University of Pennsylvania Press, 1989.

Swales, Martin. *The German Bildungsroman from Wieland to Hesse*. Princeton: Princeton University Press, 1978.

Tennyson, G. B. "The *Bildungsroman* in Nineteenth-Century English Literature." *Medieval Epic to the "Epic Theater" of Brecht*. Ed. Rosario P. Armato and John M. Spalek. Los Angeles: University of Southern California Press, 1968, pp. 135–46.

Thompson, E. P. *The Making of the English Working Class*. New York: Vintage, 1966.

Todd, Janet, ed. *Jane Austen: New Perspectives: Women and Literature, Volume Three*. New York: Holmes, 1983.

Todorov, Tzvetan. *The Fantastic: A Structural Approach to a Literary Genre*. Trans. Richard Howard. Cleveland: Case Western Reserve University Press, 1973.

Vopat, James B. "*Evelina*: Life As Art: Notes Toward Becoming a Performer on the Stage of Life." *Essays in Literature* 2, no. 1 (1975): 42–52.

Wagner, Hans. *Der englische Bildungsroman bis in die Zeit des ersten Weltkrieges*. Bern: Francke, 1951.

Works Cited

Watt, Ian. *The Rise of the Novel: Studies in Defoe, Richardson and Fielding*. Berkeley: University of California Press, 1957.

Whipple, Edwin Percy. "Novels of the Season." *North American Review* 67 (October 1848): 354–60.

Williams, Linda. "When the Woman Looks." *Re-vision: Essays in Feminist Film Criticism*. Ed. Mary Ann Doane, Patricia Mellencamp, and Linda Williams. Frederick, Md.: University Publications of America, 1984, pp. 83–99.

Williams, Raymond. *Culture and Society: 1780–1950*. 1958. New York: Columbia University Press, 1983.

Wilt, Judith. *Ghosts of the Gothic: Austen, Eliot, and Lawrence*. Princeton: Princeton University Press, 1980.

Wollstonecraft, Mary. "Animadversions on Some of the Writers Who Have Rendered Women Objects of Pity, Bordering on Contempt." *A Vindication of the Rights of Woman: An Authoritative Text, Backgrounds, Criticism*. Ed. Carol H. Poston. New York: Norton, 1975, pp. 77–115.

Woolf, Virginia. *A Room of One's Own*. 1929. New York: Harcourt, 1957.

Yeazell, Ruth Bernard. *Fictions of Modesty: Women and Courtship in the English Novel*. Chicago: University of Chicago Press, 1991.

Zagarell, Sandra A. "Narrative of Community: The Identification of a Genre." *Signs* 13, no. 3 (1988): 498–527.

INDEX